If You'd Just Let Me Finish!

Jeremy Clarkson began his career on the *Rotherham Advertiser*. Since then he has written for the *Sun*, the *Sunday Times*, the *Rochdale Observer*, the *Wolverhampton Express & Star*, all of the Associated Kent Newspapers and *Lincolnshire Life*.

If You'd Just Let Me Finish!

The World According to Clarkson
Volume Seven

JEREMY CLARKSON

MICHAEL JOSEPH
an imprint of
PENGUIN BOOKS

MICHAEL JOSEPH

UK | USA | Canada | Ireland | Australia
India | New Zealand | South Africa

Michael Joseph is part of the Penguin Random House group of companies
whose addresses can be found at global.penguinrandomhouse.com

Penguin
Random House
UK

First published 2018
001

Copyright © Jeremy Clarkson, 2018

'The Fire Inside' by Bob Seger © 1991 Gear Publishing
Company (GMR). Used by permission.

The moral right of the author has been asserted

Set in 13.5/16 pt Garamond MT Std
Typeset by Jouve (UK), Milton Keynes
Printed and bound in Great Britain by Clays Ltd, Elcograf S.p.A.

A CIP catalogue record for this book is available from the British Library

HARDBACK ISBN: 978–0–241–36673–8
OM PAPERBACK ISBN: 978–0–241–36674–5

www.greenpenguin.co.uk

MIX
Paper from
responsible sources
FSC® C018179

Penguin Random House is committed to a
sustainable future for our business, our readers
and our planet. This book is made from Forest
Stewardship Council® certified paper.

Contents

The contents of this book first appeared in Jeremy Clarkson's *Sunday Times* column. Read more about the world according to Clarkson every week in *The Sunday Times*.

No time for the stodgy bits any more, so scroll down to the bottom of the page

There's an especially marvellous moment in the wonderful film *Planes, Trains and Automobiles* when Steve Martin turns to John Candy and says, 'When you're telling these little stories, here's a good idea: have a point. It makes it so much more interesting for the listener.'

I was reminded of it last week as I read a story in *The Times* about a chap called Dan Jarvis. Today Dan is a Labour MP and the Shadow Justice Minister but back in the day he was a Special Forces major. He parachuted over enemy lines in Afghanistan and Iraq and saw service in Kosovo and Sierra Leone. So we are talking about a man who knows how to handle himself in a tight spot.

Anyway, late one night our all-action hero was at London's King's Cross station, travelling down a long escalator, when he noticed a drunk at the bottom waving a bottle.

'I gave him a wide berth,' Dan said, 'but he lunged towards me. I kept going but he squared up to me and then said, "Give me your f****** wallet or you'll get this f****** bottle."'

'That's not going to happen,' said Dan, with a steely-eyed determination.

This is excellent. A drunken would-be mugger has picked on the wrong man this time. Dan looks like a weedy businessman but underneath the suit this father of three is a trained killer. His back is like a sack of writhing pythons. His buttocks are like ostrich eggs. He's twelve stone of sinew and muscle and righteous indignation.

We can barely contain ourselves. We are desperate to know what happens next. Ready? Right, here goes. Dan turned and walked away.

He did. He walked away. So we have the best build-up in anecdote history and it completely fizzles out at the end. Dan said the incident made him think about the nature of society and the treatment of crime. Whereas it made me think: why can't some people tell a story properly?

I have one friend who is completely hopeless. He starts out by saying, 'I was on my way to work this morning,' but then interrupts himself to add a raft of detail that is simply not necessary. 'You know I'm working on the high street now because, well, I couldn't get on with my old boss. My dad was the same. He used to argue all the time with his boss when he worked at the colliery. But you could back then . . .'

So he had identified the starting point for his story as his trip to work but then instead of going forwards he had reversed down memory lane to a South Yorkshire mining town in the 1920s. The only solution at this point is to take an imaginary phone call. Or to gouge your own eyes out.

The trick when regaling friends with a story is to remember that everything is better if it's shorter. Well, not everything, obviously, but you know what I mean.

I used to work on a television show called *Top Gear* and every week the films were edited to a length that felt right. They felt balanced. They felt good. But every week there simply wasn't the time to fit them into the programme – so they'd have to be shortened. And without exception they were better as a result.

In journalism college the lecturers would often call us students back at the end of the day to give us a story that had to be turned around immediately for the 'late news' section that local papers had in those days.

One time they told us that a train carrying nuclear waste had crashed in a residential area and that we had to get the story across in no more than seven words. I loved doing that.

It's why I love Twitter today: because it forces people to be concise, to think how they can say a lot without saying much of anything at all. Twitter is making the world a funnier, more interesting place.

It's why I adore tabloid newspapers. Anyone can say, 'Mr Paddy Ashdown, Leader of the Liberal Democratic Party, today admitted to an extramarital affair.' But it takes a special type of wit and brilliance to come up with 'It's Paddy Pantsdown' and cover the whole damn thing in three words.

This ability to get your message across quickly is going to become a lot more important in the future because a whole generation is growing up with an intolerance for wasted time. They see no point in sitting through the whole of the Battle of Britain when they can go on YouTube and just see that good bit where the German's goggles fill up with ketchup.

Many see the sudden and dramatic increase in the amount of entertainment that's available online as a bad thing. They reckon that without record company bosses to filter out the wheat from the chaff and editors to decide what's worth printing and what isn't, the world will become a sea of beige.

I disagree. Because when everyone has the same platform on which to launch a musical career, people will have to work doubly hard and be doubly brilliant to get noticed. Waffle will be an early casualty.

And as a result I shall get straight to the point with an anecdote of my own from this rather turbulent week. Most of us have woken up after a night at a charity ball to find an empty wallet and a signed rugby ball on the kitchen table. So we're all familiar with the sense of: 'Oh no. What have I done?'

Well, it was worse for me on Friday morning because I woke up after a night at a charity do to be told by my lawyer that someone had uploaded a video of me using choice language to describe bosses at the BBC. He was very stern and I had to look at my shoes like a naughty boy.

But it was all meant in jest and, anyway, it worked. By being brief and controversial and a bit sweary, I woke the room up, and the auction prize I was offering – one last lap of the *Top Gear* test track – raised £100,000.

22 March 2015

I'm having another baby. But I can't tell you what it will look like

As you may have heard, the BBC has taken my gun and my badge, and I must admit it's all been a bit of a shock. For more than twelve years *Top Gear* has been my life, completely. It was an all-consuming entity, a many-tentacled global monster that was dysfunctional and awkward and mad, but I loved it with a passion. I loved it like my own child. Which in many ways it was. But then, one day, I read in Her Majesty's *Daily Telegraph* that my contract wasn't going to be renewed and that they were going to give my baby to someone else.

I felt sick because, after I'd lost my home and my mother, I'd thrown myself even more vigorously into my job and now, idiotically, I'd managed to lose that too. The sense of loss was enormous. I used to think about *Top Gear* all the time. It was a black hole at the centre of my heart. I woke every morning worrying about every single line. And I went to bed at night worrying that the changes I'd made during the day were wrong. Friends would talk to me when we were out and, though I could see their lips moving, I couldn't hear what they were saying. My mind was always elsewhere. I was comfortably numb.

Two days before the 'fracas', I'd been told, sternly, by my doctor that the lump on my tongue was probably cancer and that I must get it checked out immediately. But I couldn't do that. We were in the middle of a *Top Gear* series. And *Top Gear* always came first.

The hole it's left behind seems to stretch for eternity. And eternity is a big place. Imagine a ball of steel the size of the

Earth. Now imagine a fly landing on that ball once a day, and then taking off again. When it has eventually worn the ball of steel away to nothing, that is just the start of eternity. And I've somehow got to fill it.

Playing Patience on my laptop is not the answer. Because when you get bored, and you will, it's still only eight in the morning and you can't even think about going to the pub for four more hours. And then you have to decide not to go to the pub because that's the road to ruin and despair.

So you watch the lunchtime news and it's full of Ed Miliband doing his new Dirty Harry act and David Cameron in a hospital with his tie tucked into his shirt and his sleeves rolled up, and it's still five hours until the start of *Pointless*. So you go to the shops, and for the first time you are aware that every penny you spend is coming from a pot that's no longer being topped up. So you decide not to spend anything at all.

The only good thing is that my son is currently living with me in London, doing A-level retakes. Which means I can spend, ooh, about sixteen hours a day reading about the Cold War and helping him with his creative writing coursework. But soon he will be gone, and then the yawning chasm will open up once more.

We read often about people who live on benefits, and it fills us with rage that they are sitting about with a plasma television we bought, eating chocolate biscuits that aren't bloody well theirs. Yet after a couple of weeks in the same boat (well, all right, mine's more of a liner), I'm beginning to develop a bit of sympathy. Because what the hell do they do all day to stay sane?

I suppose it helps when all your friends are on the dole as well. You can all hang out in the bus shelter together. But selfishly, most of my friends have jobs, which means that until eight at night I have almost no one to play with.

This means I have to make everything last for hours. I have set aside this afternoon to fill in the membership form for a local tennis club. And then I shall use all tomorrow morning to take it round. The afternoon? Not sure yet. I may organize my jumpers.

And so we get to the nub of the issue. When you are thrust into the world of early retirement, it's no good living from day to day because then you're just a twig in a stream. You just get stuck in an eddy till you rot. You need to have a long-term strategy. You need something that will fill the void.

But what? Squash? Really? I'm fifty-five years old, which means that long before I become good, my knees will explode and my ears will fill up with hair. Fishing? Hmm. I'm not certain, when you've spent a life being chased across the border by angry mobs and shot at in helicopter gunships, that you can fill the hole by sitting on the bank of a canal, in the drizzle. It's the same story with gardening. When your Maserati's done 185mph you're not going to get much of a thrill from a rhubarb growth spurt.

One of my friends, who shall remain nameless, save to say that his name begins with R and ends in ichard Hammond, decided to fill his enforced leave by training his dog. And now, after just a couple of weeks, he reports that the dog in question hates him and hides whenever he comes into the room.

Things will only get worse, because recent studies have found that people who retire early stand an increased chance of developing dementia. They also live in a constant state of anxiety and will die nearly two years sooner than they might, had they stayed at work.

At fifty-five, then, you're in a limbo land where time is simultaneously with you and against you. You are too young to put your feet up but too old to start anything new.

Which is why I have made a decision. I have lost my baby but I shall create another. I don't know who the other parent will be or what the baby will be like, but I cannot sit around any more organizing my photograph albums.

Especially as most of the pictures I have are from a fabulous chapter that's now been closed. The child is grown. The dream is gone. I have become uncomfortably numb.

19 April 2015

The only answer to the Med refugee crisis: unfold your sofa bed

Life for people in these countries is extremely difficult. Because one day you're on a hillside looking after your goats and the next you're on fire on the internet. The locals could just about handle Muammar Gaddafi and Saddam Hussein, and so on. But the new lot? No. So they are giving their savings to God knows who and boarding escape boats, most of which then sink.

Those that don't sink reach Europe, where the wretched souls on board are greeted by Nigel Farage, who says they must go back from whence they came and be beheaded. Because our primary schools are full.

And now we have yet more Western leaders climbing on to their soapboxes and saying the people traffickers are committing 'genocide'. In Italy they are talking about being 'at war' with smugglers. And this is worrying because Italy has been at war with smugglers before, and it didn't go well.

It was the 1990s. Albania was in chaos. A mad tyrant had been replaced but life was still so tough that thousands of Albanians decided to flee across the Strait of Otranto into southern Italy.

They would hand over their hard-earned cash to smugglers, who very generously offered a two-for-one deal. If they were caught and sent back to Albania, they would get the next trip for nothing. The traffickers could afford to be generous like this because the number of refugees being caught was about nought.

As a result, refugees from all over the Middle East and

Africa were soon flooding into Albania to buy a two-for-one speedboat ride over the strait, until eventually the EU decided enough was enough. 'Enough is enough,' it said to the Italians. 'You have got to do something to stem the tide.'

The Italian border patrol instantly responded by buying some new sunglasses. And then it went out and got Fabio Buzzi, a brilliant powerboat designer, to create a range of fast and stylish patrol boats.

Its officers then hung around in various Mediterranean ports, in their new sunglasses, pulling girls. This infuriated all the other Italian police departments. The carabinieri said it wasn't fair that the border patrol had new Ray-Bans and a flotilla of fast patrol boats when they had to make do with crummy Foster Grants and a Fiat Uno.

So they got themselves some boats as well, which made the finance police and even the forestry police hop about and raise merry hell until they too each had a nice seventy-foot launch with a couple of thousand-horsepower turbodiesels in the back.

When I visited the southern port of Brindisi back in 2001, the harbour looked as though it were hosting some kind of mad *GQ* fashion shoot set amid a futuristic boat show for oligarchs. All of which meant that Italy had the men and the equipment to take on the smugglers. And they certainly had the sunglasses. But there was a problem . . .

Because let's just say you're out there, in the Strait of Otranto, in your fifty-knot patrol boat, when you see a refugee boat heading to Italy. You catch up and tell it to stop. It doesn't. So you then . . . you then – what? Open fire? You can't. Not on a boat filled largely with innocents.

The issue had been highlighted tragically in 1997, when an Italian naval vessel, the *Sibilia*, reportedly rammed an Albanian boat full of refugees, capsizing it with the loss of eighty-three lives.

There was another problem too. Italian electrics. I went out one night with the border patrol and, as we reached our station, halfway between Italy and Albania, the radar packed up. As the ship's technician used bits of silver foil from his cigarette packet to fix the fault, we could hear but not see the Ribs – rigid inflatable boats – tearing past in the darkness.

And even if we could have found them, all the captain could do would be to follow them to the shore, where the smugglers would drive straight up on to a beach and everyone would scarper. Yes, the boat would be a write-off but, hey, they'd simply nick another, or – using their vast profits – go out and buy a new one.

Or if it looked as if they might not make it, they would simply throw all the refugees over the side and skedaddle back to Albania. 'That happens a lot,' said the captain.

So it's all very well politicians today hosting summits and sending warships to address the people-smuggling problem, but it will all come to nothing unless someone comes up with a realistic non-lethal plan for stopping a boat that doesn't want to stop. Throwing nets in its path to disable the propeller? Yup, that'd work, probably, but then you have to offload the cargo, and where do you take it? Back to the hellhole from which it escaped? Or onwards to Europe, where it was going anyway?

Or how's this for a novel idea? We accept that the people who are fleeing Libya and other countries where ISIS is running amok are human beings and that they are not coming to Europe because of our benefits system or our health services. They are coming because they don't want to have their heads cut off with a rusty kitchen knife. And here's the thing: if we are human beings too, we should let them in.

Look at it this way. If your neighbour's house burned down, you wouldn't tell him that your house was full. Even if you neither liked nor trusted him very much, you'd make up the sofa bed and invite him to spend the night. Or is that just me?

26 April 2015

So what if Tom Cruise worships lizards? Lots of us have weirder beliefs

Whenever someone discovers that I once spent a day with Tom Cruise, they always do the same thing. They adopt a serious expression, inject some gravitas into their voice and say, 'You know he's a scientologist, don't you?'

Of course I do. There are three facts that everyone on the planet knows without knowing how they know. One: Princess Anne once had a Reliant Scimitar. Two: a swan can break a man's arm. And three: Tom Cruise is a scientologist.

It's odd. Many things are interesting about Tom Cruise – his teeth, for example – and many questions need answering. Why did you think you could play Jack Reacher? Did you know when you were making *Top Gun* that it would do for the air force what the Village People did for the navy? And Les Grossman from *Tropic Thunder* – where the hell did that idea come from?

And yet it's this scientology business that seems to fascinate people most of all. Because being a scientologist is a bit like being a murderer: you can't tell by looking at someone that they once killed a man but, when you find out, it changes the way you think about them.

Scientologists are billed as being a cross between the Moonies and the mafia. We're told they will let their wives die during childbirth and that, in their world, an abortion can only be performed with a spoon. We've even heard that they've carved symbols into a remote desert that can be used to guide lizard aliens to Earth. We're also told that if anyone actually makes these claims in print, they get sued and followed by sinister characters in G-man suits.

So the message is clear: behind the ready smile, Cruise and all of the others in his weird church are lunatics.

I'm really not sure why. Because if you go to the scientology website, it seems to be a jolly sincere thing, helping people all over the world to get off drugs and working to improve human rights. Though, as is the way with all religions, if you dig a little deeper, the founding principles do sound a bit bonkers.

They believe, for example, that 75 million years ago a chap called Xenu, who ruled a confederacy of seventy-six planets, froze billions of his people using alcohol and then flew them in a fleet of DC-8s to Earth. After they'd all been killed by hydrogen bombs placed in the planet's volcanoes, he captured their souls on an electronic ribbon and made them spend thirty-six days in a 3D cinema until they were fully indoctrinated by nonsense, and they they latched on to humans, which is why humans are stupid, unless they're scientologists, who get rid of the age-old indoctrination using money.

This is obviously mad. But is it more mad, I wonder, than worshipping a man who could apparently walk on water? Or celebrating the life of a woman who told her gormless husband that God had made her pregnant? Or wailing at a wall? Or growing a beard underneath your face and driving around Pennsylvania in a horse and cart?

At least scientologists don't come round to your house when *Pointless* is on to ask if they may have a bit of your time. But this, say the detractors, is because they are not interested in your time; only your cash.

Worse, because scientology is officially classified in many countries around the world as a religion rather than a glorified *Star Trek* convention, it is tax exempt, so it keeps all the vast sums it receives from 'gullible fools' such as Mr Cruise and John Travolta.

Hmm. Is that so different from the plate that is passed up and down the pews by Hector the Rector at evensong? I'm not saying the Church of England uses menaces to raise its cash. That would be stupid. But it certainly did in the olden days. 'Give us your money, you potato-faced old crone, or you will go to hell when you die.'

And then you have the Catholic Church, which insisted that the world's best artists created masterpieces that it then kept for itself.

Islam isn't self-funding either. All those mosques have to be paid for by someone, and it isn't the prophet himself who's writing the cheques.

As you may have gathered, I'm not a religious man. I believe that there's no one in the heavens; just a lot of hydrogen. But I have absolutely no problem with anyone who believes there is.

Only last week I sat with a straight face as someone explained that God is almost certainly a horse. This does seem unlikely, as any supreme being choosing to take on the form of a living thing would, in my mind, go for something with opposable thumbs, rather than something with hooves.

Because, let's be honest: if you're going to go to all the bother of coming to Earth to spread your message of peace and goodwill, why would you choose something that communicates by whinnying? And that is frightened by a paper bag?

She listened to these reasoned arguments and said, 'OK, then. Maybe He isn't a horse. Perhaps He's a tree.'

There's nothing wrong with this theory. It's harmless. She believes that the creator of all things is rooted to the spot in a Peruvian jungle, unable to prevent earthquakes in Nepal or a Miliband victory in Britain, and that's OK. If she wants to give all her money to the Westonbirt Arboretum, that's her lookout, and it affects the rest of us not one jot.

It's the same story with scientologists. If they want to give their cash to a group that believes the rest of humankind has been brainwashed by an outer-space dark lord called Xenu, fine. It's no worse than a little old lady giving the vicar 10p from her pension to help repair the church roof. Which was damaged by a lightning bolt that God couldn't prevent because He's quite literally rooted to the spot in Peru.

So, the next time someone says, 'You do know Tom Cruise is a scientologist, don't you?', I shall be forced to explain that it could be worse. He could be a supporter of Ed Miliband.

3 May 2015

Call me Jezza Slobovic – I'm fat, I have a tennis bat and I will win Wimbledon

My friend Jodie Kidd, who doesn't want a job on *Top Gear* and hasn't been asked, dropped round last week to say she had recently spat in a jar and then sent the sample away for DNA testing. 'It's great', she said, 'because they've worked out that I'm genetically averse to exercise.'

Of course, I don't need to go to such lengths because one glance at the greeny-brown docker's oysters that I produce every morning is enough to tell even the most untrained observer that I too should not think about going for a run or joining a gym. Any form of exertion is plainly going to be beyond the capability of a lung that is gummed up with what looks like a *Doctor Who* special effect.

And yet I am fifty-five years old and well aware that unless I take steps soon I shall become like one of those ashen-faced Americans you see at airports, weeping tears of regret as they glide past a McDonald's on a motorized scooter, surrounded by oxygen tanks, with tubes going up their noses.

I'm on the way already. I get out of breath pulling on my socks. My knees ache after scaling a doorstep. I get dizzy if I have to carry a six-pack of wine back from the corner shop. And my gut is now so enormous it looks like I have accidentally swallowed a space hopper.

The solution is obvious but impossible for someone with the determination and drive of a teenage cannabis enthusiast. I've tried the gym and it doesn't work. It hurts me. And I've tried running but so far I haven't made it out of the drive before collapsing. I just have no willpower. And my pain barrier is so low only single-cell entities could get underneath it. If I were to be tortured, I would reveal the attack plans and the location of our base if the baddie even so much as mentioned the word 'pliers'.

I looked recently at all those people doing the London marathon in open-mouthed awe because to me running twenty-six yards is out of the question. I would sooner gouge my own eyes out with a spoon than run twenty-six miles.

To me the notion of doing exercise for the sake of getting fit is completely alien. Running when you've nowhere to go and you're not late is impossible. And so is spending an hour in a room full of mirrors and priapic businessmen picking things up and putting them down again. It's not that I don't want to do that. I just can't.

Sport, though, is different. If you join a local football team, you have some fun with your mates while trying to win a game. You get out of breath, up your heart rate and there's a point to it, most notably in the pub afterwards.

But I can't do football because I'm useless at it. Once I tried to take a penalty and – I'm not making this up – the nearest the ball got to the goalmouth was when it was on the spot. From the moment my foot connected with it, it was somehow moving away.

It's the same story with snooker. People look at me for a while, and you can hear them muttering to their mates, 'Oh dear. There's something wrong with him.' There is. To me, snooker proves there is such a word as 'can't'. And anyway, I'm told it's not really a proper sport.

Tennis, though, is different. I'm good at tennis. Really good. Apart from the small fact that I cannot for the life of me do a forehand. When it comes to serving, I'm a tower of power with a hint of slice. Backhands? I'm your man. I can whack the bloody thing right into an opponent's testes. I can chop or add topspin. I'm a backhand wizard.

But forehand? No. It either hits the net, or it loops in a crazy arc off the racket and into the neighbour's vegetable garden. And not being able to do a forehand in tennis is like not being able to sing if you're the singer in a band. It's an issue.

So in an attempt to get fit while doing something I enjoy, and which I can mostly do, I have joined a local tennis club. It's a fabulous place, set in a few acres of 1952. There are some grass courts and a bar where one can enjoy a refreshing glass of lemonade. There is also a coach whose beauty is so extraordinary many of her clients have been known to faint. And 'portable' telephones are banned.

For my first session, I dressed in what I thought was a suitable uniform. I had a white T-shirt, a pair of what I understand are called 'tracksuit bottoms' and some shoes I bought for no reason at Dubai Airport in 1987.

I then needed a bat. But that's fine because I have one. It's been in the boot of my car for eight years in a snazzy and very modern-looking bat wrap. However, unfortunately, when I removed it for my inauguration session, it turned out to be a Dunlop Maxply that looked like an LP that had been left on a radiator, in the sunshine, for about a century. 'Warped' doesn't quite cover it. Rolf Harris is warped. This was something else altogether.

After much thought I decided not to turn up at my new tennis club with a bent racket, especially as I was wearing a pair of shoes that were the same colour as my teeth. So I borrowed what was necessary when I got there and soon I'd used my forehand to send all of the balls on to Holland Park Avenue. This was a good thing because after twelve minutes I was completely exhausted.

However, I had enjoyed it very much and tomorrow morning I have my first lesson with the very beautiful Eastern European coach. In my mind, by teatime, I will look like the bastard love child of Willem Dafoe and Jon Bon Jovi and I'll have won Wimbledon by mid-July.

I won't bother reporting back on my progress. You'll know.

10 May 2015

Money's no object and men don't count when a woman has a horse

Socialists will tell you the country has gone mad because it has just voted for more cuts, more austerity and a smaller, more efficient NHS. UKIP supporters, meanwhile, will tell you the country is insane because their party received almost 4 million votes but won just one seat. And Liberal Democrats will tell you the nation is bonkers because that nice Mr Cable did a Kevin Phillips Bong.*

I agree with all of them, but for different reasons. I know the country is completely off its rocker because, collectively, we own nearly half a million pet horses.

There are so many that now, every weekend, every field in the land is hosting some kind of show to which thousands and thousands of people will turn up with their nags and stand about trying to decide which is the best. This in itself is a sign of madness because horses are like milk bottles: they are all exactly the same.

But the problem runs deeper than that, because the people who own horses lose all sense of reason. And let's be clear on this: when I say 'people', I mean 'women'.

Men see horses as a tool for gambling, or possibly food, whereas women see them as deities with an ability to cure all known illnesses.

Got a cold? You'll be told to go for a ride. Got a drink problem? There are places in Arizona that use horses to cure you. Are you a burglar? Well, statistics in *Horse & Hound*

* Polled no votes at all. © *Monty Python*

have shown that 107 per cent of people who sit on a horse never reoffend, and never get cancer either.

A riding enthusiast will tell you that a horse invented the steam engine long before James Watt got involved and that it was simply unable to convey this important discovery to others.

And as a result she will treat horses with a respect that's borderline idiotic.

If, as a man, you decided in the night not to bother getting up to go to the loo and simply emptied your bowels into the sheets, you can be fairly sure that your wife would be extremely cross. This is because you're not a horse. A horse can do a big, steaming turd in its bed and she will cheerfully put on a pair of rubber gloves and change its sheets with a big-hearted smile.

It's the same story at breakfast time. When the horse is led into its paddock, it will do a number two right in the middle of its breakfast, which will also need to be cleared up. You try doing that on the bacon and eggs she's made and see what happens.

Then there's the question of violence. If your dog were to attack a child, you would be horrified and would at least consider having it put down. It's the same story with your children. If they get into a fight, you put them in their room with no supper.

But when a horse kicks an eight-year-old with such force that its head comes off, you take the poor thing's weeping parents to one side and scold them for letting their child get within range. 'Now look. You've upset the horse.'

One day your horse will be spooked by a paper bag, or a van, or a puddle, or a bit of rain, or a gust of wind, or the scent of a fox, and it will throw you to the ground. You will sustain fractured ribs and a broken collarbone, and somehow this will be your fault.

Another interesting thing about horse ownership is that

you must never have just one. You will need two or eleven or several hundred, some of which you will lend out to friends and family.

No one does this with cars or cooking appliances or children. No one says, 'Here, have one of my dogs. I've got loads.' But horse people do, because they are mad.

There's more. When your children's shoes have seen better days, you tell them that money's tight and that they'll last another term. You may even tell them off for wearing them out so quickly. But your horse? Crikey, no. The damn thing gets a new set of shoes every six weeks.

This is not cheap. Nothing's cheap with a horse. A saddle will be £1,500. The horse will need blankets, and they're £150 a go. Then there's a bridle at £150, and that's before you start buying food. Hay costs more these days than rocket, and over a year it'd be cheaper to buy the damn thing a nicely togged eiderdown duvet than keep it in straw.

You may even need to buy it a paddock from the local farmer. And the going rate for an acre these days is whatever the farmer wants. And because the farmer knows the horse woman has lost all connection with reality, he'll want about £300,000. Then you'll need to build your horse a house, which will cost more than yours did.

Oh, I nearly forgot. The horse will then need its own enormous car, full of bedding and plumbing, which will be driven on bank-holiday Mondays by a teenage girl at 4mph. These cost more than most Bentleys.

Eventually the breadwinner in the family – horse people never have jobs because they have the horses to look after – will consider sneaking out at night and lacing the horse's food with some kind of lethal drug. But this is unwise, because when a horse is dead the costs really start to run out of control.

You can't sell it to Tesco any more and nor can you rent a bulldozer to dig a big hole and bury it. That's because your wife will be sitting there, in her wheelchair, wailing through her voice synthesizer that such barbarity would make her cry and that crying will hurt all her broken bones.

So you'll need to organize a proper burial, with a vicar and so on. And don't think you can sneakily call the local hunt when the nurse is putting your wife to bed, because a) she'll hear their chainsaws as they chop it up, and b) even that will cost £300.

It's strange. We've arrived at a point where, if horses were treated like husbands, the RSPCA would make accusations of cruelty and come round with arrest warrants.

And if that isn't indicative of a nation's madness, then I'll eat my pigs.

17 May 2015

Smile, joke, sing about your ding-a-ling. Then Britain will rule again

For many years Britain has had a global reputation for being the font of comedy. The world sent us Volkswagens and Coca-Cola and bananas and in return we sent them Benny Hill and Norman Wisdom and Mr Bean. Occasionally we even produced something that was actually funny. Such as British Leyland.

But I worry now that our sense of fun has become eroded to the point where it's a withered and gnarled old stump. I wonder if we are not funny any more. Many say the problem started more than ten years ago when, in an attempt to silence hate preachers, the government drew up a clunkily written law that by accident also forbade comedians to poke fun at people.

This in effect outlawed every joke about the French and the Germans, and if the butt of your story was homosexual or black, you'd better have a good look over both shoulders before starting out. Because it is illegal to say or do something that is abusive or insulting 'within the hearing or sight of a person likely to be caused harassment, alarm or distress'.

Obviously, today, that's extremely draconian because, thanks to social media, everything that everybody does is within the hearing or the sight of everyone else. The other day a comedian told a funny joke about me. He said, 'Jeremy Clarkson is like Marmite: disgusting.' I wasn't at the event but, thanks to Twitter, I heard about it, and if I were lily-livered and weak, I could have asked the Old Bill to kick the poor chap's front door in at six o'clock in the morning.

So here we are. It takes only one fat, illiterate, greasy-haired pikey to say she's offended by something someone said on TV, and that's it. The newspapers leap to her defence, ignore the fact that it was obviously a joke and poke the police into action. And pretty soon the person who said it is in the dock, facing charges that are completely subjective. It's ISIS justice with a smiling face, really.

You couldn't run a modern-day equivalent of *Not the Nine O'Clock News*. It wouldn't be tolerated. And remember the Germans coming to *Fawlty Towers*, or *The Life of Brian*? You can no longer have any of that. Even Benny Hill chasing a nurse is not allowed, although, that said . . .

But you've heard all this before, mostly from Rowan Atkinson. What has not been said, however, is that for some reason it's not just in comedy that the spark of fun is going out. We see the same sort of seriousness infecting music.

You listen to all those shop assistants singing their little hearts out on *Britain's Got a Weight Problem* and not one of them smiles. And then you have all the earnest new bands who work really hard and practise playing their instruments in the hope we will consider them talented.

Well, we thought Meat Loaf was talented, but that didn't stop him bringing out 'Paradise by the Dashboard Light'. We knew for sure that Chuck Berry was talented, but he still went right ahead and did 'My Ding-a-Ling'. That doesn't happen any more. Where's the modern-day equivalent of the Bonzo Dog Doo-Dah Band? Why have Kasabian not sung us a song about their penises, or Princess Anne's sousaphone?

On the streets we have policemen who now have no sense of humour at all. Not that long ago the newspapers were always filled after various national events with bobbies having their helmets knocked off by jubilant youths. Try that now and in a jiffy you'll be sharing the cells with a chap who told his mates about an Englishman, a Scotsman and an Irishman.

In any public building, there are signs everywhere saying abuse of staff will not be tolerated. This in effect outlaws any witticism you may be thinking of making.

Only recently a friend told staff at East Midlands Airport that the security could do with a rocket up their backsides (which they could, by the way) and she was banned from flying that day.

Of course, there are still funny films, but mostly these are American efforts called *Horrible Wedding Crashers Go Nutz 2*. On this side of the Pond things are tragic. In the 1960s Britain released 106 comedies, whereas so far this decade we've done 18. And of these, 11 aren't funny.

Which brings me on to the newspapers, which are full of writers who want to be seen as serious and wise. They seem to think that being funny is a sign of weakness. Happily, this one has A. A. Gill, who can spend two whole columns ricocheting around 'Pseuds Corner' but then right in the middle of a discourse on pre-Byzantine architecture make a laugh-out-loud joke about turds.

He's rare, though. Because think about it: when was the last time you read anything in the *Daily Mail* that was funny? Or, apart from Matt, in the *Telegraph*? Yes, the *Grauniad* is funny, but usually not on purpose.

On mainstream television almost all the laughs come with an American accent. I am an avid fan of *Countryfile* but I've never split my sides while watching it. Or *Springwatch*. And there hasn't been anything funny on *Newsnight* since Jeremy Paxman's weather forecasts.

In the commercial breaks things are no better. Where's the combover in the photo booth? Or Ray Gardner's black-currant Tango rant, or the Carling Dambusters? John West once made a funny advertisement that showed a man kicking a bear in the plums. It was brilliant, but today in serious, austere, easily offended Britain it would not even get off the drawing board.

What annoys me about all this is that behind the scenes, in pubs and around dinner tables, comedy is still alive and well and offensive and brilliant. You may not be able to say much in public in case you are branded a racist or a homophobe or a frivolous fluffy nonentity, but in private there are millions of us who can split a man's sides at forty paces.

Only last weekend I was with my younger daughter, talking about Rupert Brooke. 'If I should die,' I said. 'Oops, spoiler alert,' she replied.

24 May 2015

Dismantle Palmyra and rebuild it outside Padstow. That'll fox Jihadi John

When Saddam Hussein was running the show in Iraq, we all knew that he was waging a cruel and bloodthirsty war with Iran. We knew too that he was using nerve gas on his own people and allowing his son to feed those who survived to his pet tiger. And let's be brutally honest, we really weren't that bothered.

Later, we were told by Mr Blair that Saddam had amassed a huge stockpile of nuclear weapons and that these would definitely be raining down on London in about forty-five minutes. And immediately, a million banner-waving people took to the streets of the capital shouting, with one voice: 'So what?'

Eventually, we got the Arab Spring, during which a number of despotic leaders were replaced by a bunch of lunatics. In Libya, they cornered Colonel Gaddafi in a storm drain and reportedly pushed a scaffolding pole up his bottom. In Syria, it turned out that one anti-regime commander had started eating government soldiers.

Then came the beheadings and the hangings and the public incinerations. Homosexuals were being thrown from tall buildings, and you could be stoned to death for having the wrong sort of sandals. This was all completely unacceptable and, as a result, we decided to do nothing at all.

But then, last week, we heard that the forces of darkness had captured the Syrian city of Palmyra and were planning to destroy its two thousand-year-old Roman ruins. This sent us all into a state of shock. 'Nooooo,' we all cried. 'They can't destroy Palmyra. Nigel and Annabel went there on holiday a couple of years ago and said it was lovely.'

The argument is a bit unpalatable. But the truth is there are billions of people in the world so we don't really care if a complete stranger is pushed off a tall building. But there's only one Palmyra. There's only one Angkor Wat temple. There's only one Highclere Castle. And you won't like this but, given the choice of losing a stranger who lives on the other side of the world or the house where they film *Downton Abbey* . . . well, I'm sorry, but we all know the answer, don't we?

I've been to Palmyra. We filmed part of the *Top Gear* Middle East special there. You may remember the sequence: Richard Hammond and I dressed in burqas and James May fell over and had to go to hospital, suffering from more madness than usual.

While he was in there I had a couple of days to mooch around and I learned absolutely nothing at all about the mile upon mile of columns or the palacey thing on a nearby hill. I couldn't tell you who built it all, or why, because I wasn't that bothered.

But I did think, as I gazed from my hotel window, that it was jolly impressive so much was still standing after such a long time. And as a result, I do think now that something must be done to make sure a bunch of disaffected computer-game enthusiasts from Middlesex don't run amok out there with the Semtex. But what?

At present we have the United Nations, which lists all sorts of things as 'important' but then does absolutely nothing to stop them being destroyed. It didn't send in 'peace-keepers' to protect those buddhas in Afghanistan and they are doing the square root of bugger all to protect what remains in Palmyra. They simply shrug and tell us that what could be moved has already been moved to Damascus. And that the fate of what couldn't be moved is now in the hands of Jihadi John and his mates.

That won't do, so I've hatched a plan. The UN needs to draw up a list of the things that really are more important than a few lives and then steps must be taken to ensure that no harm can come to them, ever.

Obviously, we can't use troops because I fear there'd be a bit of a public relations backlash. 'Why are you sending soldiers to protect a few old stones when you won't use them to look after all the people?' That wouldn't sound good on the evening news.

And there's more, because it's hard in this day and age to know where the troops would be needed. Who could have predicted five years ago that Kurdistan, eastern Ukraine and Syria would be no-go areas for Johnny Westerner? So where's next? Nobody knows. You could put troops in Egypt to protect the pyramids, only for it to kick off in Petra or Athens.

There is, as I see it, only one solution. We cannot hand the responsibility of looking after these things to the Americans because they have a very poor grasp of history and no sense at all of the need for preservation. The Italians, on the other hand, are good at nurturing the past, but I'm not sure I'd want to entrust the world's most important jewels to Luigi and Pietro. As an Italian colonel once told me, 'Our soldiers like to make love, not war.'

No. The job must be given to the British. We like the past so much we live in it most of the time. But don't worry. I'm not suggesting that we ask our troops to risk their limbs and lives to protect the world's ruins and temples. My solution is way more elegant than that. It's this: we send engineers out into the world now and bring all the world's treasures to Britain.

Piece by piece, stone by stone, we dismantle the pyramids,

ship them to Britain and build them again in, say, Leicester-shire. We then scoop Petra out of the mountain and rehouse it in Cheddar Gorge. Angkor Wat? I see that in Oxfordshire. And who wouldn't like to see the Great Wall of China sep-arating England from Scotland?

This would not only ensure that these wonderful things are safe for all of time but also it would enable history enthu-siasts to see everything that matters in a week, rather than in a lifetime.

So let's get cracking. Let's get out to Palmyra and bring the columns to Britain. And if the local historians start to make a fuss, we can simply point out that if Lord Elgin hadn't brought those marbles back from Greece, they would now be gone for good.

31 May 2015

Gotta get a job – then I can give up elderflower cordial and live again

I went last week to see a brilliant new documentary about Amy Winehouse. Made by the same chap who directed *Senna*, it uses cameraphone and home-movie footage to tell the gut-wrenchingly sad story of a talented woman drinking herself to death.

Then, of course, there's poor old Charles Kennedy, the former Liberal Democrat leader, who died last week at fifty-five – exactly my age. He was an affable soul who liked what I'm sure he would have called a tincture, and a family statement says the post-mortem showed his death 'was a consequence of his battle with alcoholism'.

It's strange, isn't it? Alcohol seems to be such a cruel and tiresomely predictable mistress. It's blamed for a part in the demise of Janis Joplin and Keith Moon and Jim Morrison and George Best and many others, and yet most still think drinking it in vast quantities is amusing.

That's probably because alcohol makes fully grown men fall over, which is always hysterical, and it makes women from the north of England fall out of their dresses, which is even better. Alcohol removes the inhibitions and calms the nerves. It breaks the ice and soothes the soul. Alcohol brings colour and depth to our lives, which is why, here in northern Europe, where the skies are grey and the scenery is largely dull, we drink such a lot of it.

Weirdly, though, I'm surrounded these days by people who are jacking it in. Maybe their doctor has pulled one of his special serious faces, or maybe they've realized that each year passes more quickly than the last and that soon they'll be in an oven. Whatever, the fact is that I regularly spend the evening at a party where no one's drinking a thing.

Last week Katie Glass, my colleague from the shiny end of *The Sunday Times*, wrote a very funny piece about giving up drinking. And a few days later a chap in the *Telegraph* wrote about much the same thing.

Now it's my turn. While I try to find a job, I've reassessed my drinking strategy. Californians have a habit of ringing at 11 p.m. and I realized that I couldn't think as straight as they do with their leaves and mineral-water existence if I was halfway through my third bottle of Léoube.

I would love to tell you that after a couple of weeks I feel sharp and on it, but that's not true. I feel exactly the same, only fatter because, instead of drinking in front of the television at night, I nibble endlessly on party packs of Cadbury Fruit & Nut. I'm also more weary because I can't get to sleep at night and then wake up, raring to go, at 5 a.m.

More distressingly, I find myself extremely dreary. When I'm drunk I'll have a stab at an anecdote and hope for the best but, when I'm not, I over-analyse the story I have in mind and invariably decide it's best not to say anything at all.

This has had an effect on my social life. Only last week a mate I've known for ten years held his stag night. He has just written to me explaining why I hadn't been invited: 'I thought you'd find it boring as you aren't drinking.' I knew what he meant, though: he and his mates didn't want to spend the evening with a miserable old sod sipping elderflower cordial.

Worse, when I do go to parties where everyone's drunk, they all look and sound so stupid with their big, beaming faces and their flirtatious ways. I just want to sit in a corner and read a book. There's a scene in the Amy documentary where she's trying to go straight and is overheard telling a friend at a gigantic awards ceremony that without stimulants it's just so boring. I felt for her, I really did, because I know what she means.

Perhaps the biggest effect, though, has been on my wallet. Because I'm not spending forty quid a day on wine and another forty on taxis to run me around, I'm saving more than £500 a week. But because I'm now driving everywhere, I'm spending that, and a lot more besides, on parking tickets. That's a side effect few people ever mention.

I suppose I should make it plain I have not given up drink for ever. I couldn't face the thought of living with the dullard in my own head for the rest of time. And I never want to be that guy at a party who spends the evening with a holier-than-thou attitude and a supercilious face.

I want to emerge from this period of abstinence as a social drinker who can whoop it up with the best of them at an all-nighter but then stick to the effing elderflower cordial when it's a Wednesday and I've an early start.

More importantly, if you can't enjoy a glass of wine on a lovely sunny day then you have removed one of the tent poles of civilization from your life. You have become no better than a cow, or a rabbit.

Which brings me back to Amy Winehouse. How many times in her distressingly short life must she have made a steely-eyed decision to quit? How many times had she written a cheque that her mind simply couldn't cash? How often did she promise to get the brakes on after two glasses and then wake up fourteen hours later full of regrets?

You may think it's a salutary lesson but it isn't really, because Amy's life was very odd. She had too much money and too much spare time and she was imprisoned by the paparazzi. Which meant she was stuck at home with nothing to do but drink more.

It's a shoulder-sagging tale. Such prodigious talent, wasted. But the truth of the matter is this. And it's worth remembering if you're thinking about taking up a life of absolute sobriety. What killed Amy was something far more dangerous than alcohol. It was the same thing that killed Janis and Keith and Jim and George and all the others. It's probably what really killed good old Charles Kennedy too: fame.

7 June 2015

It's a simple rule, PM: you stop my ration of sex and pork pies, I park for free

A few weeks ago I came here and explained how I'd taken up tennis. The plan was simple. I'd learn how to do a forehand, work a bit on my rather weak second serve and then enter Wimbledon. And I must say, all was progressing extremely well until, inevitably, I put my back out.

The pain was substantial. 'Searing' is the only word I can think of that describes it. Imagine the scene in *Marathon Man* when Dustin Hoffman has his teeth drilled without anaesthetic. Now imagine, as he sits there, that his testicles are attached to the mains. Well, you're nowhere near the agony I was having to endure.

I couldn't even think straight, which is why I agreed to have a massage. I have never believed that such things can cure anything, except if you are in Thailand and you're a businessman and you are lonely.

Massages, as far as I can see, fall into three distinct categories: annoying, ticklish and painful. But since it was impossible to imagine that my back pain could be made worse, I agreed to let a woman do some rubbing.

As is usual, I was made to fill in a form that asked all sorts of questions about my general health and medical history. This is not because the masseuse needs to know. It's to give the impression that what she's about to do is scientific in some way.

Then she spent an hour or so hurting me, and afterwards she sat me down and gave me a list of things I must and must not do to make myself better. When sitting down I must use a hard kitchen chair and avoid a soft, comfy sofa. I must drink lashings of water. And I must do star jumps when waiting for the pelican crossing lights to go green.

Diet? Yes, she had views on that too. I must avoid pretty much everything that I like and stick to magnesium, zinc and various alloys that as far as I can tell are to be found only in the gearbox housing of a Chevrolet Corvette.

And as she sat there, painting a picture of the bleak and miserable life that lay before me, I started to think that there is something wrong in the world and that it needs to be fixed.

It's this. No one with a serious face and a suit ever tells us to have fun, to go to the seaside, have a flutter on the horses and eat an ice cream. We're never instructed to go to the cinema and eat popcorn or look at internet pornography or get a nice suntan. It's quite the reverse, in fact.

We are told not to smoke and, when some of us replace the devil's delivery system with an electronic alternative, we are told that this is just as bad and we can't use that either. We are told to drink responsibly, by which they mean one schooner of sherry a year. We are told to drive slowly and practise safe sex.

They tell us eggs and milk are bad for our hearts and beer is bad for our livers. They tell us salt is worse than arsenic and we must stop drinking Coca-Cola immediately or our penises will become like press studs. Not that we need them for anything other than urinating these days.

And that's before we get to the environment. Here we are told that we must eat our cars to stave off back pain and save the polar bear, that we must wear old jumpers and recycle our poo. Barbecues, pork pies, motorcycles, central heating, soap . . . in fact, every single thing that makes us happy and comfortable is a no-no.

If we lived our lives in the manner prescribed by eco-mentalists, doctors and the government, we'd get up early, eat some yeast with our ethically sourced children, run up and down some stairs, cycle to work, grab a handful of weeds at lunchtime, work more, go to the gym to pick things up and put them down again and then cycle home for an evening of self-improvement, fitness and a spoonful of thin, organic broth.

Later, in the bedroom, having filled in consent forms in the presence of a lawyer and two witnesses, we would wrap ourselves from head to foot in cling film and be allowed a few moments of light relief with our partners before turning out the light and going to sleep at 9.30 p.m.

The upshot of all this is simple. Fewer people would become fat or ill, and as a result the nation's hospitals would become empty, which is good news for the NHS and its cash-strapped managers. What's more, the Earth would be habitable for another 4.6 billion years as opposed to 4.59 billion years.

But to be honest, neither of these things is a good enough reason for turning our lives into dreary and painful fat-free expanses of tummy-rumbling nothingness. I want to be happy, not thin. And you can't be both.

Which brings me on to a plan I've hatched. Governments are bound to meddle and lecture. It's in the nature of those who crave power to exercise that power; then their goal has been achieved.

So they are never going to sit back once they're in office and say, 'Hey, guys. You're all sentient beings. Do what you want.'

They're going to keep on telling us to dispose of our chewing gum thoughtfully and not put Fairy Liquid in the municipal fountains. And that's fine. But we should insist on a new rule that introduces a bit of balance.

So, if Mr Cameron wants to tell us to wipe our bottoms

more carefully, he must follow that up with an instruction for us to get drunk and spend a fiver on the 3.30 at Lingfield.

If he wants to put a tax on fizzy drinks, he must then say, 'And next Thursday no parking tickets will be issued.'

He needs to understand that we aren't here for the benefit of the state or the long-term future of the planet. He is, but we're here to have fun. And putting your back out isn't.

14 June 2015

Jo'burg turns to man's best fiend – but he's no match for my twelve-bore

A motorway on the outskirts of Johannesburg. It's ten at night and up ahead the hard shoulder is a discotastic blizzard of blue lights. As we draw near, we see three police cars, a lorry and quite a lot of uniformed men leaning on things.

My driver, a policeman from nearby Pretoria, has already heard from his colleagues what's happened. 'They found three guys in the back of the truck and there was a gunfight and they are dead,' he says.

With that, we sweep past the scene at an uninterrupted 70mph and go back to the hotel, where I spend a little while thinking, because can you imagine what would happen if the policemanists in Britain shot three people on the hard shoulder of the M1? It would be closed for a month. Nearby towns would be evacuated. And everyone would be running about, waving their arms in the air, for about a year.

And yet in South Africa the motorway was not only kept fully open but in the newspapers the next day I could find no mention at all of the incident. Three guys shot? In a country where you can shoot your girlfriend through the bathroom door and be out of jail by teatime, who cares?

The next day I was looking at some bones at the Cradle of Humankind, a spot in the Bush where it's said monkeys first became men. And over a cup of coffee a local bone professor was telling me that crime in South Africa was not that bad. 'Out here,' he said, 'it's fine. I've never been the victim, apart from three burglaries, and my wife was mugged at gunpoint.'

Violent crime is so common that it doesn't trouble the

seismograph needle. 'Busy day at the office, dear?' 'Not really. My secretary was murdered, but other than that . . .'

South Africa takes the concept of 'stoic' to new heights. It's a country with balls, where eyewitnesses don't stand there weeping. There's a Blitz spirit that I admire hugely. Apart from one thing . . .

Last year a friend of mine awoke in the night at his farm about forty minutes from the centre of Jo'burg to find three armed men in his bedroom. He and his family were tied up as the place was ransacked. Usually the victims are then shot, as dead people make poor witnesses, but my friend was lucky. Today he lives in the centre of Johannesburg to be safe. Well, it was that or Palmyra.

Last weekend I met the man who now lives in his house and asked if he was worried the burglars might come back. 'Well, they may,' he replied. 'But I'm OK because I have a couple of tactical dogs.'

Now in Britain we've heard of guard dogs and in America I have encountered an attack dog. But tactical dogs are different. Tactical dogs are Terminators, trained only to do one thing, which is: kill everyone.

It seems that in every ten litters there will be one puppy that's capable of becoming a hunter-killer. The rest will go off to be pets and seeing dogs and guard dogs, but this one – at a cost of about £3,000 – will be turned into a furry torpedo.

An attack dog can be controlled. You can say 'kill' or 'sit' and it will do as it's told. But a tactical dog will not. If it sees a human it doesn't recognize, even if it's a three-year-old child, it will kill them. You can stand there shouting in your special stern voice, 'No, Fenton. Bad dog. Put the baby down.' But it will make absolutely no difference.

As a result, it's easier to own an assault rifle or a fighter aircraft. By law, your tactical dog cannot be allowed to go for a walk. Nor can it be permitted to stroll around the house, because if your neighbour pops round to borrow some sugar she'll go home with no throat. A tactical dog cannot even be kept in a cage. It has to live in a crate.

It all sounds very scary and, given the choice, I'd probably not burgle a house that contained such a thing.

Or would I? Because tactical dogs can be dealt with by a poison that is known in South Africa as 'Two Step'. Invented by Union Carbide, it's an unholy substance that you put into meat and throw over the fence. The dog eats it, takes two steps and then is not even remotely tactical any more because it's dead.

Or you can simply walk up to the crate in which it's kept and shoot it. Or hit it over the head with a hammer. And what's the point of owning an expensive and hard-to-maintain weapon that can be rendered inoperative by something a burglar can buy from B&Q for £9.99?

I get the distinct impression that these dogs are owned by people who were never in the army but want, passionately, you to think they were. I suspect that many may be paintball enthusiasts who take it all a bit too seriously.

And I don't mind any of that. If someone wants to crawl about in the undergrowth, with a not very convincing Special Forces beard, a dagger tattooed on each of his right biceps and a worrying bulge in his trousers, that's his lookout. But how on earth can we live in a world where these people are allowed to turn a dog into a battlefield nuclear weapon?

I'm not a weird-beard animalista, but I can't see the point in keeping a dog in a crate when for a lot less money you could buy a shotgun, which is more effective at dealing with burglars, is more wieldy and as a bonus cannot be poisoned or neutered with a hammer.

And, yes, it can be black and fearsome to behold. It doesn't have to be fashioned from walnut and topped off with engravings of a pigeon on the brightwork.

As a general rule, I'm not really in favour of people (other than me) owning guns. But you have to admit that in a country where everyone really does need protection, they're better than turning a dog into three stone of nothing but teeth, muscle and a deranged mind.

21 June 2015

An Englishman's idea to stop Mao Tse Sturgeon taking the laird's land

The government of the People's Republic of Scotland reminded us last week that half the land north of the border is owned by just 432 people and that this is unfair. Right, I see. So how many people should own it? Five hundred? A thousand? A million? Or should it be divided up equally between everyone who lives there − 0.00574 of a square mile each?

They tried that in Vietnam after the war was over and it didn't go well because some people got a well-drained plot where rice would grow nicely and some people got a car park. Which is why now everyone works in a factory making training shoes.

It seems the Scottish parliament doesn't really know what the solution is either. It says that it wants a million acres in public ownership by 2020 but it doesn't say what it will do with it. Grow tomatoes? Open a tortoise farm? Charge rich Englishmen thousands of pounds to come along and shoot a deer in the face?

Probably not that. In fact, it seems to have it in for shooting, saying that by ending the tax breaks on game activities, it will raise £10 million a year. But that, in government terms, is about £3.75. Which is basically nothing at all. And the government says that if a landowner is seen to be obstructive or annoying in any way, they will be forced to sell their land.

It all seems very Orwellian, but it comes at you with a smiley face and a trouser suit. 'Scotland's land,' says Nicola

Sturgeon, 'must be an asset that benefits the many, not the few,' before adding under her breath: 'We want an anarcho-syndicalist commune with workers' control of factories . . .'

The BBC has dressed it all up as a piece of radical thinking and has interviewed all sorts of toothless and incoherent crones who plainly don't understand the concept of ownership. But don't be fooled. Everything that's being proposed – and the news that Mrs Queen's earnings from Scotland may be under threat too – is a left and a right into the heart of the better-off.

It's sixth-form politics made real. Pie-in-the-sky idealism. It's been tried all over the world and it hasn't worked, anywhere, ever. Mugabe, Stalin, Castro, Pot, Mao, Sturgeon. They're all the same.

Of course, the better-off are livid. All last week they were popping up on television to say they understand land management better than someone with a beard, an earring and a degree in the redistribution of wealth from the University of McLenin. This is undoubtedly true but, my God, they've been making a hash of getting the message across.

Here's a tip. If you are a Scottish laird and you want to tell the nice man from the BBC about how you barely eke a living from your half-million-acre estate, don't agree to be interviewed while standing in front of your massive house.

I know that, inside, everything is held together by moths and that you have burned all your pets to stay warm, but people sitting in a Glasgow tenement are going to lob a can of Special Brew at the benefits plasma and say, 'Och aye the noo. It's all right for McSome.'

Oh, and when the nice man with the microphone and the earnest face asks for a few shots of you walking through your gardens, say no, because he's stitching you up.

The viewers will hear you saying that land management and pest control are in your blood, but they will see you strolling through the hydrangeas past an ornamental lake. And you'll look like an idiot.

Best really not to say anything at all, because you'll be rational and you'll be arguing a point that isn't.

Debating with the Scottish National Party is like debating with a table. No, it's worse, because the table doesn't actively hate you and, if you have more than an allotment, the SNP does.

The good news, of course, is that over the coming months and years all sorts of legislation will be drafted and debated and none of it will work because it's so obviously ridiculous.

You can't let people become rich and then give their wealth to someone who's spent forty years sitting on his arse watching daytime television. It's just absurd.

A point that becomes obvious when you look at the goals. At present the SNP wants to take land from rich part-time residents and give it to locals. But how do you define 'locals'? Do you have to live on the land, or near it? And what's near? And why are the words 'Sean' and 'Connery' now ricocheting around my head?

It gets more complicated because what if these locals decide that now they're landowners they can sit about watching *Cash in the Attic* all day? Pretty soon, stags the size of elephants will be roaming the streets and goring children to death. And beavers will have turned the forests into a post-apocalyptic wasteland.

And then it'll get worse because of all those migrants who are currently clinging to the underside of various lorries in Calais; they're not stupid and pretty soon they'll realize that if they keep heading north they'll wind up in a part of the world where the poor are always right and the rich are always wrong.

So they will say that the local who was gifted the land is

now well-off and must consequently hand it over to them. So they can build a mosque. Which will then have to be handed over to the former landowners who by this stage will be at the bottom of the food chain.

There is another solution, of course. The Scottish parliamentarians could take a drive next weekend into the Highlands and have a mooch about. They'd see that it is very beautiful, very open and for the most part very well maintained.

They could have a picnic, make a heather daisy chain and then they could decide to do nothing at all. Because everything they have in mind will make it all worse.

But of course, they won't do this because the idea is mine and I'm English. So what do I know?

28 June 2015

I'll just run this up the flagpole: we've let the Union Jack go to pot

Last weekend a chap draped himself in the flag of ISIS and, with a young girl on his shoulders, went for a walk past the Houses of Parliament. Onlookers were, we're told, a bit surprised by this brazen act, but the police decided that he hadn't actually committed an offence and allowed him to carry on.

Naturally, the incident caused a great deal of wailing and gnashing of teeth in the *Daily Express*, with many horrified readers asking what would happen if they went about their business draped in a swastika.

The answer, distressingly, is 'not much'. Because flag-flying in most of Britain doesn't really trouble the forces of law and order. You want to decorate your Uber cab's dashboard with the flag of Pakistan, or hang a Gay Pride emblem from the window of your amazingly well-furnished apartment in Brighton? Well, go right ahead.

Oh, and if you feel moved to set fire to the Union Jack in the middle of Parliament Square, that's allowed too. You can't urinate on it, though, because then you'd be prosecuted for displaying your penis.

Elsewhere in the world, flags are a rather more serious business. If you were to damage the national flag in France, for example, you would be in a lot of bother. It's the same story in Germany. In Greece, if you argue with a policeman, he will arrest you for insulting the flag. I know this from personal experience.

Most countries have extremely strict rules on how a flag

can be displayed. In America, for example, you can fly the state flag if you wish, but it has to be to the right of the Stars and Stripes, and it can't be bigger or brighter or in a better condition.

And if a hotel wishes to demonstrate its international credentials by flying the flags of many nations outside its reception area, the Stars and Stripes must be raised first and lowered last. But it must never be allowed to touch the ground.

Flying it upside down is a really serious business, a point demonstrated with much poignancy in the recent *House of Cards* series. Do that and you're telling the world that the country is broken and urgent help is needed. But only the Philippines will come to your aid because that's the only country that recognizes an upside-down flag as an actual distress symbol. Everyone else sticks with things such as flares and people rushing about shouting, 'Help. Help. I'm on fire.'

There was a huge brouhaha in America last week after the state of South Carolina decided, in the wake of the racially motivated church shootings, to stop flying the Confederate flag.

Its fans are horrified. 'Yes,' they cried. 'We know that the young man who shot all those people in that church was photographed holding the flag in question, but we want to fly it so that we are constantly reminded that our side lost and that today we are slavery enthusiasts with a penchant for attack dogs and unnecessarily noisy cars.'

It's strange, isn't it? A flag is only a bit of material fluttering in the breeze, but it's seen all over the world as a powerful symbol of pride and history. Someone could have an iPhone 6 in his pocket and a Google Nest 'smart home' system indoors, but present him with a flag and he comes over all dewy-eyed and medieval. And it's hard to see why, because the idea of a national emblem didn't really get any traction until the middle of the eighteenth century.

Yes, Denmark's was around four hundred years before that, but Afghanistan has changed its national flag nearly two dozen times in the past hundred years. And how can the people of Romania get exercised about their flag when it's exactly the same as Chad's?

You certainly need to be very careful when you're in Canada, because its rules about the Maple Leaf are long and complicated. You can't, for instance, use it to make a cushion or a seat cover. You can't sign it or mark it in any way. And you are advised not to use it for decorative purposes.

In India it's even more complicated. The national flag may not be made from synthetic materials and can be used for carrying nothing except petals. And if you drop it in a puddle, then you have to go to prison for a year.

Things are a bit different in Britain, of course. You can turn it into a T-shirt or a pair of knickers. You can write on it and, as the Sex Pistols demonstrated, use it to mock Mrs Queen.

However, things get tricky if you want to actually put it on a flagpole, because then you are immersed in a world of bureaucracy, health, safety and planning permission issues. For example, you can fly a flag on the roof of your building but not – at least without consent – if you are already flying one from a pole projecting from the wall. It doesn't say why.

Furthermore, you can't have a flagpole that is more than fifteen feet tall. And you can erect it only after you've convinced the local health and safety executive that nobody could be injured as a result. Quite how anyone could be injured by a flagpole, I don't know, but those are the rules.

You can, if you wish, drape an English flag from the window of your council house, but only if you are prepared to find yourself being taunted on the internet by various Labour politicians. And while you are allowed to burn your flag as a protest, you may be prosecuted if it's made from synthetic materials, as they will give off a toxic smoke.

The upshot is, then, that you can walk about London wrapped in an ISIS flag and you can use a Union Jack to wipe your bottom. And if you fly it upside down, the only people who'll complain are a few elderly pedants in Tunbridge Wells.

But if you want to fly our national flag, the right way up, from the roof of your house, it's not worth the bother.

12 July 2015

Spare me the 57 varieties of Angela who think they make a better ketchup

Naturally, we are all very smug about the economic situation in continental Europe because in Britain everything is going jolly well. Or is it?

We keep being told that unemployment is low because everyone has set up their own business. But what do these businesses do? Make nuclear reactors? Smelt iron ore? Deliver anti-submarine laser weapons into a geostationary orbit?

I'm afraid not. Because so far as I can tell, every new business in Britain is selling extremely twee home-made tomato ketchup to country pubs.

You must have noticed. You've ordered the beer-battered cod, which is served, according to the six-foot-square hand-written menu, with hand-cut, twice-cooked chips and a minted pea purée and, when it all arrives, you ask for some ketchup.

It comes in a worryingly pretty little bottle with a ghastly hand-drawn trug-and-muddy-veg label, but you are assured that it really is ketchup and that it's made locally by a lovely local woman called Angela, so you spoon the contents all over your food, which will immediately render everything you've ordered completely inedible.

I admit, I am not even on nodding terms with the concept of cooking. To my smoke-addled tongue, fish tastes pretty much exactly the same as chicken. And red wine is indistinguishable from beer. But I do know this. No ketchup is a match for the real thing. And the real thing is made by Heinz.

I appreciate that there are a lot of lovely and bored

middle-aged women who've spent a lifetime becoming very good cooks. And I'm not surprised that when their children leave home, they feel the need to make a few quid from what is a labour of love. But why do these people think that they can make a better ketchup, on their kitchen table, than Heinz?

Nobody looks at a pair of training shoes and thinks, 'Hmmm. I reckon people would like a pair of home-made training shoes instead.' Nobody has ever started a business selling home-made pencils. Or home-made telephones.

We look at the iPhone and we think, 'Hmmm. Even though I can buy all the components for this at my local electrical store, I'm fairly sure that if I tried to turn them into something that can receive pornography from space, it would be a disaster.' And yet, people fork Heinz ketchup into their mouths and think, 'I can make a nicer tomato sauce than this.' Well, you can't, so don't.

I therefore say this to the nation's pub owners, if a well-to-do lady with expensive hair and summer frock comes flouncing into your establishment with a wicker basket full of stuff she's made in her own kitchen, explain politely but firmly that you're not interested.

They don't, though. They actually buy the stuff she's made because they think it's un-posh to serve stuff made by Heinz. Well, it isn't. And it's the same story with HP sauce. Nothing. Else. Will. Do. OK?

Ask Richard Branson. He knows. In the early 1990s he was approached by a Canadian outfit that reckoned it had produced a drink that was even more zesty and refreshing than Coca-Cola. Now, you know and I know that this is impossible. On a hot day, or when you have a major-league hangover, there is simply nothing to rival a cold can of Coke. The black doctor in the red ambulance is what I call it.

Sadly, however, Branson didn't know this, so he invested a

great deal of time, money and effort into launching Virgin Cola. He introduced it to America by arriving in New York's Times Square on a tank. And he made it the beverage of choice on his aeroplanes and trains. And yet, despite all this huge marketing push, it flopped. 'I consider our cola venture to be one of the biggest mistakes we ever made,' he said.

There are certain things in life – Google springs to mind here – that are nailed, things that are so good and so ingrained into the human psyche that nothing else will ever come close. And that brings me back to Heinz tomato ketchup and what I hope is a helpful idea to ensure the green shoots of Britain's ketchup-based recovery continue to grow beyond next Tuesday.

First of all, why tomatoes? If you must make a ketchup, why not use mushrooms? Such a thing is commercially available through a company called Geo Watkins, but you haven't heard of that, have you? No, and neither has anyone else, so there's an opening. Or, because mushroom ketchup does look a bit like diarrhoea, why not marrow ketchup? Or carrot ketchup? Or sweetcorn ketchup?

Or why not make household-waste ketchup? Simply pour the contents of your under-the-sink bin into a vat of vinegar and lots of sugar and stir it all up until it has the texture of wallpaper paste. And then – here's the really clever part of my plan – serve it in a bottle that harks backs to the Heinz original.

We in Britain love stuff that doesn't work. Red phone boxes. The original Mini. The House of Lords. And we miss having a sauce bottle that refuses to deliver its contents. It's why we buy so many Gillette razors – because they come in a packet that can only be opened with Semtex.

Today, Heinz sells its tomato ketchup in squeezy bottles, and that's no good at all. We need glass bottles with a neck that is precisely two millimetres narrower than the width of the average kitchen knife. And the contents need to have a viscosity that enables them to sit completely still unless you hit the bottom of the bottle with a force slightly greater than the breaking point of the human trapezoid bone.

This way, everyone can sit in country pubs, delighted that they are reliving the old days, shaking away at a bottle that will never give up its contents. And as a result never finding out that the sauce in the bottle is made from old teabags, some prawn shells and last night's leftovers. Or paella, as the Spanish call it.

19 July 2015

Before you make a fool of yourself, Mr Midlife, try this for a real buzz

By and large, we do not pour scorn on teenagers for having spots and sitting about all day being sullen and uncommunicative. We understand that in those difficult years their brains are being soused by more chemicals than you'd find in the evidence room at a Bogotá police station.

And we know that it's impossible to keep a bedroom tidy or have decent table manners when you are nothing more than a life-support system for your testicles.

We are similarly tolerant of the elderly. We recognize that, as the crooked hand of winter casts its shadow in a person's head, he or she is going to smell a bit and forget stuff. That's why we don't push old ladies out of our way on the pavement or laugh at old men for wearing zip-up slippers. Because we know that comfortable footwear is simply nature at work.

And yet we seem to have no sympathy at all for a middle-aged chap who wakes up one morning and thinks instinctively, 'Right. I must have an affair with my secretary and buy a Porsche.'

When a woman of good character decides one day to go shoplifting, we sympathize. Or at least we should. Because she can't help it. She is going through the menopause.

It's the same story with periods. Every twenty-eight days a woman becomes so mad and irrational she doesn't even know she's being mad and irrational. And if anyone suggests she is, she replies by shouting and swearing and throwing frying pans at your head. And we don't get cross or impatient when this happens because it's a fact of life.

Well, so is a man's midlife crisis. He knows that he is designed to have been eaten by a lion by the time he reaches forty-five, and that it's only science and maths that are keeping him alive. He's done everything he was created to do. He's procreated and provided. And now? He's just meat.

To make matters worse, his children aren't speaking to him. His parents are drooling into their Shackletons wing-backs, his wife is out shoplifting, he can hear the Reaper's approach and he feels as though, if he's going to be kicking around for a little while, he may as well use the bits of his body that haven't stopped working.

And when he does? Well, the world turns on him and points the accusatory finger of love-rat condemnation.

This is unkind. We are horrified that Alan Turing was chemically castrated to 'cure' him of his homosexuality. And today we would be appalled if anyone told a gay man to stop being gay. And yet it is socially acceptable to openly laugh at a fifty-year-old man who's hurtling around the dancefloor at a techno club with his twenty-two-year-old secretary.

He doesn't want to be there. He hates modern music and his legs hurt. But he can't help himself. And it's not just the secretary thing either. When a middle-aged man goes to the barber and asks for a dramatic rug rethink, he knows he's going to emerge from the shop looking absolutely ridiculous.

Every fibre of his being is well aware of the fact that a thick, luxuriant barnet does not go well with a chicken-skin neck and droopy moobs, but his pant compass is saying, 'Get a hair transplant.' And it's a message that cannot be easily ignored.

I spend all day thinking that I should take up deep-sea diving. The call is powerful. I fancy myself down there in the deep, wrestling sea snakes and emerging from the surf looking like the hero in a Wilbur Smith book.

And then I have guilt when I spend the day instead playing Solitaire on my computer and looking out of the window.

The guilt is dreadful. It's all-consuming sometimes. I know that the Reaper is on his horse and heading my way at a decent canter. I know I have only a short time left and that I should fill it with as much excitement as possible. But I get out of breath quickly, and if I'm no good at something after two minutes, I give up. Which smears the sense of guilt with a veneer of shame and regret.

If I were a woman, I'd cheer myself up by stealing a ball-point from W. H. Smith, but I'm not, which is why, last week, I went canoeing. I used to like canoeing. I was even quite good at it. But, I dunno, something seems to have happened in the past forty years so that after half a minute of paddling all I could think was: 'Why doesn't this bloody thing have an outboard engine?'

Later, as I was being revived, a local man – I'm in Australia – asked me to try some of the honey he'd made. He puts his hives near the karri tree, which flowers only once every eight to ten years. And I have to say that it was the second-nicest thing I've ever put in my mouth.

'You have expensive taste,' he said with a smile. 'That stuff costs about £1 a gram.'

And that's when the thought hit me. A man enters his midlife crisis because he has been plodding along in the same direction for thirty years and he starts to believe that, unless he does something radically different, he will waste the extra time that science and maths have granted him.

Normally, what he does to relieve the pressure is try to recapture his lost youth. But instead he should welcome the onset of autumn by embracing the future. In short, he should get a hat and take up beekeeping.

It's gentle, sedate and harmless and, if you place your hives near some kind of exotic bush – bees may have a reputation for hard work but they are fundamentally lazy and will go to the nearest flower to their house – you end up with a honey that you can sell for a great deal of money.

There's a dignity to that. Which is what makes it better than spending the rest of your days trying to keep up with your new wife, who's nineteen.

26 July 2015

Splints, tick. Crutches, tick. Stuff health and safety, tick. Let the holiday begin

Judging by the absence of traffic on London's roads, you're all currently on holiday, which means that fairly soon you will be overcome with an uncontrollable urge to injure yourself. Many of you will do this by going water-skiing. Others will choose to be towed behind a speedboat on an enormous banana.

Well, you go right ahead, but don't come crying to me when you arrive home on crutches, or in a box, or with a bottom so full of water that you could double up as a fish tank.

Water-skiing is like snow-skiing. Professionals make it look so easy that after a couple of bottles of wine you too think you could do it. But here's the thing. It's not easy and soon you will have a dislocated hip.

Being on an enormous banana is very easy. So easy that after just a few moments you will decide to try to turn it over. Nobody does this when they are watching television at home, or when they are sitting in a restaurant.

Nobody thinks, 'I wonder if I can make this chair fall over?' But put them on an enormous banana and almost straightaway they will start to rock violently from side to side until over they go. And then they are in a hospital with a head wound.

What's really odd is that the need to try to turn the banana over becomes particularly irresistible when you are sharing the ride with your children. They're sitting there, bouncing up and down and squeaking with delight, and you're at the back, thinking that it'd be much better if you put them in a wheelchair for the rest of their lives.

I was in Australia last week and every morning lots of people with Tarzan hair and ankle bracelets ran down the beach and leapt into the sea with their surfboards.

Within an hour most of them were in a shark, and those who weren't were back on the beach with a skeleton that wasn't joined up any more.

And I kept thinking to myself, 'Why do you do this? Why spend a lovely sunny day putting yourself in harm's way?'

If you keep going round the globe, you eventually reach New Zealand. And here things are even worse because as soon as you are off the plane you will feel compelled to jump off a bridge, trusting that the organizer, who may or may not be a little bit stoned, has tied the bungee rope properly.

And if by some miracle you survive this ordeal by gravity, you'll climb into an enormous see-through ball and ask someone to push you off a cliff. It's extraordinary. You've sat in an aeroplane for more than two days to reach New Zealand and as soon as you get there you decide to become a paraplegic.

It's not just summer holidays either where we crave a spot of light paralysis for ourselves and our families.

On a weekend break in December many parents will take their children ice skating. It all sounds very idyllic: ruddy-faced kids whizzing about, mittens on strings, and the public-address system playing a selection of heart-warming carols. But do you know why they play carols at ice rinks? It's to mask the screams coming from the first-aid room.

Well, that's what it says on the door. Because 'first-aid room' suggests it's full of nothing but a plump nurse with a cupboard full of sticking plasters and aspirin. But if you step through the door, it's like going into the aftermath of an alien attack. There are limbless corpses everywhere and the walls are papered with flesh.

What's the matter with Monopoly? Or chess? Or if you

want to get some fresh air, a spot of homoerotic volleyball? Oh, and there's another thing.

Why does everyone these days want to do a parachute jump? If you want to raise money for charity, which is the usual impetus, why not sell jam or do a sponsored walk? Why jump out of an aeroplane?

I have never jumped out of an aeroplane, and I never will. I'm sure it's a rush, standing by the door, plucking up the courage to take one last step. But after that it will be a few seconds of pure terror with a choice of two possible outcomes. Either you end up back at the airfield where you started in one piece. Or you end up back at the airfield where you started with a broken ankle.

I definitely can't understand why someone who has jumped out of an aeroplane and not broken their ankle would want to do it again. Because that's like going to a casino and betting constantly on red. It's a statistical certainty, bound by the laws of probability, that one day you're going to lose.

And yet here we all are in the summer holidays, scattered to all four corners of the globe, water-skiing and jet-biking and trying our hands at stuff for which our office-bound minds are completely unprepared. And why? Why are we risking so much for a momentary thrill?

Well, it's because of those signs in shopping centres that tell us the floor is slippery when wet. And it's because of George Osborne's high-visibility jacket. And it's because of labelling on food.

It's because we live our day-to-day lives in a big cotton-wool ball, with handrails to stop us falling over and new roundabouts to make sure we aren't knocked off our bicycles.

All this health and safety flies in the face of everything that makes us human – our playfulness, our need to explore strange new worlds and cut our knees occasionally.

Which is why, for two glorious weeks every year, we can fling off our socks and ride motorcycles in shorts and drink too much alcohol and eat too much food. Will we get a fatty liver and a broken leg as a result? Yup. Do we care? Nope.

Because soon we will be back at the airport, not being allowed to take any liquids on the plane in case we moisturize the pilot to death.

2 August 2015

This will relax you, said the prison yoga teacher as she pulled my leg off

Back in the summer it was decided by various people with serious faces and stethoscopes around their necks that I needed a complete break, and they weren't talking about two weeks in the sun, with a book and a million cocktail parties every night. They were talking about a whole month in the Stone Age.

They said very sternly that after dealing with the stresses of a dying mother and the BBC television chief Danny Cohen and a lost job and a million other things besides, I was about to become a drooling vegetable, and that I must go immediately to a prison where there would be no contact at all with the outside world.

I readily agreed because in my mind this 'prison' would actually be a businessman's retreat, filled with Scandinavian furniture and half-naked Vietnamese women who'd spend all day smearing my eyes with cucumber juice and rubbing my feet with warm stones.

It wasn't. In fact, it was an actual prison. Cell blocks. Shared dormitories. Guards. Razor wire. And to fill the yawning chasm between the 5 a.m. roll call and 10 p.m. lights out, hours and hours of what I've now decided is the absolute worst thing in the world – yoga.

You may have heard from people who admire Jeremy Corbyn and go to Goa for their holidays that it's wonderfully relaxing and an excellent way to stay in shape. But it's neither of those things, I can assure you.

First of all, an instructor with the voice of a mouse and

National Geographic magazine centre-spread breasts invites you to lie on the floor in a room full of whale song that is played at exactly the volume necessary to make her instructions inaudible.

Occasionally you pick up a snippet in which she is saying, very softly, that you should adopt a position called the downward dog, or the pigeon or the crow, and you have no clue what any of this means. Of course you don't. Yoga is designed to be unfathomable, like golf, so that old hands can roll their eyes when a new boy mistakes the pigeon for the crow. Or accidentally becomes a dog.

The only way, really, of knowing what you're supposed to be doing is by looking across to see what your neighbour's up to, but I don't recommend this, as the position they've adopted is almost always either impossible or disgusting. Once, I noticed the woman next to me had cut herself in half and was using her tongue as a set of shoelaces.

My biggest problem, however, is that my body can only really be body-shaped. Lying on my tummy with my legs pulled over my head so that I look like a treble clef is therefore extremely uncomfortable. This is why I spent the first ten minutes grimacing and swearing.

Eventually the mouse woman came over to see what was wrong, and I explained that I hadn't been as unrelaxed since I was in a Hawker Hunter that was tumbling in an inverted flat spin towards Wiltshire at about 400mph.

'May I touch your body?' she said soothingly.

'Yes,' I grunted.

And with that, she gently pulled my leg back until it came off. The pain was excruciating, so I got to my foot, hopped out of the room and spent the next few days with a pronounced and uncomfortable limp.

We're told yoga was first practised five thousand years ago, as though this somehow makes it acceptable. Well, it doesn't. Human sacrifice was practised five thousand years ago, but that doesn't give you carte blanche to spend your afternoons plunging a sword into the nearest virgin.

I used this argument, out loud, on the prison guards, who pulled sympathetic faces and said that in future I could do meditation instead. This is much easier. You sit on the floor, with your index finger and thumb joined together, and hum.

The benefits? None at all, so far as I can see. I'm told it's so that you can live 'in the moment'. But how, if you are living in the moment, do you ever work out what's in the fridge for supper or whether you need to go to the lavatory or how to structure your next business deal?

The simple answer is: you can't. So we can safely say that those who do meditation don't have jobs that matter. And don't really understand how the world works. Many, I imagine, are committed socialists. And all will have extremely dirty bottoms.

'Do you not like it?' said the mouse woman incredulously.

'Oh, I don't mind any of this new-age stuff,' I said. 'It gives ugly people something to do.'

After this I wasn't invited to her classes any more and was made to spend several hours a day talking to a horse. Or standing on my head in a swimming pool. Or doing something called Zumba. At one point I was given a stone that, the lecturer said, would help me stay calm in difficult situations. That night, I rubbed it a lot.

And then one day I found something that was even more useless and annoying than yoga. It's called t'ai chi, which makes it sound exotic and moodily spiritual, but in fact it's nothing more than slow-motion kung fu.

Seriously, you tiptoe through a garden very slowly, as though you are playing Grandmother's Footsteps, and every so often you stop, turn and do a karate chop that takes about fifteen minutes to complete. For sheer stupidity, it's up there with ley lines and astrology.

Its enthusiasts tell us that thousands of years ago people had inner peace because they used t'ai chi to achieve equilibrium. But that's rubbish. They had inner peace because all they had to do all year was plant seeds and then relax while the weather turned them into food.

They sat on the floor because they had no chairs and they hummed because they had no PlayStations. And they did things in slow motion because they were never in a hurry.

We are and, yes, that does sometimes tie us in knots. But there's a cure for this that isn't uncomfortable at all. It's how I spent my last week in prison: sitting in the sunshine, chatting with friends and smoking.

4 October 2015

Chickens are safe, but Labour's Ms Vegan will leave us ripped to shreds

With all the hullabaloo about white poppies and whether he'll sing the national anthem, you might not have noticed that Jeremy Corbyn has chosen a person called Kerry McCarthy to be Labour's spokeschair on the environment, food and rural affairs.

I was very surprised by this because I thought the radio announcer had said the job had gone to Perry McCarthy, who was *Top Gear*'s first Stig. That would have been weird. But further research has revealed that actually the choice of Kerry is even weirder, because she describes herself as a militant vegan. Which means that if Labour does get elected, the person in charge of the nation's farming will not even eat an egg.

Worse, her veganism isn't something she does quietly and for her own reasons. She believes that we should all be vegan and is on record as having said that eating meat should be viewed in exactly the same way as smoking tobacco. And how would that work then? You'd have to eat your pork chop on the pavement outside the restaurant, in the rain? And on a train, you'd have to have an electronic udder on which you could vape if you wanted some milk in your tea?

Hold on, I need to be careful here because veganism is actually a disability. It's fine when you are nineteen and you hate your parents and you want to be a nuisance, but if you only eat weeds'n'seeds in later life you will become deficient in vitamin B12, which – this is true – will cause you to become ugly, uncoordinated and stupid.

Of course, a vegan will tell you that this is a small price to pay if it means the nation's chickens and cows are free to roam wild and happy. They have in their minds a country-side freed from the smothering, chemically infused fire blanket of modern farming. They dream of meadows and babbling brooks, and hirsute women in boiler suits making love to one another on a mattress of bluebells and Fair Trade Birkenstocks.

The trouble is that Ms McCarthy was born in Luton and studied Russian, naturally, at Liverpool University. Which means her only connection with the countryside is her refusal to take part in it. And that makes me a better spokesperson because I have an actual farm. Obviously, I don't do any farming as such; mostly, I drive round the fields in my Range Rover glowering at ramblers. But last weekend I did some manual labour, so now I have a pretty good idea of what Britain would look like if dear old Kerry ever found herself in the hot seat . . .

Last year I noticed that a path through one of the woods had become so overgrown it was impassable even in my car so I asked the farmer if he'd attach one of those whirry things to the back of his tractor and clear away some of the under-growth. He did a good job but just twelve months later all the plants that had been minced and smashed were back, stronger and more determined than ever.

So last weekend, because the farmer was busy spraying something important on to the fields before the weather did something crucial, I decided to have a go at clearing the path myself. I therefore rented a flail, attached it to the back of my quad bike and set off.

Now Ms McCarthy would have us believe that when nature is left to its own devices it will produce nothing but forget-me-nots and grasses that whisper in the breeze. But nature is no different from its most vibrant invention – man. Which means that the weak and the timid are overwhelmed almost immediately by the strong and the vicious. It's a jungle out there, literally.

My path, therefore, was overgrown with horse-sized thistles, nettles that appeared to be dead but which could still send a man into anaphylactic shock and thick bramble bushes with thorns like the incisors on a great white shark.

Still, I figured, none of this would be a problem for my flail, which went straight over the first bramble bush and then died in a horrible graunching cacophony of smoke, failure and expense.

This was no problem, though, because I had also rented a chainsaw that, after just four hundred pulls on the cord, began its two-stroke dance of death. Now, I've seen *Scarface*, so I know that chainsaws can deal with human bone, no problem at all. I've also seen shows on lumberjacking in Canada, so I'm aware that they can take down even the mightiest redwood. But after just three seconds in an autumnal Cotswold bramble bush the chain came off and that was that.

Feeling a little fed up, I realized I'd have to clear the path using old-fashioned branch cutters so, having parked the quad bike, the flail and the broken chainsaw in a nearby stream, I began to wage my one-man war with Kerry McCarthy's vision of heaven.

It was extremely tough going because each end of a bramble stalk is anchored into the ground, forming a hoop that is designed to trip you up and pitch you head first into the thorns. Or you will step into an unseen badger hole. Either way, you're going down. Had I attacked my own face with the chainsaw, the end result would have been less gruesome.

But, using swearing, I was soon making progress and after three hours had nearly cleared a square yard. But then I noticed something terrifying. It turns out that a bramble bush grows by three inches a day, which means that the path you're clearing is closing behind you. Until eventually you are trapped on a shrinking island in the middle of an acre of lacerating, poisonous anaphylactic death.

This, then, is what Britain would look like under a Labour government. Badgers will knock over all the walls, allowing an indestructible, tangled forest of horror to engulf our towns and cities at the rate of three inches a day. The cows and sheep will die. Foxes will murder the chickens. And soon there will be nothing to eat but the fruit these plants of doom produce. Which will turn us all into twitching, yellow-faced morons.

11 October 2015

Dear hotel manager, get off of my smalls. Yours, Keith Richards

According to leaked paperwork, the Rolling Stones are demanding that all the hotels in which they stay provide extra butlers, a twenty-four-hour bar, after-hours dry-cleaning services, a plentiful supply of Marlboro cigarettes and clearly written instructions in every room on how the television works.

The message then is clear: these ageing rockers have spent so long in the platinum-branded, super-pampered section of cloud-cuckoo-land that they've completely lost touch with reality. 'Doubtless,' you will scoff, 'they also want to shower each night in the tears of an angel.'

Yes, but just for a moment put yourself in the leopardskin shoes of Keith Richards. You've been on stage for a couple of hours, belting out an approximation of all your best-known hits, and now it's eleven o'clock at night and you're in your seventies and you're tired. It's possible, though photographs would suggest otherwise, you are also hungry.

Well, you can't go to a restaurant because the waiter, for a laugh, will eject some bodily fluids into your supper. And then ring a local newspaper to say that Keith Richards has just wolfed down a plateful of your – let's be kind, let's say – saliva. Garnished with a couple of the chef's dingleberries.

And there will be photographic evidence of this because every other person in the restaurant will have spent their entire evening sneaking pictures on their telephones. They may even end up with a snap of you apparently picking your nose that they will then sell for £100.

So. Since you're an old man and you don't want to eat saliva or be humiliated in the newspapers for apparently picking your nose, you'll be forced to retreat to your room to watch a bit of television. Which as we all know is now impossible in every single hotel in the world because the controls are completely unfathomable.

There will be several remotes on the bedside table that you have to match up to all the equipment using nothing but guesswork and swearing. And eventually the television will stop playing the 'Welcome Mr Ken Richard' message and will become a forest of hash accompanied by the sort of white noise the CIA uses to make its captives go mad.

While stabbing away at the wrong remote to make the volume go down, you will first of all open the lid of the DVD player and then you will turn the screen into the sort of menu you could understand only if you were a senior programmer at Microsoft. HDMI 2.0 and Aux mean nothing to a man who is a) seventy-one and b) drunk.

Eventually, of course, you will get the television to show some kind of moving image. And since it's usually a woman with massive breasts talking Klingon to a completely orange man with Silvio Berlusconi hair while foam is hosed into the shrieking audience, you will give in and call for assistance.

But when you are a member of the biggest rock band in the world, you can't do that because the hotel staff will sell you out. But then you already knew that because the perfectly reasonable request you made for written instructions on how the television works has been leaked.

Maybe then you could do a spot of laundry. Oh no, you can't, because no one can be arsed with that form in which they ask you to count how many items you are submitting and then has a column in which they are allowed to give their number. And guess what? Yup. Their number is always lower and always tallies with the amount of things they are returning.

That's a problem we all have, but for Keith Richards things are much worse. Because the chambermaid isn't even going to get to the lift before she's tipped your dirty smalls into a pile, whipped out her iPhone and shown the world that you don't wipe your bottom properly.

I'm not making this up. I am not Keith Richards but, after I checked out of one hotel in Australia, its management rang the newspapers and told them exactly what I'd done since I'd checked in. Some hotels won't shop their guests to the press. But a lot do. And you can never tell which is going to do what. So you have to plan for the worst, which is why the Stones have 'demanded' – newspaper talk for 'politely requested' – special dry-cleaning services.

But how come, you may be wondering, these brilliantined old stick insects can't even make it to the tobacconist's for a packet of fags? Why have they asked the management to provide a supply of Marlboros?

Right. Fine. Let's assume that you are in a petrol station, paying for your fuel, when who should breeze in but Keith Richards himself. You're going to stare, aren't you? And wonder if it'd be OK to ask him for a selfie . . .

Happily, while you're deciding, someone else will jump in first. 'I'm sorry to bother you, Keith,' they will say, 'but I'm your number-one fan. I saw you once in Leeds and . . .' They will go on for some time before asking for a photograph. This will involve passing their phone to a stranger who will not know how it works, so they will take a picture after five agonizing minutes of their own eye.

And now everyone in the petrol station is thinking the same thing. If Keith has demonstrated his willingness to have his picture taken, surely he won't mind doing one more . . .

They've all got a back story. They've all got a reason for wanting a picture. They're all number-one fans and they've all got different phones that no one else can work. All of which means that Keith, who just popped out for a packet of Marlboros, is going to be ninety-five by the time he gets back to the broken television set in the room.

And doubtless you're now scoffing again, pointing out that you paid for Keith's lavish lifestyle so you're entitled to take his picture and read about his every move in the *Daily Mail*.

But wait a minute. You also paid for James Dyson's lifestyle. But you don't demand he comes out of the back office and gurns into your camera every time you buy a vacuum cleaner, do you?

18 October 2015

Sorry to be a bore but we must drill a great hole through Blackpool

We keep being told that, thanks to various capitalist banker-bastards who all want second homes, property prices in provincial Britain are now so high that people – or 'hard-working local families', as politicians like to call them these days – simply cannot afford to put a roof over their heads. I don't doubt for a moment that this is true.

So what about all the refugees who burst from the back of vans on the M20 every evening and disappear into the under-growth? We have to presume these poor displaced souls do not continue to live on embankments, feeding on berries and scrumped apples, and that they end up in some kind of house. But how can they afford to do this?

Well, it turns out that Britain is playing host to an increas-ing number of what officialdom calls 'houses in multiple occupation' (HMOs). You probably know all about this phenomenon, but since I divide my time between Chipping Norton, Holland Park and the business lounge at Terminal 5, I did not.

The idea is simple. Landlords, especially in seaside towns such as Blackpool, buy a large guesthouse that hasn't been used much since people realized it was cheaper and sunnier to holiday every summer in Spain. They then rent out each room to whoever comes along. And they don't have to worry about the rent not being paid because, thanks to housing-benefit rules, they are guaranteed a steady income from Her Majesty's Government.

So everyone's a winner. Poor people in the town, whether

they're refugees or down-on-their-luck locals, get a super-cheap room they can call home; the landlord gets a return on his investment; and the government gets people off the streets for next to nothing. Lovely.

Except, of course, it isn't lovely at all, because the people who end up in HMOs tend not to be what you'd call 'house proud'. And many are enthusiastic users of heroin or Stella Artois, which means that even if they try to tidy up a bit, it all goes wrong and they end up in the middle of the floor under a pile of broken furniture, gently marinating in a puddle of their own ordure.

Soon, people in the street who are house proud and do not use heroin or Stella Artois tire of the smell and the begging and the crime and the noise and they sell their house to a landlord, who fills it with yet more lost souls. Until pretty soon the whole area is a cesspit of awfulness and disease.

It really is. A BBC reporter told us last week about the state of various HMOs in Blackpool and it was all too disgusting for words. There were cookers that looked as though I'd been using them, deformed pets, mattresses bearing stains you don't want to think about and flies the size of your hand feasting on the grimy stickiness of every flat surface.

You looked at the pictures and you couldn't help thinking, 'Jesus H Christ. How bad was your life in Syria for this to be better?'

Needless to say, local councils have got it into their heads that landlords – or 'greedy landlords', as we must call them these days – are entirely to blame and, as a result, rush about the place in a blizzard of hi-vis vests and clipboards and over-the-top hazmat face masks, ordering them to make improvements or else.

Right. I see. So let's just assume for a moment that the greedy capitalist banker-landlord-bastard employs a team of decorators to run amok with the Farrow & Ball. Does the council think that the heroin and Stella enthusiasts will come home that night and think, 'Ooh. This smells lemon-fresh, so I shall immediately give up drink and drugs and become a plumber'?

Because that doesn't happen. What does happen is they continue to come home from the off-licence every night, with yet another deformed pet and a wheelbarrow full of heroin, which they consume until all the new paint is stained with yet more vomit and effluent.

The council then blames the Tories and the private sector and uses taxpayers' cash to create its own accommodation, which must meet such high health and safety standards that the drug addicts and the drunks end up on the street, selling themselves to whoever comes along. Until they are finally given a clean bed, by a doctor, so they can at least die with the dignity life was so unwilling to provide.

It's hard to know what to do about all this. The private-landlord idea works well economically, but life in the conditions it creates cannot be much fun. The council-run schemes, like all Soviet thinking, sound great on paper but don't work at all. And still the refugees keep on coming. And property prices keep on rising, and young, hard-working families in rural areas keep being driven into town centres to look for jobs.

Happily, however, there does seem to be a solution, especially in some of the worst-affected areas of Britain: fracking. All these terrible HMOs in places such as Blackpool and Morecambe and Lancaster sit on a freak of geological good fortune: the rocks are full of gas that can be extracted and used to reduce Britain's dependence on Russia for its lighting and warmth.

We know this. We know too that we have the technology to extract this gas quietly and safely. And we know that, if only we could get on and do this, Lancashire would become as rich as Saudi Arabia. There would be jobs and cash and shimmering skyscrapers where all the run-down guesthouses stand now.

Amazingly, however, we are not able to get the fracking ball rolling because Friends of the Earth and its frizzy-haired mates in other eco-organizations are fighting the proposals every step of the way.

Because of the desire of these groups to live in a medieval mudbath, hard-working families in Blackpool and desperate refugees who have fled their own countries for their lives are being forced to endure conditions that are truly inhumane.

I do not know what clean-living, bicycle-riding, smoke-free environmentalists die from. But if there is any justice in the world, it would be shame.

25 October 2015

Beneath the splinter in my foot lies the key to all human endeavour

In the closing stages of last weekend's American Grand Prix, a man called Nico Rosberg was well out in front. And all he had to do to keep his world championship chances alive was drive round a few corners without making a mistake. It should have been easy.

Except it wasn't, because with just a handful of laps to go he suddenly became June Whitfield. He got his feet all muddled up, pressed the wrong pedal and slithered on to the grass verge in an uncoordinated mud-brown soup of Reginald Molehusbandry. His teammate swept past, and that was that. A year's work up the Swanee.

It's strange, isn't it? Nico is a talented driver. He could drive round and round a track all day without making a single mistake, and yet, when the chips were down and the pressure was on, he blew it.

We see the same sort of thing going on in penalty shootouts. In a Sunday-afternoon kickabout, any big-name player could score a hundred times out of a hundred. But in a World Cup decider, even the best striker becomes a big wobbly octopus and hoofs the ball into the next postcode.

All of which raises a question. If a footballer at the top of his game is capable of using his mind to become completely useless, then why can't someone with no skill at all use his or her mind to become a leading goal scorer at Manchester United?

Back in 2004 I went to see the mighty Wasps rugby team play an amateur outfit from Solihull called the Pertemps Bees. On paper the part-timers looked as though they didn't stand a chance. They were fork-lift-truck drivers and plumbers taking on a team that featured God knows how many England players.

And yet, while the Wasps had all the skill, the Bees had all the heart. And as the final whistle blew, the mind had triumphed over the much heavier, faster and more muscular matter. Yup, the Bees won.

And it's not just in sport that we see this. There are documented cases of people with quite serious illnesses getting well after taking a Smartie once a day for a month. They'd been told they were testing a new type of chocolate-flavoured drug and, because their mind believed this, their body got better.

Last weekend I was in Warsaw and I somehow managed to get a splinter in the ball of my foot. I'm not one to make a fuss or exaggerate, as you know, but I was in screaming agony. And yet on Saturday night I walked on to a stage in front of 50,000 people and for the next two hours I completely forgot about my gaping wound. It was as though it wasn't there.

This morning I'm getting a cold. I know it. I can feel the telltale signs in the back of my throat, and there's a heaviness to everything I do. I know for a fact, however, that it will not actually become a cold because tomorrow morning I'm flying to Seattle to do an Important Job and I have told myself that I cannot therefore have a runny nose.

This will work. It always does. If you really and truly cannot spare the time to lie in bed watching *Cash in the Attic*, then the cold will simply lie there, dormant, twiddling its thumbs, waiting for you to go on holiday. Then it will arrive. In spades.

I have never, not once in all my life, taken a day off work because of illness. And I have never, not once in all my life, had a holiday that hasn't at some point been spoiled by a bug or a chill of some sort.

It's not just me either. A group of Tibetan monks amazed doctors recently in an experiment in which they were placed in a freezing-cold room draped in wet, cold sheets. None shivered. They just sat there, concentrating on increasing the heat generated from their bodies until, after just a few minutes, the sheets were dry and warm.

Apparently, they do this as a regular competition: seeing who can dry the most sheets in a single evening. Well, what else is there to do when you're a monk? 'Come on, lads. Let's see which of us is the best at being a tumble dryer.'

All of which makes me wonder. Is it really worth going to Mars? Yes, man has an insatiable desire to know what's over the next hill, and what sort of lizard bats live at the deepest parts of the ocean. But surely the most valuable bit of exploration not yet done is to the centre of our own heads. And no, don't worry. I'm not going to toe the Hollywood line that we use less than 10 per cent of our brains and that we could all be Iron Man if only we could unlock the rest. I'm well aware that we use more than 10 per cent of our brains just to ball our fists.

However, while we know how a brain works – we know which bits are flickering away when we run or read or watch pornography – we don't know how the wiring works when it decides to ignore the pain of a splinter or to cure the common cold.

We know it can do this. We've all heard about farmers who walk miles carrying the arm that's been torn off by their tractor. We've all read those Victoria Cross citations about pilots who landed their shot-up plane even though they had 164 bullet wounds, and we've all experienced it ourselves: the ability to forget discomfort when there are more important things to be getting on with.

Imagine, though, if we could wire ourselves up so that we

could do this at will. Illness would no longer matter. We could all be Wayne Rooney. We could all be Nico Rosberg. And, unlike him, we wouldn't bottle it at the last moment. It'd be brilliant. But instead of working this all out, we're busy mapping the sea bed and digging up pharaohs.

1 November 2015

Vite, vite, Johnny French. We can't wait much longer for a nuclear roast turkey

When the nuclear power station at Chernobyl blew up, everyone ran about, waving their arms in the air and saying millions would die from the radioactive fallout. Farmers in Wales said their sheep had turned green and many had grown a new head. Ukraine, said the experts, would be a desert until the end of time.

Well, I went to Chernobyl last year and spent a day mooching about in the nearby city of Pripyat. The trees were full of fruit. The woods echoed to the sound of wolf cubs playing joyfully in the sunshine. And so far I have grown no warts.

It's a similar story in Fukushima. A tsunami caused what's described as a 'level 7 event' and, once again, the experts were to be seen on television, wailing and gnashing their teeth and explaining how everyone in Japan would die a horrible death within weeks. And yet, so far, the number of people who've died from radiation exposure is, er, nought.

This is the problem with the debate on nuclear power. Every scrap of information we receive comes from the mongers of doom. We read phrases such as 'level 7 event' and we're scared, even though we don't know what level 7 actually is. Nor do we know how nuclear power works.

We think there is some kind of rod made possibly from uranium. Or maybe plutonium and that it needs to be cooled somehow. It's hard to be sure and there's no point consulting the internet for more information because that has been hijacked by the disciples of Monsignor Bruce Kent.

I'm not a disciple of God Luddite. I get my opinions from

a well of something called reason and it goes like this: we need to generate electricity and we can't use coal and gas because we can chip and chisel and frack as much as we like but one day both will run out. And we can't rely on new-age alternatives such as sunshine or wind because neither can produce anything like what we need. Which means if we want to drive electric cars and charge our phones and make tea, we must go nuclear. There is no alternative.

But, oh my God, there simply has to be an alternative to the way we go about delivering it . . .

Britain was the first country in the world to open a nuclear power station, but then we adopted the same philosophy that we saw with the Mini and the Land Rover and Concorde and the red phone box. We invent something . . . and then never develop it.

In 2006, however, Tony Blair decided to put that right. He declared nuclear power was 'back on the agenda with a vengeance'. But there was a problem. There were no nuclear physicists in Britain. Not one.

So it was announced we were getting into bed with the French, who a year later said the people of Britain would be cooking their Christmas turkeys using lemon-fresh nuclear power by 2017.

In 2008 all was going well. Our French friends announced there would be four new plants in Britain, all of which would use the European pressurized reactor system. But then in 2010 disaster struck.

Engineers scouring one of the sites, at Hinkley Point, in Somerset, found a colony of badgers. They applied to Natural England for permission to move them and, having submitted detailed plans of how this might be done, the licence was granted. But that wasn't good enough for a bunch of women who, in their heads, were still chained to the fence at Greenham Common. 'This is how they'll treat people,' they wailed. 'You'll be tranquillized in the night and put in vans.'

So much time and effort was put into Badgergate that no one noticed another problem. We had the design for a new reactor. We had a badger-free site. We had government approval. But then someone looked in the bank and, uh-oh, there was no money to build anything.

While everyone sat around wondering what on earth they were going to do, the wave hit Fukushima and everything was halted while the design was analysed to make sure it was safe. Which, since Fukushima was a totally different design, is a bit like halting the production of Bedford vans because a Boeing 747 has crashed.

It was May 2011 before anyone realized the Bedford van is nothing like a Boeing 747 and there will never be a tsunami in Somerset. Which meant everyone could go back to scratching their heads about money.

Happily, Chris Huhne, then Energy Secretary, forgot that he'd once said the government must stop putting time, effort and subsidies into nuclear energy and decided to use cash earmarked for green projects to, er, subsidize the new power plants. Maybe his mind was on other things . . .

But whatever, with the subsidies in place, the French applied for planning permission. And as anyone who's tried to build a conservatory knows, this is never easy. Indeed, owing to the rules on newts, bats and badgers, their application ran to 55,000 pages.

It was such a complex job that it was March 2013 before permission was granted. By which time the costs had run amok and more money was needed. Which meant that six months later the government agreed to pay Johnny French £92.50 for every megawatt-hour of power – twice what electricity normally cost at that time. And we'd be paying it for the next thirty-five years.

And it still wasn't enough. By May last year all they'd built was a new roundabout. And now here we are, just twenty-five months away from when we were supposed to be cooking our turkeys with nuclear power, and still nothing is finalized. Even though the Chinese are now involved, the French are still doing that shruggy thing after they've been asked an awkward question such as 'When?'

I'm not surprised, really, because the actual answer is that we can't afford nuclear power. And we can't afford not to have it either.

So here we are. It's nearly ten years since Mr Blair said nuclear power was back with a vengeance and all we have to show for it is a new roundabout and a family of rather confused badgers.

8 November 2015

Labour's little leftie does not deserve the abuse. But I know a man who does

After Labour lost the election and Ed Miliband went off to begin an exciting life of obscurity, the party needed candidates for a new leader and lined up a selection of milk bottles. There was a milk bottle in a suit called Andy and a milk bottle in a dress called Yvette and some other milk bottles whose names I can't for the life of me remember.

And then someone thought, quite rightly, that party members should perhaps be given the opportunity to vote for someone who wasn't a milk bottle. They wanted someone from the Industrial Revolution, someone from the past: a churn, perhaps, or a pail.

So they put forward a little beardy bloke from the hard left who didn't sound or look anything like the other production-line politicians. And of course, against all the odds, the little beardy bloke won. It was a storyline that could easily become a Hollywood film.

Everyone was delighted. The huge number of young people who'd joined the party specifically so they could vote for the little beardy bloke danced in the streets with joy. I was delighted because his appointment would keep his party out of the hot seat for a few more years, and for much the same reason the City, businesses and ordinary 'hard-working' families up and down the country were delighted too. 'Phew,' we all said.

Since then, though, the little beardy bloke seems to have become the living embodiment of evil. Everything he says or does, or wears, is seen as yet more conclusive evidence that he is basically the Ebola virus on a bicycle.

Last weekend, at the wreath-laying events in Whitehall, he was the centre of attention. He'd said in the past that the whole Remembrance thing was 'mawkish', so everyone reckoned that he'd spoil the event somehow by staging some kind of potty sixth-form protest.

Many thought he'd wear a white poppy or turn up in a donkey jacket. Perhaps it would say 'NUM' on the back. Maybe he'd go the whole hog, rock up in cycling Lycra and then give a Black Power salute during the 'Last Post'.

But no. He wore a normal suit and a sombre tie. He stepped forward properly and placed some correctly coloured poppies in the right place at the right time. Apart from the beard, he looked like all the other milk bottles who'd turned out on that unseasonably warm Sunday.

And for the young people who'd voted for him and who were undoubtedly hoping he'd goose the Queen and vomit on the Cenotaph, he'd prepared a clever little statement saying he was there to remember soldiers who'd fought for peace, and those who'd helped rebuild lives in countries such as Sierra Leone, and not just the gung-ho commando sergeants who'd stormed a Jerry machine-gun nest armed only with a teaspoon. So well done, little beardy bloke. You kept everyone happy on what is an important day.

Except he didn't in fact keep everyone happy at all because, after he'd laid the wreath, many decided his bow wasn't reverential enough.

The coverage of this slight was extraordinary. It's yet another example of shoddy behaviour, everyone said, from a man who plainly hates his country. We were then reminded for the fortieth time of how he'd turned up at a Battle of Britain service with his top button undone and then not sung the national anthem.

And how, when he was supposed to be meeting the Queen,

he'd gone on a walking holiday in Scotland. Well, of course he had. He's an anti-royalist. We know this. He loathes privilege. And it would be revoltingly hypocritical if, after spending a lifetime dissing Mrs Queen, he suddenly decided to put on a white tie and crawl about on his hands and knees in her presence.

It's the same story with Remembrance Sunday. This is a man who's deeply anti-war. He has said that he would never push the nuclear button, and it's clear he'd still be trying to negotiate a peaceful settlement with ISIS even when he was dangling, naked and upside down, from some scaffolding in Trafalgar Square.

So he's not like the milk bottles who turned up on Remembrance Sunday to pay their respects. They wanted to be there. He didn't. He'd rather mourn all the cyclists who've been killed on the streets of his constituency. But he was there and he did what was necessary, which, in my book, is good manners.

Let me put it this way. How deeply do you think Mr Cameron would bow if he was asked to lay a wreath for all those who had fallen while fighting for workers' rights?

I'm getting a bit bored with the endless criticism of Labour's little beardy man. And embarrassed, actually. Because he seems a nice chap, and endless criticism of every single thing he does will be driving him mad with despair.

I don't like that and think that if we want to bully someone, we should stick with his deputy, Tom Watson, who deserves everything you can throw at him, up to and including the tractor unit of a Scania lorry.

You can argue, of course, that Jeremy Corbyn wants to become the prime minister and that it's only right and proper that the voters are aware of who he is and what he stands for. But we know that already. He's from the loony left. He thinks everyone should be poor, ugly and on a bicycle.

The fact is, though, that because of all this and because of his beard, he is less likely to become prime minister than my dog. I think he knows that. I think he also knows he won't even be given a shot at the top job because long before that happens the milk bottles will kick him out.

So I'm going to set an example here and try my hardest to leave him alone from now on. Easy though it may be – and fun – to kick him and tease him and bully him, I shall remember that he is keeping the red flag in a drawer for now and in future stick to abusing his ghastly little nasal sidekick Watson.

15 November 2015

The snooper's charter is a danger to us all. A man in the pub told me

So you're walking down the street one day when you encounter a young chap with a ready smile and a clipboard. He's conducting a poll and, since you're in no particular hurry, you readily agree to answer his questions.

Of course you do. It's nice to be singled out and asked for your opinion. It makes you feel important. You may even find yourself standing a little taller as the question begins . . .

'Does it worry you that deep packet inspection probes could soon be used when communications service providers refuse to submit data, even though it's expected that most would maintain data about users in unencrypted form, from which contact information could readily be separated from content?'

At this point Captain Clipboard looks up and, with much gusto, says, 'This, of course, would circumvent SSL encryption during transmission.'

So what's your answer? Are you a) very worried about that, b) not worried in the slightest or c) unable to answer because you have absolutely no clue what he's on about?

Well, you're in a minority because, according to YouGov, which did a poll on this subject, a whopping 71 per cent of people in Britain are very unhappy about the prospect of these deep packet inspection probes snouting about in their ISP's SSL – secure sockets layer – encryption programs.

This is because the actual question was more like: 'Are you happy to let policemen rummage about in your emails and your internet browsing history?' Put it like that, and everyone who's had a peek at some online sapphic action is going to say: 'Whoa, there. Just a cotton-picking minute . . .'

But now let's translate it another way. 'Would you like the police to be able to prevent some kind of terrorist atrocity on the streets of London?'

This not only exposes the big problem with opinion polls – you always get the answer you want – but also highlights the dilemma in the current 'snooper's charter' debate about individual liberty and freedom and the Big Brother state.

On an individual level none of us wants our thoughts and our dreams and our sexual fantasies to be available to the forces of law and order. But we do want the security services to be able to access the electronic secrets of the weird-beard loner at No. 43.

I've been trying to work out where I stand on the issue, and it's not easy because we simply don't know what's possible already. We hear from Tom Clancy and others of his ilk that if you use the word 'bomb' or 'gun' while on the phone, government-run tape recorders in limestone caves are automatically triggered and will record the rest of your conversation. But is this true? We have no idea.

We're told that shadowy figures can work out exactly where we are on the planet because our mobile phones are trackable even when they're turned off. But are they?

Likewise, we have learned by watching films and television that the security services run a fleet of geostationary satellites that can read the sell-by date on a strawberry-flavoured yoghurt. Is this for real? Again, we don't know.

We do know the police can gain access to every text message you've sent – and possibly every email as well – within a certain time frame. But we don't know what kind of permission they need to telephone Vodafone and say, 'Hand over the info.'

We learned after the Russian airliner was brought down in Egypt recently that Western intelligence agencies were able retrospectively to identify chatter on social media that hinted at an attack. But were they? Or is that just a bit of PR to make us more inclined to support those deep packet inspection probes?

This murkiness is of course important. Because if we don't know what our security services can do, then the terrorists don't know either. That's why it's important to keep on filling the internet and the nation's pubs with claims and counterclaims and conspiracy theories.

I sat next to a cyber-security expert at dinner the other night and he said that if you gave him a laptop and an aerial he could kill any diabetic with a hi-tech insulin pump in about twenty minutes. When I asked him about people with pacemakers, he said, 'I wouldn't even need the aerial.'

Is medical wi-fi security really that lax? I only have his word for it. It is said North Korean agents managed to hack into Sony's emails. And they were using nothing but two beetroots and some coal. So what can the CIA do with all its cloak-and-dagger hi-tech wizardry? More? Who knows?

Did you know that you can switch someone's phone on without them knowing? Well, you can. Apparently. You send it a text that turns on the microphone. So then you can listen to every word its owner is saying, even though the screen is dark and silent.

Certainly, it's very easy to hack into an Android phone. Though when I say 'certainly', what I mean is 'probably'. And before iPhone users get all smug, let's not forget what happens when you put your nipples on iCloud. Next thing you know, they're on YouPorn.

Time and again we are told that by far the safest way to hold a conversation in secret is while playing electronic games on a PlayStation. Do you believe that? Or is it a clever scheme dreamed up by Messrs Bond and Bourne to get disaffected Muslim youths to converse openly on a channel that appeals to them and that in actual fact is as secure as a piggy bank?

Which brings us back to the so-called snooper's charter. It worries me, if I'm honest, because if the government sets out exactly what's legal and what's not, all the murkiness and subterfuge is gone. This means that Johnny Terrorist can work up a strategy that allows him to remain in the electronic shadows.

Far better, surely, to maintain the mystery. To keep him guessing. To force him to communicate with a pen and paper and a stamp.

Though there is even a danger there, because forcing him to return to the Stone Age is kind of what he wanted in the first place.

22 November 2015

Come on, Charles: put Frankenfish and bio bees in your world peace plan

Oh, how we laughed when Charlotte Church went on *Question Time* recently and told the audience of lunatics and lefties that the conflict in Syria was caused by global warming. But it turns out that she has a powerful ally – the future king of England.

Yup, Prince Charles will head to Paris tomorrow to tell a conference on climate change that the city was attacked recently because of your local pub's patio heaters and that the Russian jet was brought down last Tuesday because so many people are now driving around in those Range Rover thingies.

Well, Your Royal Highness, I've done some checking and it turns out that the Su-24 was actually brought down by an AIM-120 Amraam missile fired from an F-16 Fighting Falcon aircraft. My Range Rover had nothing to do with it.

But let's say for a moment that the powerful double act of Charles and Church is correct and that global warming is to blame. This of course means that we have to forget the problems caused by Winston Churchill drawing up borders in the Middle East with no regard for Sunni and Shi'ite sensibilities.

We must also forget the woeful idiocy of George Bush Sr, who went all weak-kneed in the first Gulf conflict, and the astounding stupidity of George Bush Jr and Mr Blair, who eventually did remove Saddam Hussein, even though they had no plan for any kind of replacement.

Other things we must forget are the rousing rhetoric of Western leaders, who a year ago were ready to support any group that wanted to overthrow Syria's regime and who are now dead set on keeping Bashar al-Assad in the hot seat, and the tribal issues, which are as old as the hills.

And the Kurds. And the mysteries of Islam. And the sense among Muslim youths that America is somehow out to nail anyone with a tea towel on his head. Yes. We must forget all that and assume that all was well in the region until 2007, when the summer was a bit warmer than usual.

This, according to Charles and Charlotte, meant the crops failed, and that meant people who lived off the land were forced into the towns and cities, where for reasons that are a bit unclear, if I'm honest, they decided life would be better if they threw a homosexual off a tall tower and set fire to their next-door neighbour.

And that in turn led to Turkey's Roy Lichtenstein shouting, 'Fox three,' and pressing the Fire control that unleashed his Amraam into the back bottom of the poor comrade's Su-24.

If you squint a bit and don't think too hard, you can just about see that this makes sense. But what exactly are we supposed to do about it? Sell our patio heaters and Range Rover thingies in the hope the world cools down and the ISIS fighters put away their AKs and go back to a life of goats? I'm not sure that's realistic.

Or are we supposed to draw a lesson from what's happened in Syria and resolve to peg climate change where it is? Because if things stay as they are, the farmers of, say, Devon will never be compelled to come to London one day to set fire to Graham Norton.

Nor would the good people of Cardiff wake one morning to find the streets have been taken over by a load of disgruntled sheep farmers who've been driven from the high ground and are now embarking on a life of bank robbery and global terrorism.

This is what Charles and Charlotte seem to be saying: that when simple country people have a bad year on the farm, they are filled with an overwhelming desire to explode in a Belgian shopping centre.

Well, if that's the case, Charles must stand up in Paris and tell the delegates that, if we want to prevent another country from falling into the clutches of a lunatic mob, scientists must be allowed to develop genetically modified food that can grow to be strong and delicious with very little water.

After the audience has taken this in and the applause has died down, he must adopt a serious face, look straight into the camera and tell Greenpeace activists to stop rolling around on these crops every time they are tested and, to hammer his point home, he should then hold aloft a genetically modified salmon that in one of the farms throughout Panama and Canada became fully grown and ready for the pot in half the normal time.

Then he needs to eat it, possibly with a bit of hydroponic lettuce drizzled with some biotech corn oil. Afterwards, he should grin and rub his tummy and say: 'Yum, yum.'

He needs to say that last year in the United States 94 per cent of all soya beans, 96 per cent of all cotton and 93 per cent of all corn was genetically modified in some way. And then, to show he cares, he must make a plea for this incredible engineering to make its way to the poorer parts of the world as soon as possible.

Because who's going to buy a manky Syrian goat when for half the price they can buy a tasty in vitro burger that – and I'm not making this up – was never part of an animal? It's made from meat that was grown in a Petri dish, in a lab.

Charles needs to be spooning the stuff down like a five-year-old at a jelly party as he tells the audience how meat made by Brains out of *Thunderbirds* rather than by Farmer

Giles requires almost no land, how there's none of the methane you get from cows and how it would end the debate on factory farming. He needs to sell this stuff as though his life depended on it. Which, if you share his views, it does.

In short, Charles and Charlotte need to stop telling us about all the problems we're creating. And start promoting, enthusiastically, all the solutions.

Of course, he will say it's absurd to suggest global terrorism can be ended by science meat and a genetically altered bee. But he was the one who started it by saying the attacks in Paris were caused by my patio heater.

29 November 2015

Officer, arrest that man – he's all too easily offended by Fury's piffle

A friend was burgled last weekend. And stand by for a shock because by Wednesday a suspect had been arrested and was in a cell. I thought that sort of thing didn't happen any more. I thought the police no longer even investigated burglaries because they were far too busy interviewing people who'd said something that someone else thought was horrid.

We learned recently that a boxing champion of some sort called Tyson Fury had said in an interview that the devil will come to the Earth and do what devils do just as soon as abortion, homosexuality and paedophilia are all legalized.

The thrust of his argument was that in the 1950s nobody would ever have believed that one day it'd be legal to do sex with someone of the same genital grouping. In the same way as, now, we cannot believe that kiddie-fiddling could one day be considered acceptable. But that maybe . . . who knows?

As a result, many people vowed to not buy Mr Fury's calendar this Christmas. Others went further and tried asking the BBC to make sure he was not shortlisted for a gong at the annual Sports Personality of the Year bash.

That's an absurd idea because all Fury has done is tell the world that he's a bit dim. And if the BBC were forced to shortlist only those with a reasonably high IQ, the Sports Personality of the Year could be a held in a shed.

One person, however, decided that trying to get a dim man banned from appearing in the same room as lots of other dim men and women was nowhere near harsh enough. He reckoned that Mr Fury needed bringing down a peg or two so he reported him to the police, who confirmed last week that the boxing and Jesus enthusiast will now be questioned.

Yup. A chap whose job is to beat other men to a pulp is going to be questioned by officers because officially one man – one – was upset by something he'd said. Whatever happened to sticks and stones?

I've been in Mr Fury's shoes. A number of years ago I said while appearing on *Have I Got News for You* that I run over foxes for fun and the next thing I knew two burly police-menists were sitting in my conservatory, drinking a half of pale ale and scratching their heads.

Someone had complained to the Met and the Met had asked the CNPD (Chipping Norton Police Department) to dispatch Starsky and Hutch to my house for a bit of a shake-down. They'd arrived in a bit of a fluster because they weren't quite sure what was going on.

Were they there to see if I really had said I'd run over a fox for fun, which we all agreed was a bit pointless because anyone could clearly have heard and seen me saying it on television? Or were they there to see if I actually had run over a fox for fun?

If I hadn't, then is it a crime to say that I had? And if I had, is that a crime at all? We weren't sure. Certainly, we all agreed that it would be jolly difficult in a court to prove that the fox-flattening incident was for fun or because the stupid thing was crossing the road without looking. In the end, we filled in lots of forms that were sent back to the Met in London and then . . . nothing happened.

I can pretty much guarantee that this is what's going to happen with Mr Fury. Two policemen will arrive at his caravan. They will ask him if he really did suggest that homosexuals are the same as paedophiles and then, after establishing that he did, or didn't, they'll fill in a load of paperwork, get his auto-graph and a couple of selfies and that will be the end of that.

We need to be clear on something here. There is a very big difference between an angry mob in Ku Klux Klan head-dresses chanting and parading outside the house of a homosexual couple and a God-bothering sportsman tarring gays and paedophiles with the same brush.

Let's be frank. He wasn't urging gangs of young men to grab a selection of shovels and pickaxe handles and maraud around Soho looking for Julian Clary.

He wasn't suggesting that homosexuals should be castrated or put into a camp of some sort. He was simply saying that, as a Christian, he found the notion of legalized gay sex repellent.

You may not agree with that. I know I don't. But it is Mr Fury's right as a citizen of this country to express his views. And it is your right to stick your fingers in your ears and go, 'La-la-la-la-la-la-la,' if you don't want to hear them.

It is also your right to telephone the police and make a formal complaint. And then it's their duty to send two constables round to see what's what. And that's the problem. Because Mr Fury plainly wasn't inciting any form of hatred. I've listened to the tape, and all he was doing was spouting a load of religious gobbledegook. Go down to Speakers' Corner in Hyde Park on a Sunday morning and you'll hear far worse.

Plainly, then, something needs to be done, but what? We need a law that prevents so-called hate preachers from urging extremely impressionable young men to explode in a shopping centre. But that law cannot be used to stop Jimmy Carr telling jokes about rape. Or Mr Fury being anti-gay, or me saying I ran over a fox for fun.

Happily, I've come up with a plan. It's very simple. If, after questioning Mr Fury, no action is taken, the police should then go round to the house of the man who made the complaint and arrest him for wasting police time. And to help them out with that, his name is Ian Sawyer. He's fifty-five. He's from Manchester. And he looks a bit like a potato.

This is the only way to make the professionally offended think twice before picking up the phone. They have to understand that, if they make a complaint and they're wrong, they are going to get punished for being a crybaby.

13 December 2015

The signs said New York but it looked just like London and felt like hell

At this time of year many people decide that they should go on a Christmas-shopping trip to New York. And, having given the matter some serious thought in the past couple of minutes, I'm fairly sure it's the stupidest idea in all of Christendom.

Unless you are one of those pouting imbeciles with expensive hair whose sole ambition is to appear in the *Mail Online*'s sidebar of shame, Christmas shopping is not even on nodding terms with the concept of fun. It's too hot because you are wearing a big coat. And because you are wearing a big coat, you knock a lot of stuff off shelves. And then you end up with too many bags and the handles are digging into your fingers so you think you have gangrene, and your car's parked miles away and it's raining and the pavements are full of people moving at one mile an hour and you are racked with guilt because you have bought your daughter's boyfriend some corn-on-the-cob forks and he's going to know they cost only £2.99 and your daughter's going to know it too and then she isn't going to speak to you until Easter Monday.

So why, when you know it's going to be like this, would you choose to do it in New York, where the people move even more slowly and the shops are even hotter and you can't work out what anything costs and you can't have a cigarette anywhere and, on top of all that, you've got jet lag and you want to go to bed, even though it's only four in the afternoon?

There's another problem with New York. You get to the airport in London, you let someone take a photograph of your breasts, you get undressed and they take away your Nivea in case you decide on the flight to moisturize the pilot to death, and then finally you are allowed into the perfume shop that stands between you and your gate.

And by the time you've done all this, you could have completed all your Christmas shopping in your local town, gone home, wrapped everything and watched half of *Pointless*.

Instead, however, you are facing a seven-hour flight, seven hours in a queue for immigration and a seven-hour taxi ride to the wrong address in the wrong part of the wrong borough because the driver couldn't understand a word of what you were saying and had arrived in America on the flight before yours.

Eventually, though, you will find yourself in Manhattan, rumbling 'through the concrete canyons to the midtown lights, where the latest neon promises are burning bright'. I think that's from a song. But no matter, because shortly afterwards you'll emerge, blinking, into the brawl that is Fifth Avenue, where you will find that all the shops are familiar. That's because you passed every single one of them on the long and dreary trudge from security to the gate at Heathrow. You also passed them the last time you went to the Village at Westfield. And when you were on holiday in Marbella.

It doesn't matter, though. There are so many people on Fifth Avenue doing their Christmas shopping that you have about as much of a say in where you go as a Pooh stick. Which means that pretty soon you'll find yourself pinned against some kind of diddy skating rink, much like the one at Somerset House in London.

You hope that you'll see a fully grown man fall over, but none does, and then you are jettisoned from the eddy and, if you're lucky, you'll end up at your hotel, which almost certainly will be owned by a British company and staffed by British people.

The next day you'll head into SoHo, where you will be carried past shops such as Jo Malone, Stella McCartney, Ben Sherman, Barbour and Dr Martens, until you end up in Greenwich Village at Myers of Keswick. Or the Spotted Pig. Or maybe back where you started, at Soho House. (Branches in Shoreditch, Notting Hill, Chiswick and Chipping Norton are also available.)

I noticed this phenomenon the first time I went to New York. Adrian Gill took me to see the 'real' America. Which involved staying at a British-owned hotel, taking tea with Robbie Williams and meeting lots of people I dimly remembered from drinks parties in South Kensington.

I went there again last weekend and the London connection was even more pronounced. In two days I went to the opening of Lloyd Webber's new show, *School of Rock*, and then to a party where I bumped into the chief executive of *The New York Times*, who's called Mark Thompson and used to run the BBC, and Shaun Woodward, who was an MP for various parties until recently. Oh, and the jewellery designer Theo Fennell. Desperate to hear an American accent, I went back to my hotel, where sitting at the bar was the former BBC presenter Richard Bacon.

I do not know of two cities anywhere in the world which are as similar as New York and London. Moscow, Sydney, Vancouver, Buenos Aires, Rome – they're all different. But New York and London? No. One's a bit taller than the other and one is wider. But that's it.

Both have pronounced and quite small districts that come with different smells and a different vibe. Both hum with pent-up energy. Both – these days, at least – have taxi drivers who are useless. Both are filled with people from everywhere else. Both are financial hubs and shopping centres. And both are located on islands off the coast of America.

Choosing to do your Christmas shopping in New York, then, is like driving hundreds of miles this morning to buy your copy of *The Sunday Times*. What's the point when the one available right on your doorstep is exactly the same?

Well, not exactly. New York may be full to overflowing with British people and British shops and British businesses and British hotels, but when you ask for a cup of tea, the staff are still baffled by the recipe. Which means that after an hour or so you'll get a cupful of lukewarm water with a small bag of what appears to be bark.

20 December 2015

Hallelujah, Reverend! This hymn hater has seen the happy-clappy light

I woke last Tuesday with a heavy heart because I had to spend the morning lying on my back with a man in my mouth, and the evening in a church, listening to Hector the Rector prattling on about the virgin birth, like it really happened.

I would love to tell you that the dentist wasn't as bad as I had feared. But I can't. Because it was. But the church service was a revelation. It was fantastic. I actually sang, loudly and lustily, and I clapped, and when it was over I was sad because I wanted more.

School for me was ruined by two things: Shakespeare and God. Mostly God, because on a Sunday morning I would have to get up at crikey o'clock and put on a suit and a tie so that I could spend an hour worshipping someone who never wore much more than a loincloth.

I hated the hymns very much, apart from 'Jerusalem', which isn't a hymn at all, but what I hated most of all was the seriousness of it all. We were all gathered together to talk and sing about a fairy tale but anyone caught laughing, or smoking, or having a good time in any way was given a detention. Which meant sitting in a room the following weekend reading more bloody Shakespeare.

I vowed when I left school that I would never set foot in a church ever again. But of course, things didn't work out that way because there would be weddings and christenings and now, I'm sad to say, funerals. Not that you can tell any of these things apart.

They're all just as miserable as one another. Because you're in a suit and you have to mumble while someone mangles his way through the hymns on the organ, and then an old man gets into the pulpit and gives you a Form I V B interpretation of some tiny passage from the Bible, during which you are invited not to find any joy at all.

I went recently to a Catholic memorial and oh my bloody God. On and on went the priest, about the lamb of God and how we were all basically evil and only for about four seconds were we allowed to celebrate the life of the poor man whom God had killed, because let's not forget that, alongside all the bright and beautiful things he created, he also invented cancer and mites that eat children's eyes.

At this point, I should say that I have no problem with those who choose to believe or even those who put a hat on and waddle down to their local church on a Sunday to do a bit of mumbling. They are old and they are clinging to the prospect that when this life is over, there will be another, in heaven. There's no harm in that. Mostly.

But I do have a problem with the way the established churches are run in this country. There's too much lecturing and too many giant thermometers in the graveyard urging us to help God's accountants pay for a new roof. Why does it never occur to them to get Michael McIntyre or John Bishop into the pulpit to give their spin on how the meek will inherit the Earth?

Why don't they try, just once in a while, to make us happy rather than guilty? And at this point we get back to where I began, on Tuesday evening, at the first church service I have ever enjoyed.

It was full, as is usual, of lots of middle-aged and elderly people in suits. And naturally, there were a few bored-looking children with side partings and school coats, wondering why they couldn't have been left at home to play *Grand Theft Auto*.

However, up at the front, where you would normally expect to find an old man in a frock, there was a gospel choir. Which was made up of what I can only describe as several sets of lungs with hair. God, they were loud.

Of course, because the audience was white and middle class and middle-aged, we had no idea what to do. I guess many of us had seen a gospel choir in a film and I don't doubt that, like me, we had all thought, 'How quaint.' But here we were, face to face, and we had no idea what to do.

They were giving it the full Aretha Franklin and we wanted to bop along, but we were in a church so, obviously, that wasn't allowed. Except it was, because after the first song one of the singers turned round and, in so many words, said, 'Come on, everyone. Why don't you get off your bony white arses and join in?'

So we did. We belted out 'I Say a Little Prayer' and 'I Can See Clearly Now' and, yes, at one point I was even up to eleven while singing something by Boney M. By the time we got to the encore, which was 'O Come, All Ye Faithful', we were louder than AC/DC.

Gospel has its roots in Africa, where song is based on a system of call and response. The singers give you a line, and then you repeat it. Which is ideal if you can't afford a hymn book or you can't read. And because they could afford no instruments, they used the human voice for the music, and clapping for the rhythm section.

As you would imagine, it was decried, when it first surfaced in America, for destroying the dignity of songs that were written to serve God. I think that's rubbish. I think songs are often enhanced with some gospel-inspired backing vocals. Blur. Madonna. U2. They would agree with that.

But you judge for yourself. Next Christmas, if you feel obliged to worship the baby Jesus in some way, don't bother with Rick the Vic and his wonky organ. Say no to the uncomfortable pews and the old ladies in hats and try a bit of happy-clappy gospel.

I would go even further. The Church of England is in dire trouble. Visitor numbers are falling. Congregations are dying, literally. And there seems no hope. But there is. Simply make the next Archbishop of Canterbury black and let him fill his churches every Sunday with some Boney M and Johnny Mathis. It'll be standing room only.

27 December 2015

Pipe down, mudslingers. It was Frank, not Phil, that soaked the north

As the north of England gradually sank beneath the swirling brown torrent, we learned that Sir Philip Dilley, the boss of the Environment Agency, and therefore the man responsible for the nation's flood defences, was sunning himself in Barbados.

Naturally, we were invited to sneer at this ne'er-do-well who takes our money to do a job and then buggers off to the Caribbean whenever the weather turns iffy.

But hang on a minute: let's just say for the moment that Sir Dilley had cancelled his winter-holiday plans. Let's say that, instead of heading for Gatwick to board a plane to Barbados, he'd got on a train and headed instead for Carlisle. What difference would that have made?

The rain would still have fallen. The rivers would still have burst their banks. A thousand DFS sofas would still have been ruined. And Robert Hall would still have been on the news every night, in his logo-less wellies, telling us about northern grit.

When it became obvious that a street was in danger of being submerged, did the shopkeepers stand quivering in their store rooms saying, 'We have no idea what to do. If only the boss of the Environment Agency was here to offer some kind of guidance'?

When that bus became trapped in the torrent, did the fire brigade rush about in panicky circles, waving their arms in the air, saying, 'Everyone onboard will surely die because Sir Dilley is not here to tell us how to inflate our dinghies'?

Actually, I should imagine that the people on the ground were quite grateful that he was in Barbados, because if he'd turned up in his gabardine, and his new Christmas jumper, they'd have had to stop rescuing people and make him a cup of tea.

We saw this with David Cameron. He was in flood-hit towns, shaking hands with various flood-relief workers, who, because they were shaking hands with the prime minister, were not doing any actual flood-relief work.

It's therefore better that politicians and civil servants stay away whenever the weather girds its loins. Their job is to sit down after the flood waters have gone away and the DFS sofas have been replaced to work out how best such problems can be prevented in future.

For evidence of this you need look no further than the Lake District when the first storm came roiling in from the west. I can't remember its name. Eunice, probably. Or Brian. Whatever, a local engineering company immediately dispatched its men and its heavy equipment to solve the problem, which they did in short order.

A couple of days later the town was threatened once more, but this time the boss of the local engineering company was told by police chiefs obsessed with health and safety that it was too dangerous for his men to work. So, because these police chiefs were on the ground, and not on holiday in Barbados, thousands of people spent their Christmas scraping raw sewage from their plug sockets and cooking their turkeys with a candle.

Exactly the same thing happened again this week when Storm Frank came barrelling over the Pennines. Homeowners were told to stop protecting their property with sandbags and leave the area immediately. The chief constables were running around as if a giant meteorite was on its way. 'There is a danger to life,' they shrieked.

This is the first thing Sir Dilley should do. Tomorrow morning he should hold a meeting in his office with various people from the police and the Met Office. And he should tell them in a special stern voice that in future they've got to calm down and stop pretending that above-average rainfall is an extinction-level event.

Afterwards he should ask local councils if they'd offer grants to any homeowner who's put decking over their back garden and turned their front lawn into a car park if they'd put it all back as it was, to give the rainwater a chance to soak away before it gets to the greengrocer's.

Sadly, though, Sir Dilley will not be able to take any of these practical steps because on Monday he will almost certainly be in a headhunter's office, having lost what the *Daily Mail* calls his '£100,000-a-year, three-day-a-week cushy number at the Environment Agency'.

This, I think, is actually the biggest problem facing Britain today. Whenever a problem arises, the boss is invariably blamed and then sacked before he has a chance to make sure it doesn't arise again.

It's all rooted in a disease that causes rational people to hate anyone who is moderately successful or lucky or beautiful. We're invited to rejoice if we see a spot of cellulite on Kate Moss's thighs. We are encouraged to laugh openly if a lottery winner loses his fortune in some way. And we are invited to sneer if a politician has the temerity to go on a foreign holiday.

You may be aware of the 'Rich Kids of Instagram' feed. It's a place where children of the well-off post photographs of themselves drinking champagne and wearing watches the size of a medium-sized tortoise. If I were a teenager and I looked at all those pictures, I'd be inspired to get a good job and work hard. But no. Instead of thinking, 'One day I shall be able to provide all that,' the disease makes us think, 'Right.

What can I do to make sure they lose their watches and their champagne?'

In short: money, if you've earned it, is bad enough; but money, if you haven't, is unforgiveable.

All of which means that just a day after Sir Dilley got back from his holiday in Barbados, he was described on his Wikipedia page as an 'upper-class twerp'.

He certainly isn't a twerp, because he gained a first-class honours degree in civil engineering. And I'm not sure about the upper-class bit either, because his only political contribution has been £2,000. To the Scottish Labour Party.

All I do know is that we pay him to do a job. And now we must leave him alone so that he can get on and do it.

3 January 2016

Kim has a bomb. No need for panic – just fire up the Roman candles

It was a tremendous week for the glorious leader of the Workers' Revolution Party, who, using cunning and guile, stunned the world by taking three days to reorganize his Cabinet.

Meanwhile, in North Korea, another glorious leader of another Workers' Revolution Party went one stage further and, in a deep pit near the Chinese border, set off a hydrogen bomb.

Or did he? North Korea's Fiona Bruce, who delivers her news bulletins by shouting while wearing a nylon baby-doll ballgown, certainly seemed to think so. She said the country had successfully detonated an H-bomb, and then, after a short commercial break in which stirring music was shown over a fetching picture of Kim Jong-Corbyn, she announced that America was an imperialist dog. Only less delicious.

Naturally, all the Western leaders were very cross about this new development. 'We are very cross about this,' said Philip Hammond, Britain's Foreign Secretary. Chinese leaders were cross too, because the blast had caused cracks to appear in a school playground on their side of the border.

And that, really, is when the penny started to drop. 'Hang on,' thought the world's experts. 'If this really was a hydrogen bomb, then surely it would have caused more damage than cracks in a school playground.' 'Yes,' said the world's seismologists. 'It caused only a very small shudder. Our needles would have rocked more if a fatty such as Kim Jong-un had fallen down the stairs.'

At this stage it's important to understand the difference

between a simple atomic bomb – the sort that was dropped on Japan towards the end of the Second World War – and the much more fearsome hydrogen bomb, which uses a normal atomic explosion to trigger a far larger, thermonuclear reaction.

Russia has set off a thermonuclear bomb with the explosive force of 50 million tons of TNT. Detonate one of those a thousand feet above London and the windows in Cairo would rattle. Whereas North Korea's bomb only managed to crack a school playground a hundred miles or so away. Boffins are saying it was a device of about six kilotons, which in the West is known as a 'firework'.

As a tool for scaring its enemies into acquiescence, then, Fatty-un's bomb is about as effective as a pair of slippers. But then along came a former British ambassador to North Korea, who told the *Daily Mail* that this was just the start. He said that if the bomb could be made to work, and that if it could be militarized so that it would fit into a missile, and that if that missile could be loaded into a submarine, then Jong-un's glorious navy could sail undetected through the Solent and, with no warning at all, damage school playgrounds all the way from Ringwood to Buckler's Hard.

That sounds very terrifying, but there are a lot of 'if's, chief among which is this submarine business. We were told last year that North Korea had indeed launched a nonnuclear test missile from a sub, but it later emerged that actually it had been from a submerged barge.

The North Korean navy appears to be not very good. It runs two fleets, one on the west coast and one on the east. This is because the vessels it has are not capable of getting from one side of the country to the other. When it stages manoeuvres, one or two ships usually sink.

Some, however, sink on purpose. These are submarines.

Mostly they are tiny little things that have been abandoned by most navies for being completely useless. But there is talk that North Korea has built itself a much bigger vessel based on a 1960s Yugoslavian design.

Hmmm. I once flew across Cuba in a 1950s Russian aircraft that had spent most of its life in the Angolan air force, and that was pretty ropy.

But a Yugoslavian-designed submarine that was built in North Korea. It's hard to think of anything less likely to work. Especially after the chef has loaded up the larder with several dozen excitable spaniels.

Let's say, however, that it does. And let's say that they manage to fit it with a tube from which this thermonuclear missile can be fired. Does anyone seriously think it'll be able to sail all the way from the Sea of Japan to the Solent without being detected?

It runs on diesel power, which means it has to stay on the surface most of the time. And what are people on cruise liners and cargo ships going to say when it burps and belches its way past them? 'Ooh, look, a big dead whale with a weird metal erection.'

This is what the world always seems to forget when it comes to nuclear weapons. You may be able to build one, but then you have the problem of getting it to explode over the city of your choice.

During a recent bout of tension between India and Pakistan, I asked an Indian chap if his country's nuclear missiles would be capable of hitting Islamabad. 'I'm not even sure they could hit Pakistan,' he replied.

We saw only recently four Russian cruise missiles sailing over their targets in Syria and landing hundreds of miles away in Iran. And somehow we are expected to believe that North Korea is on the verge of developing a missile that can be fired from underwater and will then guide itself to Wilton Avenue in Southampton.

Well, I don't, which is why I sniggered when Philip Hammond responded to Fatty-un's underground firework explosion by saying he would be pushing for a robust response.

What form will that take? A strongly worded letter? Or is he saying we should order one of our subs to wipe Pyongyang off the map? I suppose we can take comfort from this: at least we have a choice. If Comrade Corbyn ever gets into the hot seat and Trident is abandoned, we won't.

10 January 2016

I stand before the Twitter Inquisition, guilty of not worshipping Bowie

As you may have heard, David Bowie is dead. And all week we've been told very forcefully that he was an inspiration, a genius and a force for good in a troubled world. Flowers were laid outside his New York home. There were outpourings of grief all over the world. And the television schedules were cleared to make way for hastily prepared look-back documentaries. David Cameron didn't actually interrupt Parliament to say Bowie was 'the people's pop star', but I bet it crossed his mind.

The next day every newspaper carried page after page of thousand-word think pieces from anyone who had access to a computer. 'I once stood next to him at a urinal and remember well how thoroughly he washed his hands afterwards.' 'I saw him driving a car once and it struck me then how down to earth he was.'

I was caught up in the mood of the moment and opened Twitter to say something respectful and emotive. But here's the thing. I was too consumed by sadness about the death of Ed 'Stewpot' Stewart to think of anything sensible.

It's not that I didn't like Bowie. I did. 'Modern Love' is the only song that can get me on a dancefloor. I chose 'Heroes' as one of my Desert Island Discs. And *Hunky Dory* is one of only two albums yet recorded on which I like every single track. The other is *Who's Next*, in case you're interested.

But of course you're not interested because, even now, a week after Bowie's death, I bet you're still running around with a lightning bolt on your face, playing 'Ashes to Ashes' over and over and weeping as you plan your candlelit vigil outside his dad's former home in Tadcaster, North Yorkshire.

Furthermore, I bet you're still reeling from my claim that I'm more shocked and saddened about the death of Ed 'Stewpot' Stewart. I am, though. Ed Stewart was the sound of my childhood. I once asked him to play 'Clair' by Gilbert O'Sullivan for my sister on his *Junior Choice* show and he declined. Even then he could see that a song about a fully grown man's love for a small girl was somehow wrong.

Sadly, though, I am unable to wax lyrical at any length about dead Ed because that will be seen as disrespectful to Bowie. And this is my big problem.

My colleague Camilla Long fell into a similar trap. As people headed off last week to Brixton, Bowie's south London birthplace, with hopeless little tea lights and *Spiders from Mars* scarves, she spoke out on Twitter about the need to 'man up', commenting that all the grief was 'deeply insincere', and was widely condemned.

At dinner on Monday I said I'd been more upset when Clarence Clemons from the E Street Band died, and immediately there was a stunned silence. Even if I'd vomited in their food, the other guests couldn't have been more horrified. 'You can't say that,' said one young woman after she'd been brought round with an adrenaline shot to her heart.

But I can say that. And I did. Because who says we must all have a hive mentality? The problem is widespread now. If you were to go on to Twitter or FaceCloud or whatever and say that you didn't give a stuff about Syria's refugees, you would be torn limb from limb. The queen bee has decided that we little worker bees will be sympathetic to their plight, and that's that. We are.

It's the same story with David Cameron. No one is allowed

to say out loud that they like him. In the same way as no one is allowed to say they don't like Judi Dench.

Cycling is a good thing. And all cyclists are saints. Someone decided that this is so, and somehow it has now become the law. And anyone who dares to flout that law will find himself in the court of YouTube, where he will be sentenced to spend the rest of his life as a quivering hermit.

There used to be something called political correctness, which was an invisible force field around race, gender and sexual orientation. In many ways it wasn't a bad thing. But now its tentacles have become endless and have spread into pretty much every aspect of our lives.

Being fat? That's not allowed. And neither is being thin. Being rich is evil. Being poor is noble. Being rich and giving your money away to the poor is Bono-ish and therefore to be sneered at. Suggesting quietly that paedophiles have an illness and should be treated for it rather than set on fire is idiotic. Being a paedophile is the worst thing in the world.

All rape is exactly the same. Anyone who drives an expensive car is fundamentally bad. McDonald's is wrong. Starbucks is the devil. Taylor Swift isn't. Global warming is definitely caused by man. Sean Penn is a hero. Donald Trump's a moron. All nurses are angels, all hospital managers are bunglers, supermarkets are money-grabbing bastards and the EU is a complete waste of everyone's afternoon.

These are all rules. You may not disagree with any of them. If you do, within earshot of someone else, you will be beaten with sticks.

Much the same fate now awaits anyone who says, 'I mourn David Bowie's passing but I didn't like some of his music and I thought that most of his outfits were pretentious twaddle. And, while I'm at it, what was *Merry Christmas, Mr Lawrence* all about?'

Try saying that in public and pretty soon you'll learn what it's like to drown in spittle.

The fact is, though, David Bowie wasn't in the prime of his life, speeding through a tunnel, and neither was he in an open-top Lincoln on a sunny drive through Dallas: he'd run his body ragged with a rock'n'roll lifestyle, and he died from cancer, aged sixty-nine, which until quite recently would have been considered a ripe old age.

It's sad that he's died, but please don't demand that I wander about in public shedding tears that aren't real.

17 January 2016

Transgender issues are driving me nuts. I need surgery on my tick boxes

Now that women can vote and homosexual couples can marry, you might imagine that the world's student activists, trade union leaders and environmentalists would pat themselves on the back and break open a bottle of sustainable elderflower juice to congratulate themselves on a job well done.

But no. They have decided that we must now all turn our attention to the plight of people who want to change their name from Stan to Loretta, and fight for the right for men to have babies.

I'll be honest. When this issue first began to surface a couple of years ago and we had pop stars such as Sir John running about, talking endlessly about the transgender cause, I did roll my eyes a bit. Because in the immortal words of Reg, from the People's Front of Judea, 'Where's the foetus going to gestate? You going to keep it in a box?'

As far as I was concerned, men who want to be women were only really to be found on the internet or in the seedier bits of Bangkok. They were called ladyboys, and in my mind they were nothing more than the punchline in a stag-night anecdote.

I wasn't alone either. Only recently I was chatting to a doctor about how people can now demand gender-reassignment surgery on the NHS and he said, 'I get lots of people in my surgery with a Napoleon complex. But I don't buy them a pointy hat and a French army uniform.' I found that funny.

But there's a distinctly unfunny side to the coin. Just recently some friends of friends were having one of their eight-year-old daughter's school chums round for a sleepover. As the day approached they received a call from the girl's parents, who said, 'Er, she's not actually a girl.'

She had been born a boy but had insisted from the age of three that she had a girl's name and wore girls' clothes and, later, that she went to a girls' school. And her parents had simply indulged this whim.

I was horrified. I wanted to seek them out and explain that they were free to live a lunatic life, washing their armpits with charcoal and liking Jeremy Corbyn's thoughts on how ballistic nuclear submarines must be built by the comrades and then used as flower pots. But they must not, and I was going to emphasize this with spittle, be allowed to poison the mind of a child.

When I was five I wanted to be Alan Whicker, but my parents didn't buy me a blazer and send me to hospital to have my adenoids sewn up. Other kids wanted to be super army soldiers or astronauts. It's what kids do: dream impossible dreams.

You don't actually take them seriously. You don't take them to a hospital when they're ten and say, 'He wants to be a girl, so can you lop his todger off?' Because what's going to happen five years later when he's decided that being a man isn't so bad after all and he's in the showers at the rugby club?

And there's more. Only last week we received news from the *Daily Mail* that at Isle of Wight prison nine inmates have decided they would like to be women and now want the NHS to stump up £100,000 for the necessary procedures.

Transgender enthusiasts talked with serious faces about how this demonstrated the scale of the problem and the horror of being a woman trapped not just inside a man's body but inside a man's prison as well.

Yes, but hang on just a cotton-picking minute. When I was

at school, I announced that I would like to be confirmed as a Christian. This was seen by teachers and my housemaster as a sign that I was growing up, so they happily agreed to my request.

And from that day on I was allowed to skip compulsory chapel on a Sunday morning – where you were checked and ticked off on a register – and go instead to the early-morning village communion service, where you weren't. Which meant I didn't have to go to church at all and could therefore spend all weekend with my girlfriend.

Can't anyone see, I wailed, that this is what's going on in the Isle of Wight nick? They tell the screws they want to be women, they get a bit of make-up and some breasts to play with and they are then transferred to a women's prison, where they can spend the rest of their lives being a lesbian. It's every man's dream.

To try to calm down a bit, I turned to the BBC for guidance, and there I was told there are 650,000 people living in Britain today with some kind of gender 'issue'. Well, I just sat there shaking my head, because the simple fact is: there aren't.

We are told that one in ten of the population is gay, that one in ten has cancer, that one in ten supports ISIS, that one in ten thinks Corbyn's doing a good job, that one in ten has a criminal record, that one in ten is living below the poverty line and that one in ten was born elsewhere, and now we are expected to believe that one in a hundred are transgender. Well, if that's so, it means that – according to my maths – fewer than three in ten are healthy, straight, honest, British people who don't want their genitals altered. And that's obviously rubbish.

But then I thought of something. Let's just say for a moment that one in a thousand are transgender. Or one in a hundred thousand. Or even that it's actually just one. Let's say that there is one person out there who is a woman living in a man's body, or the other way around.

I started to imagine what life might be like for the poor soul. It would be dreadful. Absolutely awful. And all they seem to want to make their life better is a third gender-option box on official documents. That's not really the end of the world for everyone else, is it?

24 January 2016

Utter even a kind word and the lefties' digital vitriol is instantly fizzing

Ever since the tie was invented, gentlemen of means have sent their sons away to a good boarding school where they would forge lifelong friendships with like-minded boys who'd go on to become useful-to-know captains of industry and world leaders. It was called 'the old boys' network'.

It didn't really work for me, if I'm honest. I don't see my school's magazine very often but the last time I looked, there was a letter from one of my former classmates saying he'd become a manager at United Biscuits. Another had written to say he's now a policeman.

However, the friends I met at school did introduce me to other friends, and now I have an address book that's full of people who have jets, and can get tickets to things, and generally make my life that little bit easier.

The old boys' network, however, is rather more than the professional equivalent of Disney's queue-jumper pass, because it meets in dusty clubs and it sorts out all kinds of political and strategic stuff that makes it easier for the privileged to keep on being privileged.

Those on the left have never had that luxury. Largely, they went to local state schools, where they met local people who could only dream of moving to Tamworth and becoming the manager of a biscuit company. They knew that out there, in the world, there were other people who shared their views, but as they never went on shooting weekends, they could never actually find them.

And when they tried to get organized and national, and

came up with secondary picketing, along came Mrs Thatcher, who said, 'Not on your nelly, comrade.' And banned it.

But then, all of a sudden, there was Twitter. And because of it, the lefties had a means of communication. Of finding one another. They had a network to rival the clubs of St James's and the picnics at Eton.

Today, Twitter is said to be in trouble and lots of people have come up with all sorts of reasons why rival social media sites such as Snapchat, which is where young men post pictures of their poos, and Instagram, where young women post pictures of their dogs, are powering ahead.

I used to like Twitter a lot. It was a fun place where clever people such as Giles Coren could condense their thoughts into a literary amuse-bouche. But now it's being policed by people who are furious about everything and everyone who isn't Jeremy Corbyn. As a result, it can often be very unpleasant.

Last week, in this column, I said that in the olden days I used to find the whole transgender issue either funny or annoying. But I concluded by saying that it must be awful to be trapped inside the wrong sort of body and that if these unfortunate souls want a third gender-option box to tick on a passport application form, no one should really mind.

And with wearisome predictability the *Mirror* completely ignored the conclusion and ran a story saying that I was a bigot who'd filled my newspaper column with transphobic invective. It uploaded this to the internet and that was that.

As is the way with modern media, the story spread rapidly, until by lunchtime Twitter had accepted it as fact and then carpet-bombed my phone with abuse. It was weird. I'd said very clearly that I sympathize with transgender people. I'd said they could have my support in their quest to be recognized as a third gender. And yet, despite this, I was drowning in their vitriol.

I'm not alone, of course. There was that woman who sent a tweet saying she was boarding a plane to Africa and that she wouldn't get AIDS while there because she was white. By the time she landed, Twitter had got her sacked.

Only last week Twitter noticed that the Christian names of Wayne Rooney's three children began with the letter K. This meant he was definitely a member of the Ku Klux Klan and as a result he must be taken out and shot as soon as possible.

I'll give you a dare. Go on to Twitter now and say something mildly right-wing. Say there are too many immigrants in Britain or that patio heaters didn't cause those sperm whales to beach themselves in Norfolk. Or that you've shot a badger. By teatime you'll have been made to feel like Hitler and it'll feel like the whole country wants you to commit suicide.

Of course, you can block users who are abusive, but that's like standing in a Bangladeshi sewer after Ramadan finishes. You can flail about as much as you like and wail loudly about the importance of free speech. But ultimately, you're going to get covered in excrement.

This is Twitter's big problem. It's being policed by the Stasi. And of course, when they react angrily to what you've said, the *Mirror* and the BBC and the *Guardian* see this as evidence that you've done something wrong. So they run a story saying, 'Twitter has reacted with fury . . .' which then causes the whole site to become angrier still. Really, they should drop that bird logo and replace it with an endlessly spinning red flag.

This, then, is not the sort of platform where advertising can thrive. Praise a restaurant or a shop, and there will be an immediate assumption that you've been paid off, using money that should have gone to a refugee, you bastard.

In this anti-capitalist world of Twitter's secret police, any attempt to market a good or service is met with derision. Sponsorship? Don't make me laugh. It would have been easier to get Leonid Brezhnev to wear a McDonald's badge on his hat. And as a result, trying to monetize Twitter is like trying to monetize Arthur Scargill's hair. It's not possible.

I think it's a shame. Twitter's a good idea. But these days it sounds like a sixth-form common room after the head-master has announced the guest speaker at tomorrow's assembly will be Katie Hopkins.

31 January 2016

Yo, kids, this morning's anti-drug message is brought to you by ISIS

In the beginning there was the war on drugs, and then after that hadn't been won, there was the war on terror, which isn't going terribly well either. And now everything has become very complicated because it seems the terror and the drugs have joined forces.

Reports suggest that ISIS is feeding its foot soldiers with an amphetamine called Captagon, and there's evidence to back this up. Last November Turkish anti-narcotics police confiscated a staggering 11 million pills that they say were on their way into Syria.

Apparently, if you take Captagon you feel invincible and wide awake and strong. And the effects are even more pronounced if you don't drink, which we must presume applies to the ISIS mob. In fact, you feel so awake and so invincible that you will happily strap some dynamite to your chest and then blow it up.

Well, now, I'm sorry, but how do the ISIS top brass make this sound attractive to their men? 'Come on, comrades. Take one of these pills and within the hour you will be human wallpaper.' If I were sitting there cross-legged on the floor, I'd put my hand up and say, 'If it's all the same to you, sir, I'd rather not.'

I see this problem with all drugs, in fact. Because who looks at someone who has ingested cocaine and thinks, 'Yes. I'd like to be boring and self-obsessed, so I will have some of that'? And who looks at people who've smoked weed and thinks, 'Yes. I want to find toothpaste funny and I want to be so hungry that I'll eat a sherry trifle sprinkled with frozen peas, so pass it over'?

On a recent trip to Burma I was taken to a party in a remote mountain village where everyone had taken something called yaba. Roughly translated, this means 'madness drug'. It is made from a mixture of caffeine and methamphetamine and was originally given to horses that were pulling heavy carts.

But then one day someone thought, 'I know. I'm going to put one of those horse pills in my mouth. And then I'm going to swallow it to see what happens.' What happened is that he turned, immediately, into a swivel-eyed lunatic. He became a rampaging bundle of taut sinew and spittle, massively angry about absolutely everything and extremely violent.

If you see someone who you think has taken yaba, here's a tip. Don't spill his pint. Especially if you are in Burma's Shan state, because here he will be furious – and armed with an AK-47.

Now, you would have thought that if you'd been in a bar, watching someone banging their head on the wall and shooting anyone who looked at him funnily, you'd think, 'Crikey. I must remember not to take what he's had.' But no. They didn't. For some reason they thought it would be fun to shoot their mother for putting too much milk on their cereal and tucked in.

I've never tried a Quaalude, but those I know who have done talk about it as though it's some kind of perfect nirvana. They go all dewy-eyed and misty about 'Ludes in the way that you and I go all dewy-eyed and misty when we recall childhood picnics and first kisses.

And I struggle to see why, because I've now seen *The Wolf of Wall Street*, and Leonardo DiCaprio made it very clear that actually Quaaludes cause you to crash your Lamborghini and roll around on the floor with what appears to be cerebral palsy. This looked a pretty good anti-drug message to me.

However, anti-drug people think they know better and are forever showing us pictures of dead drug runners in Colombia and comatose teenagers who've eaten some dodgy ecstasy at a nightclub in Preston. Obviously, this isn't working. Then you had Nancy Reagan with her famous 'Just say no' campaign, and that didn't work either, because what teenager would take a lecture from a woman who looked as if two crows had crashed into her face?

The most recent anti-drug push in America was even more hopeless. It used emojis, which, Grandad, are those little pictures you put at the end of a mobile-phone message if you want your text to be billed as a picture and you don't care because your parents are picking up the tab.

To you and me the anti-drug message just looked like gibberish. There were pictures that included a 'donut', a bee and a man putting something in a wastepaper basket, and none of it made any sense. But to a teenager the message was very clear. And what it said was: 'I do not have to be trashed to have fun.'

Amazingly, earnest charity people thought kids would see this and think, 'Ah. Whoever wrote that and put it on a billboard in Times Square understands my language, so next Saturday night, instead of smoking a joint with my friends, I shall go to the library and read some Hugh Walpole.'

There was another emoji ad that – if you were under thirty – said, 'I'm tired of drinking to fit in.' I'd love to see them run that in Newcastle.

Except I wouldn't, because it would be pointless and stupid. As pointless and stupid as showing kids how they will look if a drug takes hold of their life.

Because teenagers don't think much past tomorrow afternoon, which means they simply cannot see the possibility that one day they'll be turning tricks in a back street for a rock of crack.

'It won't happen to me' is what kept everyone sane in the trenches. And it's what keeps the lavatories packed at most nightclubs.

Far better, surely, to show them the Quaalude scene from *The Wolf of Wall Street*. To show them what drugs do in the here and now, not in twenty years' time and not to some low-life in a cartel on the other side of the world.

And I can think of no better place to start than Captagon. 'Take this and you'll be overcome by a need to go to a shopping centre and explode.'

7 February 2016

If you want the Oscar, Ridley, better start shooting *Blade Limper*

If you look carefully at all the people who've been nominated for a big award at the Oscars ceremony later this month, you will notice that none of them – not one – is a conjoined twin, or a man who's really a woman, or a dog. There's no one there whose mum took thalidomide, and none was born in Yorkshire. But everyone seems to have a bee in their bonnet about the single fact that none of them is black.

There was a photograph of all the hopefuls in the newspapers last week, and it was just a lot of rich people with one head each and four functioning limbs. It was billed as 'the white face(s) of Hollywood', and lots of people were very cross.

Some even pointed out that in the awards' near-ninety-year history only twelve non-US films have won Best Picture. And eleven of those were British.

But if you stop and think for a moment, you have to conclude that the silver screen is just about the least white place on Earth. You look at the really big film stars these days and for every Tom Cruise you have a Will Smith. For every Robert Downey Jr there's a Denzel Washington. And that's before we get to Morgan Freeman, Cuba Gooding Jr, Jamie Foxx, Forest Whitaker, Don Cheadle and Samuel L. Jackson. Oh, and this year's Oscars host, Chris Rock.

And while none of these guys is up for a big award this time round, you can hardly accuse the Academy Award judges of institutional racism or naked Trumpery because in 2014 it was a two-horse race between *Dallas Buyers Club*, which was about AIDS, and the eventual winner of Best

Motion Picture, *12 Years a Slave*, which was about being a slave for twelve years.

In 2006 *Crash*, which was an excellent film about racism, beat *Brokeback Mountain*, which was about homosexuality. In 2009 *Slumdog Millionaire*, which featured no white faces to speak of – not even Ben Kingsley's – walked off with the top gong, and in 2011 it was the turn of *The King's Speech*, which was about disability.

It's obvious, then, that the judges love a cause. They like a film that addresses issues and rights wrongs. And don't say they avoid giving the Best Actor award to a black man, because they gave one to Washington, Foxx and Whitaker, not to mention Sidney Poitier.

However, they have never once given the top gong to a superhero film. And a blockbuster in which a rock is heading our way never gets a look-in, although, that said, the alien-fest *District 9* was nominated. Mainly, I suspect, because actually it was about apartheid. This is my big problem with the Oscars. Anything even remotely populist is dismissed as being no better than the popcorn or the Palace Tandoori commercials.

And that brings me neatly on to Ridley Scott. He's an Englander and the son of an army officer and the list of films he's directed boggles the mind.

There was *Alien*, which we all know is a masterpiece. Then there was *Gladiator*, which managed to be huge and engrossing even though one of the main actors died halfway through the shoot.

Black Hawk Down, Black Rain, Hannibal, Thelma & Louise, Blade Runner, American Gangster, Robin Hood – you've seen them all many times. They form the spine of the DVD shelf in your sitting room. They are to the world of cinema what *Rumours* and *The Dark Side of the Moon* are to your record collection. And Ridley did them all.

You probably walked right past *Matchstick Men* one Sunday afternoon in your video-rental shop, assuming that because it starred Nicolas Cage it would be impenetrable nonsense. But it was an extremely good film about a chap with obsessive compulsive disorder. And it was the same story with *Someone to Watch Over Me*. Yes, it starred Tom Berenger, who came and went in *Platoon*. But, again, it was excellent. And they were Ridley's too.

Of course, there are some wonky moments in his back catalogue. *The Counsellor*, which starred absolutely everyone, was a bit of a mess, and I've tried many times to understand *Prometheus*. But it's like long division. I just don't get it.

Judging Ridley on these failures, though, would be like judging Paul McCartney on 'Ebony and Ivory', or Terry Wogan on 'The Floral Dance'. Because the fact is he's a staggeringly good and versatile director who makes films people want to see over and over again. And he's never won an Oscar.

He's up for Best Picture at the end of the month for *The Martian*, and I can pretty much guarantee he won't win, because it's too exciting and too funny and too popular. So he'll have to sit there and gurn as someone else goes on to the stage, and I don't doubt he'll feel gutted.

But cheer yourself up, Ridley, with something Jilly Cooper once said: 'Jeffrey Archer and I would trade all our sales for one prestigious literary award. In the same way that people who win prestigious literary awards would trade their statuette for a tenth of our sales.'

In a much smaller way, I know what she's on about, because Bafta never gave *Top Gear* an award. The great and the good from the world of British TV never thought our efforts were worthy of recognition, and I had to sit there in my frilly dinner shirt as someone who'd made a programme about social workers in Oldham was given the gong by someone who'd presented *Britain's Heaviest Paving Stone*.

I could smile, though, and I did, because our show was really popular with the viewers. And that's who we made it for. Not a dame from Islington.

The Revenant may win Best Picture. And Best Actor will probably go to Leonardo DiCaprio, who has never won before, probably because he's never been forgiven for being Jack Dawson in *Titanic*. That's fine. It's a good film and I enjoyed it.

But I enjoyed *Avengers: Age of Ultron* even more. And that hasn't even been nominated. An omission that, it should be noted, has nothing to do with the fact that Samuel L. Jackson is in it.

14 February 2016

I'm aching like billy-o and dying for a fag. It's a fat man's holiday

Very rich people are able to control their lives extremely well. They are able to control their sightlines and their address book and even the droopiness of their breasts. They never have to look for a parking space or pop to the shops for milk or sit next to someone on a plane. And they don't have to worry about how their children are doing at school, because whatever happens, they'll be fine in the end.

If you invite a very rich person to your house for dinner, they may well accept, but that doesn't necessarily mean they will turn up, because very rich people may decide at eight o'clock, when they should be getting ready, that they'd rather watch *Ray Donovan*, or go to St Moritz.

Very rich people are always doing precisely what they want to be doing at all times of day and night. And the moment something starts to be dreary, or damp, they just start doing something else.

However, there's one thing they can't control: their health. They can make sure that they are surrounded at all times by perfect people, perfect weather and perfect food and wine, but they cannot do a damn thing to stop one of their cells deciding one day to become cancerous.

Very rich people, however, will not accept this. They have it in their minds that because they breakfasted, in Rome, on an otter's nose, smeared with the still-warm earwax from a famous horse, that of course they can control their bodies too. So they go mad.

When a normal person goes on holiday, they get up in the

morning and immediately lie down again, in the sunshine, with a book. They relax until it's time for lunch, after which they find some dappled shade and go back to sleep again. Until it's time for dinner and bed.

Very rich people, however, do not see the typical holiday as a time for relaxation. They see it as an opportunity to stop their hearts bursting and their livers breaking down and their lungs becoming black and scabby and tumorous. They see holidays as an opportunity to buy a bit of 'extra time' at the end.

There's a small island in the Caribbean called Mustique, where very rich people get up in the morning, do exercise and then walk up and down some very steep hills. Read a book? Not a chance. Not when you could be on a tennis court, or a horse, or a treadmill.

The treadmill is almost certainly the world's biggest killer of very rich people. Some die because their designer clothes get caught in the rollers and they're strangled. Some because they fall over and hit their head. And some because their heart goes, 'What the hell are you doing?' and then explodes.

And so they lie there, having their faces rubbed off by the still-functioning belt, thinking in their dying moments that it's impossible. 'I bought my neighbour's house because I didn't like the sound of his children playing. I can control sound. So why am I dying?'

That's broadly what I thought this morning. I'm spending a few days with friends in Barbados and we are now at a stage in life when we too think that if we actually move around all the time, we'll buy ourselves a little bit longer in an old people's home.

And so this morning, instead of lying down with a book about a secret agent called Clint Thrust, I was to be found hurrying through a small fruit salad so that I could make it to my fitness session on time.

It was all quite jolly to start with. We made jokes and pulled faces as we were made to jump up and down and stretch bits of elastic. But after ten minutes it stopped being jolly and we started to hate our instructor, who was a bit like that drill sergeant in *Full Metal Jacket*. After another ten minutes I started to wonder what he'd look like without skin, or a head, and I may have said this out loud.

For the final ten minutes none of us made a sound. We were too exhausted even to grunt. And then we had to do the wind-down, which involved adopting a series of extremely unnatural positions and leaning this way and that until it hurt. The position I wanted to adopt most of all was called 'the Private Pyle'. I really did want to be on a lavatory with a mad stare and an M14 rifle.

An hour has elapsed since I gave the sergeant-major a fistful of dollars and I still don't even have enough breath to light a cigarette. And I'm thinking, 'I've been here for three days now and I've done nothing but play tennis and pick things up and put them down. I even went on a golf course yesterday and gave myself a cricked neck by repeatedly swinging my bat into the ground near where a ball was lying.'

And what has been achieved, exactly? Well, I ache everywhere. My buttocks, in particular, feel as though they have caught fire. My arms are so numb they can't even pick up a glass of wine, and for what? So that many years from now I can suffer from Alzheimer's for just a few more days.

You may imagine that I will at least have a less ridiculous-looking body as a result of these exertions, but I've just seen it in a mirror and I thought I was staring at a weird picture of a six foot five inch beluga whale with idiotic tan lines.

But this is the done thing today. And so when I get home I shall be compelled to employ a hundred Poles to create a vast subterranean world beneath my house that I shall then fill with bits of equipment that can be used to break my heart and my neck.

Except I won't be compelled to do that. Because what this break means is that I've earned the right when I get back to spend a few nights on the sofa, watching television with a takeaway curry and a delicious bar of Cadbury Fruit & Nut chocolate.

21 February 2016

The NHS new towns are Nazi nonsense. We need *Call of Duty* garden cities

Having established that it's jolly good at mending broken legs and even better at getting mildly political songs to number one in the hit parade, the NHS has decided it would like to start designing towns.

So it's trying to sell us a vision of newly created urban areas where health is put at the top of the agenda. There would be no fast-food shops near schools, and children would be encouraged to go for a walk rather than sit at home shooting aliens and terrorists on their games consoles.

'Virtual' care homes would be created so elderly residents could speak to nurses and one another without going outside. And roads would be designed with special signs to help those suffering from dementia.

Of course, we've seen this sort of thing before. The Dutch have been building Camberwick Green-style cycling-friendly towns for years, and before that Hitler built the Prora resort, where German workers could go to the coast and do star jumps from dawn till dusk.

But it's the first time that 'strength through joy' towns have been contemplated in Britain, and already ten areas have been identified as potential sites. I hope and pray, however, that none comes to fruition, because it's the stupidest idea since Sir Clive Sinclair decided we'd all like to drive to work in an electric slipper.

The problem is simple. New towns, or garden cities as they are sometimes called, cannot work, because they are built to address the issues we face now. Not the issues we will face in ten or a hundred years' time.

Take Welwyn Garden City, in Hertfordshire, as a prime example. A neo-Georgian town centre was erected in the 1920s, and all the roads were designed to be fringed with wide grass verges on which children could play with their hula hoops and the grown-ups could do star jumps. Lovely. But it was decided that lots of different shops would be messy and unnecessary, so just one was provided. Yup. One.

Then you had Milton Keynes. It came along in the 1960s, and by then planners had realized that more than one shop was a good idea. They'd also worked out that people didn't want to do star jumps all day long and that they'd rather drive a car instead. So the town was chopped up into little pieces by a grid system of dual carriageways that had 70mph speed limits.

And there would be no pesky traffic lights. Every main junction was a roundabout so you could whizz about in your Humber or your Austin more speedily. I rather liked Milton Keynes. And I still do. But I think everyone else would argue that building a new town around the car isn't really what we want today.

And that, as I said, is the problem. When they built the Tower of London, nobody sat back and thought, 'Right. We've got the dungeons and we've got the portcullis, but what if, one day, we need to open a gift shop?'

And when the Romans decided Bath needed a communal swimming pool, did anyone say, 'Yes. But what if one day everyone's house has its own bathroom?'

Which brings me neatly to the outskirts of Poundbury, in Dorset, the Prince Charles creation where people can live in a town-sized tin of eighteenth-century healthy-living shortbread.

The idea is that it's a complete mishmash, with no separate

zones for shopping, business, the rich and the poor. Everyone lives, works and buys their groceries in one big potpourri
of 'Morning, Constable', 'Morning, Reverend', Enid Blyton,
Cider with Rosie awfulness.

This means you wake up next to a family of Romanian
squatters and walk to the factory that makes organic birdseed breakfast cereal, and then you pop out at lunchtime for
a hearty ploughman's that takes four hours to buy because
the shop selling the crusty bread is two miles from the shop
that sells crunchy pickle, which is half a mile from the shop
that sells manky apples full of dead wasps. And you can't
drive, because that's bad for the polar bear, and you can't buy
the whole thing in one go from the supermarket thingy
because supermarkets are horrid.

If you want that kind of thing, fine. But I guarantee that
within ten years all the shops selling crunchy this and organic
that will have gone out of business and the Romanian squatters will have nicked your bread oven and you won't be able
to get any sleep, partly because Prince William keeps landing
his helicopter in your back garden and partly because of all
the Amazon and Ocado lorries bumping over the organic
sleeping policemen.

It's going to be the same story with the eco-towns that are
currently very popular with planners. Yes, the houses all have
new-fangled central-heating systems, and windmills to get rid
of the sewage, but the time will come, very soon, when we get
all our energy needs from hydrogen fuel cells. And people
living in a house with solar panels on the roof are going to
feel pretty stupid as they huddle round a candle for warmth
and eat their parents to stave off the hunger pangs.

That's going to be the problem with these NHS towns.
They sound tremendous in the here and now, but soon they
will be made to look, by unforeseen events, idiotic.

Of course, fans of nationalization say that, unless we do something to address the issue of obesity, the NHS will go bankrupt and that these towns are therefore absolutely vital. But come on. Ten new Proras full of people with dementia crashing into people doing star jumps and children playing Hopscotch in the middle of the road isn't going to cut it.

They'll house, at most, half a million people, which means that there will be 77 million other people living in Welwyn Garden City and Milton Keynes and Bath who will continue to eat McDonald's until they explode.

Or until someone works out that all the star-jumping is giving people heart attacks and that playing *Call of Duty* is actually good for a child's mind.

6 March 2016

Call up the paparazzi army to take Brussels – and keep us in Europe

After a month of campaigning in a normal election, we are usually fed up with the mudslinging and the over-analysis and the infernal polls. But this Brexit referendum seems different, because it seems we are not.

Everywhere I go, people are asking the same thing. Are you in or out? Freed from the rich-versus-poor tribalism of a general election, everyone's listening, everyone's thinking, everyone's calmly trying to make up their mind.

Of course, it's being billed by the media as some kind of personal heavyweight showdown between Bouncing Boris and Call me Dave. Which would mean we'd have to choose between a man who has screwed up London's roads to indulge his love for a Victorian transport system. And a man whose wife we quite fancy.

Sadly, however, we are not choosing which old Etonian we prefer. It's more complicated than that and we need the proper campaigning because none of us really knows what's for the best.

I have spoken in recent weeks to super-rich businessmen who do not know what an exit would mean for commerce and I've spoken to hedge-fund managers who are similarly clueless about the effect such a move would have on the City. These guys are opinion formers. They have the ears of ministers. And they're all standing around at parties with their palms upturned and their shoulders shrugged saying, 'We don't know.'

Normal people reckon it all comes down to immigration.

Will we have more Syrians if we stay in the EU than if we leave? And no one knows the answer to that one either. Or whether it's a good thing ultimately. Or whether it's just a phase the world's going through and it'll all be over when Putin stops bombing Homs.

What we think we know is that if Britain chooses to leave, the Scottish will say, 'Och aye the noo,' and refuse to come with us. Which would mean immigrants could catch a boat to Edinburgh and then simply walk into England. Which would mean we'd have to rebuild Hadrian's Wall. Or would we? Again, I'm not sure.

I suppose that now is as good a time as any to declare my hand. I'm with the man whose wife we fancy. I'm in.

When Mr Cameron was touring Europe recently, seeking a better deal for Britain by sucking up to prime ministers from such places as Romania and Hungary, I watched on YouTube an MEP called Daniel Hannan make an anti-EU speech to a group of, I think, students. It was brilliant. One of the best speeches I've ever heard. And I'll admit it made me question my beliefs. But despite his clever, reasoned and passionate plea for us to leave Europe, I'm still in. He talked sense, but a lot of this debate is about how we feel.

Back in 1973, my parents held a Common Market party. They'd lived through the war and, for them, it seemed like a good idea to form closer ties with our endlessly troublesome neighbours. For me, however, it was a chance to make flags out of coloured felt and eat exotic foods like sausage and pasta. I felt very European that night, and I still do.

Whether I'm sitting on a railway concourse in Brussels or pottering down the canals of south-western France or hurtling along a motorway in Croatia, I feel way more at home than I do when I'm trying to get something to eat in Dallas or Sacramento. I love Europe and, to me, that's important.

But I'm the first to acknowledge that, so far, the EU hasn't really worked. We still don't have standardized plug sockets and every member state is still out for itself, not the common good. And this is the sort of thing that causes many people to think, 'Well let's just leave and look after ourselves in future.'

I get that. I really do. And after I'd watched Hannan's speech, it's briefly how I felt too. But actually, isn't it better to stay in and try to make the damn thing work properly? To create a United States of Europe that functions as well as the United States of America. With one army and one currency and one unifying set of values.

Britain, on its own, has very little influence on the world stage. I think we are all agreed on that. But Europe, if it were well run and had cohesive, well-thought-out policies, would be a tremendous force for good. I think we are all agreed on that as well. So how do we turn Europe from the shambles it is now into the beacon of civilization that it could be in the future?

Well, the answer, I think, lies with the press. Today, in Britain, an MP cannot even put a cup of coffee on expenses without being torn to pieces by the media. A duck house will get him the sack. He can't look at a pretty girl or pick his nose, and woe betide any of them who say something which is slightly at odds with what they've said before. Or what the leader is thinking.

British MPs work and play in the glare of powerful follow spots. They are monitored constantly by the newspapers . . . the same newspapers who tell us that these people are power-less because these days all the major decisions are made in Brussels.

Right. So let's switch our attention then. Let's leave the 'parish councillors' alone and concentrate our big guns on the real decision-makers in Brussels. Let's have hacks outside their houses all day long, waiting for one of them to do or say something wrong. Let's make them accountable. Let's turn them from 'faceless bureaucrats' into household names.

That is the biggest problem with the EU right now. Nobody is really concentrating on its leaders. Nobody is saying, 'Hang on a minute . . .' And this means they are running amok.

It's why we need to stay in. So our famously attentive media can try to stop them. To make them pause before they move. To make the continent work the way the continent should, as a liberal, kind, balanced fulcrum in a mad world that could soon have Trump on one side and Putin on the other.

13 March 2016

Sober Syrians we should let in; boozy Brits are too shaming to be let out

If you listen to the bleeding-heart liberals with their Baftas and their Islington postcodes, then every single one of the Syrian people currently stuck at the Macedonian border or holed up at that camp in Calais is a decent, hard-working soul who wants to come to England to start a nail salon.

Whereas if you listen to the UKIP types with their red trousers and their usual spot at the bar, then they're all terrorists and ne'er-do-wells who want to come to Britain so they can pick our pockets and burgle our houses while gorging on our healthcare system.

The truth, of course, lies somewhere in the middle. Some of the people queuing up to come to England want to explode in a shopping centre as soon as possible and some want to steal your wallet. But some are living under a tarpaulin sheet, in a field of mud, in the cold, because they grew weary of waking up every morning wondering whether they'd be blown to smithereens by a Russian bomb that day or be beheaded by a lunatic. To these people, even Rotherham looks like heaven on earth.

Not that long ago I was actually in Raqqa and Homs, the hellhole cities that vie for coverage every day with Kim Kardashian's bottom. I had a nice time there. I met lots of people who were kind and funny. They gave me tea in their shops and asked if Captain Slow – James May – was as hopeless in real life as he appeared to be on television.

It troubles me that many of these people will now be dead. And it troubles me even more that some of them are in that French dump, with their children, trying to get into Britain.

I don't have a Bafta and I don't live in Islington, so I'm not daft. I'm not going to sit here now and say, with a tear in one eye and a bit of a sniffle, that we should open the Channel Tunnel immediately because I know that's impractical. Britain is a small island and while only 2 per cent of the land mass here is actually built up – that's a fact, by the way – we simply don't have the houses for a million newcomers or the money to keep them fed, watered and healthy.

Which brings me neatly to the poolside bar of the hotel in Morocco where I was staying last week. It was horrible. The hotel itself was a giant concrete maze painted brown to make it look like an ancient fort. The pool was ringed with palm trees to make it feel like an oasis. And the people around it were the sort who were completely taken in.

They'd come away, in March, to spend a few days getting diarrhoea simply so they could go home with a red nose that would cause people at the lodge to say, 'Have you seen Brian's tan? His laundrette must be doing pretty well.'

At night I was cornered in the bar by some drunken green-grocer from Luton with an Instamatic and Dr Scholl's sandals and last Tuesday's *Daily Express* who droned on and on about how Nigel Farage should be running the country and how many languages Enoch Powell could speak . . . and then he wandered off to get some more Watneys Red Barrel and another packet of cheese-and-onion crisps and I was left thinking, '*Monty Python* was way ahead of the game on this.'

But instead of a party of Germans forming pyramids and frightening the children there was a group from – and I'm saying this because it's true – Liverpool. They had shaved heads, gym-toned bodies and voices that could crack glass on the International Space Station.

They called the waiters Mustapha and drank a seemingly endless amount of cognac and Coke. This is a drink with which I'm unfamiliar. And I hope it stays that way because it seems the more you ingest, the stupider you become. After four, one of the party said that the Gestapo were like Heinrich Himmler's Special Forces. He knew this, apparently, because he'd watched a television programme.

Their views on the employment laws of Britain were interesting too, since they seemed to think they were slaves. And that upon their return to Liverpool they would definitely be sacked.

Then they all jumped in the pool and made a lot of noise, which caused all the Brians and the Freemasons to peer over their Harold Robbins books and look displeased. And the waiters to scurry away for fear that they'd be used as a volleyball in the very near future.

And all of this got me thinking. These people are English. They have British passports. And it is their way of life that we are trying to preserve when we say no to the Syrian refugees.

But answer me this: who would you rather have living next door? This lot? Or a teetotal family from Homs who have fled from Vladimir Putin's jets and Jihadi John's knife so they can have a quiet life in the shires?

We keep talking about the citizenship test, to make sure that newcomers know the name of the national anthem and how to hold a knife and fork properly before they are given a British passport. And yet we hand them out without so much as a by-your-leave to morons who have less intelligence than the average dishwasher. Simply because they were squeezed from between their mothers' phlebitis-ridden thighs in Britain.

I'm not suggesting for a moment that we introduce a one-in-one-out policy that would mean ejecting one undesirable for every Syrian who's allowed in (although, deep down . . .), but I do think we could adopt some kind of halfway house that prevents Britain's most unpleasant souls from travelling abroad.

The fact is: we need to be careful of our image. And I'd far rather be represented on the world stage, and around its swimming pools, by someone who had the gumption to up sticks and walk across Europe with his children to find a better life than a yobbo in a football shirt who mixes cognac with Coca-Cola and thinks he's a slave just because he has a job.

20 March 2016

Shave off the beards, hipsters. Or prepare for a long wait at Gatwick

When the IRA used to run about the place, sportingly giving a brief warning before detonating a bomb, we never dignified its activities by calling the Troubles a war: the group's members were always referred to as common criminals. And we never used to let it interfere with our lives either. The IRA would blow something up and the next day we'd go to work as usual.

Today the Blitz spirit seems to have gone. We talk about the 'war on terror', which means we think of the ISIS fanatics as warriors rather than tragic, drug-addled losers who treat the world as one big *Call of Duty* game. And while we all say, after every atrocity, that we will not allow these people to interfere with our everyday lives, we then proceed to do the exact opposite.

After the Brussels attacks last week, security was immediately stepped up at airports and train stations all over the world. Theresa May, the Home Secretary, said travellers must expect extra delays as they head off for their Easter holidays, and in Argentina Barrack Obama was criticized for dancing the tango rather than speeding back to the White House.

Then came the 'experts' with all sorts of idiotic ideas about how we can prevent people from exploding in future. They've already decided that we can no longer fly with toothpaste or a tennis racket, or any kind of cream, in case we suddenly decide to moisturize the pilot to death. And they are introducing legislation that means the constabulary can have a look at the websites we have visited whenever the mood takes them. So what's next? No gloves? No electrical equipment of any kind?

It has been suggested that, in future, because two jobless halfwits blew themselves up in Belgium, people must be screened before they are allowed into an airport building. What's the point of that? You'd still have thousands of people all huddled together in one place. It's just that they'd be out-side in the rain, rather than inside, where it's dry and warm.

If you're on an Easter break now and it took you hours to get through the airport, then the criminals have won. It's as simple as that.

So what's to be done? Well, we're told that there are pos-sibly up to six hundred people in Europe right now who are happy to explode, and I'm not sure there's a damn thing we can do to stop that happening. We can't even put our hands up and say, 'OK, OK. We give in.' Because we don't really know what it is they want. Apart from us all to die.

The fact is that they are going to carry on blowing up until the recruits realize that they don't end up in heaven with a load of virgins. That they just end up dead, like all their vic-tims. And that's not going to happen any time soon.

So we have to accept that there will be atrocities in various European cities from time to time. And then we have to work out how life for most people can carry on as normal in spite of this.

I've listened all week to politicians saying that we need more EU integration and that we need less EU integration. I've heard bleeding-heart liberals say that if the Muslim youths in various run-down suburbs were given a better edu-cation and a proper job afterwards, they would be less inclined to blow themselves up. And I've heard frothing Nazis say that they should all be escorted back to wherever they came from in cattle wagons.

But because we live in sensitive times when we are not allowed to cause offence, I haven't heard one person suggest the one solution that everyone knows will work.

Cara Delevingne. Your first primary-school teacher. My children. Andrew Lloyd Webber. And everyone in the Salvation Army. At an airport, all of them have to put their liquids in a see-through bag and take off their shoes and their belts and their watches. And they all have to queue up for hours.

All of them are treated no differently from a sweating alarm-clock salesman from Homs. And why? Because we know, and the security services know, that they are not suicide bombers.

All the people who exploded this month in Belgium and Turkey were Muslims. So were those who blew up in Paris and London, and those who planted bombs in Madrid. So were those who flew the jet liners into the Pentagon and the World Trade Center.

And I'm sorry, but if you are looking for a criminal who's described as male and bearded, with a dark complexion, why the bloody hell do you stop and search a nine-year-old blonde girl with blue eyes and a My Little Pony rucksack? That's just idiocy.

But of course, we all know the problem. If Britain has two queues at its airports – one for white people and one for those who aren't – then we are going to find ourselves on the naughty step at the United Nations. Because that's racism.

Which means that we are fighting what we stupidly call the war on terror with our hands tied behind our backs by political correctness.

In the Second World War the security services didn't harass everybody. They went after those who wore lederhosen and couldn't say 'squirrel' properly. And those who were suspiciously good at cooking pasta. Nobody said that was racist. It was just common sense.

Whereas today things are so bonkers that officials in South Yorkshire didn't dare investigate a child-grooming operation because it was a Pakistani thing and they didn't want the headlines. And Dame Judi Dench is searched every time she goes abroad because it would be racist to not search her.

It's potty. And it's got to stop.

So I'll say it. If we really want to carry on with our lives – as we say we do – we need two queues at the airport. One for people who don't have beards. And one for those who do.

27 March 2016

Picking a holiday is hard when Johnny ISIS beats you to all the brochures

Last week we were shown some photographs of the Egyptian seaside resort of Sharm el-Sheikh. And it looked like Chernobyl. The swimming pools were empty and the lobbies of the vast, gaudy hotels were deserted. And while the market carpet shops were still open, the 'For you, my friend, special price' vendors were just hanging around in doorways because they had no customers.

Local tourism officials are trying to put a brave face on it, saying visitor numbers to the country have only halved in recent years, but the truth of the matter is that no one in Britain is sitting at home this morning saying, 'Mavis. How do you fancy Egypt for a summer break this year?'

Yes, the brochures still talk about balmy evenings and camel rides and sipping umbrella-shaded cocktails by the pool, but we all sort of know that we'd also get light gunfire, muffled explosions and some beheadings. These are not what we want while on holiday because it's hard to get your head straight if you're on a sun lounger and it's in a ditch two hundred yards away.

And it's not just Egypt that's no longer on the list of possible holiday destinations. With the notable exception of Morocco, pretty much the whole of northern and central Africa is now a no-go area for Johnny Brit.

Tunisia. Algeria. Libya. Chad. Sudan. The Democratic Republic of Congo. Kenya. Somalia. Terrorism and lunacy have put the kibosh on the lot. And there's no point moving west for some respite, because there you'll probably get bitten by a bat and catch Ebola.

Don't you find that staggering? Even when the world was cut in half by the Iron Curtain, you could still go to Prague or Zagreb or Moscow and be fairly certain that you'd come home with a head. But today, in half a continent, you can't.

And that brings us back to the holiday brochure. Because it's not just Africa that's a problem. Yemen. Iraq. Syria. Turkey and that whole swathe of consonant-tastic countries that stretches right the way over to India are now no longer available to the drunken greengrocer from Luton with his Kodak Instamatic and Dr Scholl's sandals.

I remember, not that long ago, seeing a map in the *Daily Mail* that explained what ISIS wanted: a huge Islamic superstate that stretched all the way from the Atlantic coast of North Africa to the Himalayas and then down through Southeast Asia to the tip of Australia.

And I scoffed because it seemed ridiculous. And yet now it doesn't seem ridiculous at all. I mean, would you go to Bali for a holiday? Exactly.

So it's Greece then? Nope. Not unless you want to share the beach with a tidal wave of migrants. And life is equally distressing in large parts of what used to be called Yugoslavia.

And that's because the creation of the Islamic superstate has caused millions of people who don't want to be crucified or pushed off a tower block to up sticks, load their meagre possessions into a leaky Rib and head for Europe. Where some have discovered that the best way of fending off starvation is by hitting holidaymakers over the head and stealing their wallets.

This time last year you'd have gone for a mini-break to Belgium. And why not? It is a wonderful place. All those cobbles and all that mayonnaise. Yum, yum. But now?

Then there's Paris. My daughter and her boyfriend went there recently for a weekend and that sounds lovely. But it isn't great any more. It's frightening. I know we are supposed to stand up to the terrorist threat by deploying the Blitz spirit, keeping calm and carrying on. But when it's your daughter on the Métro it's bloody hard to keep your upper lip stiff.

And things aren't much better even closer to home. We like to think of London as a tourist hotspot. We tell the world about Changing the Guard and the Queen and *Top Gear*. But there's no getting round the fact that the terrorist threat in the UK is 'severe'. Most of us accept that one day, sooner or later, someone's going to explode on the Central line. And that makes it hard for visitors to relax.

So south-eastern Europe, Belgium, Paris, London, Bali, the Middle East and northern Africa. You can cross that lot off the holiday destination list because of ISIS and its affiliates. Which, you might imagine, is not the end of the world because there are plenty of other alternatives.

Really? I only ask because I've spent the past week trying to find somewhere I can take the children in August, and it's all hopeless. Italy and Spain have migrant issues and terrorism threats as well and, while I love the south of France, my kids can't afford to pay €1,000 for a bottle of vodka. So that pretty much counts out the Med.

Germany? Hmmm. I'd like the plane I take to go on holiday to have been made there. But I don't want to spend my free time in leather shorts eating sausages to the strains of an oompah band. Scandinavia? Too cold. Eastern Europe? Not really. India will give you diarrhoea and, for well-documented reasons, I think Argentina is a non-starter.

Chile is lovely in every way. It's a tremendous place. One of my favourite countries in the world. But it's not realistic for a two-week holiday in what'll be winter anyway.

And that's the thing. When you bring realism into the equation, when you look for a destination that's safe, clean, accessible and cheap, there is only one viable option: America.

Which has caused me to sit back in my chair and have a Biro-sucking moment of thoughtfulness. Because we have it in our heads that George W. Bush didn't really know what he was doing when he invaded Afghanistan and then Iraq. But maybe he did.

Maybe he'd worked out that down the line, after he'd made a complete Horlicks of everything, America would become the world's only realistic holiday destination.

10 April 2016

I refuse to dry my teabags for Osama Binman

As a general rule, I'm not in favour of the death penalty. However, I would make an exception for people who drop litter. There should be on-the-spot executions for people who do that. No excuses. No trial. You drop a pizza box on the pavement and straightaway you get a bullet in the back of the head.

I went to Hatfield in Hertfordshire last week and, as I turned on to the slip road off the A1, I could not quite believe my eyes. Because the grass verges looked like a Brazilian favela. I've seen less messy downed airliners. And I'm sorry, but if I were running the council, I'd shoot someone in the town square on the hour, every hour until the culprit owned up.

Except that's not going to happen, because actually the problem of littering is in part being caused by recycling-obsessed councils. And now it's going to get worse because town-hall chiefs in Hull have just introduced a scheme that means homeowners who don't recycle properly face having their bins confiscated. Yup, the city council is saying that if you can't do it properly, you can't be allowed to do it at all. And that's probably the stupidest idea in the whole of human history.

I'm ashamed to say that I don't understand recycling. It's just not one of my specialist subjects. I'm dimly aware that if I throw away my kettle, it could one day be turned into a Volkswagen or a Boeing 737, but that, I'm afraid, is the full extent of my knowledge.

My kitchen bin is divided into four compartments. One is

for general waste, one is for chicken food, one is for recycling and the other is for recycling stuff that won't be recycled if I put it in the other recycling compartment.

All of this means that when I open the bin lid to throw away some onion peelings, I spend several minutes wondering whether the chickens would eat such a thing or whether they could be used to make a Volkswagen, before giving up and putting them in the general-waste compartment.

And now I won't be able to do that any more because my efforts will be judged by the dustbinerie. And if it decides I've put something in the wrong section, it'll confiscate my bin and I'll be forced to throw my waste out of the car window when I'm driving down the motorway.

Because I'm not prepared to do this, I decided to try to learn a little bit more about recycling. But it's too confusing for words. Council experts in Hull tell us that one or two baked beans that you've not scooped out of the tin properly can contaminate everything else in the 'blue bin', as if we know what a blue bin is or means.

They also say that a used teabag can make cardboard soggy and therefore non-reusable. So where do the teabags go? Or are we supposed to dry them before we throw them away? Because I am trying to make a new television show and I've children to raise and three newspaper columns a week to write. So I really don't have time to dry my teabags.

Retired people do have the time for this kind of thing, which is why your local tip is always full of elderly people putting everything in the correct bin. They seem to enjoy this: getting everything right and tutting scornfully at those who don't. In their minds, it's a sort of golf club.

I once saw an elderly gentleman turn up at a tip with a small plant pot full of gravel that he emptied into the bin marked 'gravel'. He then drove home, pleased, no doubt, that apart from the fact he'd driven to the tip in a Mercedes, he'd done his bit for the environment.

The rest of us, though, don't even have the time to work out what's what. Take cotton wool as a prime example. It's a natural fibre, so surely it could easily be recycled into a jumper or the sole of a training shoe. But no. My local council's website informs me that it contains fibres of some sort and must therefore go in general waste.

Doors? You'd imagine that a door could easily be turned into something else. A table? A rabbit hutch? Or maybe a new door for an immigrant? But for some reason the council will only take three. If for some reason you want to throw away four doors, you have to give it some money.

Garden waste? Apparently, this can be handled by the council's composting facilities, but not if you've put it in an actual composting bag. I don't understand that rule either. But you'd better not get it wrong because you'll be judged by the dustbin men and, if you fail, they'll take away your bin. Probably on the day they come round for the Christmas bonus.

You might imagine that while all this is annoying, it's necessary, because we can't simply chuck the refuse away. But we can, actually. The maths show that every single thing America throws away in the next hundred years – even if the population in that time doubles to more than 600 million – could be placed in a hole that's four hundred feet deep and five miles across.

In a country the size of Britain, all our waste for the next century could be buried in an area no bigger than Jeremy Corbyn's back garden.

There is, however, a better solution. We simply put a 1 million per cent tax on all unnecessary packaging. Starting with Gillette. And then moving quickly to tackle those companies that sell microscopic camera SD cards in two square feet of what feels like steel-reinforced titanium.

That's a much better idea. Instead of taking away our bins when – let's be honest – the dustbin man can't be bothered to do his job, why not take away the houses of those who create all the waste in the first place? And the lives of people who think that a single green pepper needs to be sold in its own plastic mackintosh.

17 April 2016

Coming soon to Amazon it's . . . er . . . Cary McCarface

So the votes are in, democracy has spoken and, with a crushing majority, the public has decided that Britain's new polar research vessel should be called the RRS *Boaty McBoatface*.

Organizers of the poll had hoped the winning suggestion would be the name of a famous explorer or naturalist. They had suggested the *Scott of the Antarctic* or the *David Attenborough*. But the public was having none of it. And in the end *Boaty McBoatface* gained more than 124,000 votes. Almost 90,000 more than its nearest rival.

I can't remember – ever – feeling so proud to be British, because nothing sums us up quite so well as this result. It simply wouldn't happen in Germany. Or America. But here it would. And it did. And if they roll out the idea to the Royal Navy, I'd like to suggest HMS *Vulnerable*. That's a brilliant name for a warship. Or HMS *Weak* – that's even better.

But there's a problem. The Natural Environment Research Council, which runs the new polar ship, is plainly worried that the name will cheapen the important work it does down there among the penguins. So now it is trying to wriggle out of its obligation.

The organization has looked closely at the rules of the poll and has found, to its relief, that a clause says the final decision rests with its chief executive. And it has pointed out that the former BBC radio presenter who first suggested the *Boaty McBoatface* handle is mortified by the fact that people took him seriously. So now the council is back to the drawing board, trying to think of a name by itself, and I feel its pain . . .

When I first signed up with Amazon Prime to make a new motoring show, I knew all sorts of problems lay ahead. I'd have to start a production company and find potted plants and an office to put them in. I'd have to deal, too, with insurance and health and safety and accountancy and all sorts of other stuff I either don't understand or hate. There was one problem, however, that I hadn't even considered. And it has turned out to be the biggest of the lot: choosing a name.

I spend at least six hours a day in my office – which is insured and smoke-free and resplendent with potted plants – sucking creatively on a corporate Biro as I wait for the daily 3 p.m. 'Anything yet?' phone call from Amazon in Los Angeles.

My original idea was brilliant. The show would be called *Speedbird* and the logo would be a Seychelles white tern, graceful and beautiful. It would be an image completely at odds with the hour of television that was to follow – and I liked that.

But it wasn't to be. *Speedbird* had already been bagged as a trademark by someone else in the media, so that was that. There was a similar issue with *Speedwolf* and *Ironbird* and *Wolfbird* and everything else I thought of.

Every morning, I'd make a £7,000 call to the lawyer with an idea, and every afternoon I'd get a £7,000 reply saying the name was already in use by someone in New Zealand or France or Ukraine. *Prime Torque. Autonation. Skid Mark.* Everything was a no-no.

To make matters worse, I was told the name didn't have to exactly match an existing trademark. It only had to sound or look similar in some way to become an infringement. This means every single combination of letters in the English language carries with it some risk of legal action down the line.

At the end of one lengthy – and almost completely silent – ideas meeting with senior staff, our lead director piped up with *Three C**** Driving Along*. This, it turned out, was available. But we felt we'd probably lose the family audience, so it was back to staring out of the window and trying not to throw my plant pot at James May whenever he spoke.

We tried to sound interested as he suggested *The Pink Helmet* or *The James May Show*, but then one day he struck gold with *Gear Knobs*. We all liked it. We thought it was amusing and hurriedly we put in another £7,000 call to the lawyer.

She said the trademark was available, but it would be an unwise idea, owing to the laws surrounding intellectual property. In short, the BBC not only owns the rights to the Stig and the Star in a Reasonably Priced Car and the Cool Wall, but also to any name that is remotely similar to *Top Gear*. We tried explaining there's a show called *Fifth Gear* that doesn't belong to the BBC but it was no good. Arguing with a lawyer costs more money than we had, so we hurriedly put the phone down and went back to the drawing board.

Amazon was starting to find our hopelessness funny and put out a video of James, Richard Hammond and me trying to decide on a name. But behind the scenes it isn't funny. Because we need a name that isn't in use by any business anywhere in the world and doesn't even sound or look like any name that's in use by any business anywhere in the world. And it can't even be a minor play on the words Top or Gear. Oh, and it has to be a name that's liked by me, our producer, Hammond, Eeyore and a billionaire in Seattle.

By this stage, Twitter has become involved, and every day my account is full of bright ideas from @M3man45790 and @Zpowerdude45889 and the like. One was good – *Two and a Half Pillocks* – but that fell by the wayside, partly because

Hammond, for some reason, didn't like it and partly because 'pillock' isn't a word in America, which is where most of our audience live.

We've even had to drop the working title of *Currently Unnamed TV Show* because, as someone pointed out on the internet, this could be turned into an unfortunate acronym.

And now, after this polar research ship malarkey, we've even had to shelve our plans to put the whole thing to a public vote. Because everyone would vote for *Cary McCarface*, and then we'd have to wriggle out of the whole thing by handing over the decision to our chief executive, who's German and would therefore go for something like *A Car Programme*. Because that's vot it is, *ja?*

Or maybe I'm wrong. The Germans are actually quite good at names. I know this because I'm there now, in the small resort of Wank.

24 April 2016

For me, the war is over: let Germany run everything

As you may have read, I am keen that we remain in the European Union. But not half as keen as I would be if the European Union were made up of just four countries: England, Denmark, Holland and Germany. That coalition of like-minded peoples would, I think, work well. Especially if we put Germany in charge.

Oh sure, we beat them in two World Wars and one World Cup, but after spending last week on a filming trip in Bavaria I was left with one all-consuming question: how? How does anyone beat this lot at anything?

I began the trip in a small, guttural-sounding Alpine town and, as I stood outside the hotel, blowing smoke in the general direction of passing American tourists, I noticed that every single shop was small and privately owned and fantastically neat. There was no German Home Stores hosting a closing-down sale, no charity shops and no gaping holes where Woolworths used to be.

And there was no litter. By which I mean none at all. And because there was none, I had no clue what to do with my cigarette end. Simply tossing it away would have been like taking a dump in the middle of the Somerset House skating rink. I was therefore forced by custom and example to extinguish it in a flowerbed and then put the butt in a passing American's rucksack.

The following morning, however, I received a shock. While having another cigarette I noticed that in the middle of the perfectly cobbled street there was a discarded plastic coffee stirrer. Later I told our local fixer about this, imagining she would find it funny that I'd noticed. But instead she looked shocked. 'Where was it?' she asked, in the manner of someone who was going to drive back into town to clear it up. 'It was in the street outside our hotel,' I replied. There was a long pause as she thought about that. 'It must have been dropped by one of your film crew,' she said.

We may scoff and roll our eyes at that, but what's so wrong, I wonder, with living in a country where it is inconceivable that someone would drop a plastic coffee stirrer in the street?

The next day I pulled on to a grass verge while the film crew waited for the right-shaped cloud to form and, immediately, a local person pulled over and told me that I couldn't park on the grass verge because I'd leave wheel marks and possibly squash a flower.

My natural reaction to this sort of interference is to tell the busybody to eff off and leave me alone, and I was on the cusp of doing just that. But then I thought, *She has a point*. So, with an apologetic wave, I moved on. And as I drove away I looked in my rear-view mirror to discover that, sure enough, I had left marks in the otherwise perfect grass and I had bent a couple of dandelions.

After this I decided to see whether I could find something wrong with Germany. Apart from the wine. And the pop music. It didn't take long. It has a truly lousy mobile phone network. Most of the time there's barely any signal at all, and I never once saw the 3G symbol flash up on my phone. But then, why do you need a fast data delivery service when you can leap into your car and, thanks to the autobahn speed-limit policy, be two hundred miles away in an hour?

Which brings me on to Germany's drivers, all of whom are excellent and all of whom have up-to-date car insurance, or, as they elegantly call it over there, *Kraftfahrzeug-Haftpflichtversicherung*. Then there are the roads, which are as smooth as the glass they used to make the Hubble telescope. Every repaired section is as invisible as the tucks on an ageing supermodel's face. There is not even a word for 'pothole'.

And nor does the German language cater for 'striking junior doctor' or 'fly-tipping' or 'lying police officer' or 'the football ground failed to meet safety standards'.

Nor would you be able to say: 'It seems that when he was a young man at university, our prime minister went to a party and placed his gentleman sausage into the mouth of a dead pig. So now he must resign in shame.'

Because when it comes to this sort of thing, the Germans are a lot more tolerant . . .

A couple of years ago, someone posted photographs on the internet that appear to show a younger Angela Merkel enjoying a naturist holiday with a couple of female friends. And nothing happened. There were no strenuous denials from her office. No efforts were made to take them down. Because in Germany everyone knows that they are either fake, in which case, so what? Or they're real, in which case people now know their chancellor – unlike her incongruous Barbie-doll double – once sported a 1970s welcome mat between her legs and a pair of excellent breasts. And again, so what?

In the past I've mocked German lavatories, which come with a shelf to catch your stool and a supply of lollipop sticks that enable you to examine it for defects before flushing it away. But actually, it's simply an early-warning system for colon cancer, and what's wrong with that?

It's a question that cropped up time and again as my week in Bavaria rolled by. We laugh at the Germans, but why? Because it's nothing more than a country that works.

You don't queue for security at the airports. You don't spend half an hour in your hotel room trying to turn out all the lights. The hot water arrives instantly. So does your train. And shopkeepers don't waste your morning with idiotic small talk. That's why I'd put them in charge of a new, slimmer EU. The English would then do the banking and the jokes, the Dutch would organize the parties and the Danes would make the furniture.

And think how good the football team would be, especially when it came down to penalty shootouts.

1 May 2016

Reception? Help, I need a manual on turning the light off

On average I spend two or three nights a week in hotels, and until last weekend I hadn't found one that wasn't annoying in some way, or terrible.

The worst, in the tea region of north-western Uganda, was very terrible. The bedlinen had plainly not been washed since Idi Amin went west, so I decided to discard it and sleep on the mattress. Which, when I removed the sheet, turned out to be the most revolting thing in the world. I shan't spoil your breakfast by describing the nature or hue of the unpleasant stains. I'll just say that I haven't retched quite so violently apart from the time when I was in China and I saw half a dog.

Then there was a hotel in Bolivia. I was woken up at 6 a.m. by one of the cleaners, who had come into my room without knocking. 'Buenos dias,' he said as he shuffled past my bed on his way to the bathroom. Where he enjoyed a noisy poo before shuffling back out of my room with nothing more than a mumbled 'gracias'.

The Thief hotel in Oslo was very different from this. It had a manager of unrivalled professionalism and was equipped with all the things you'd expect in a country where every child's state-sponsored micro-scooter has Swarovski crystals in its wheel hubs. My room was fabulous. It even had a fire.

And if I'd been moving in for a couple of years, I'd have been able to work out how all the features could be operated. But I was there for only a short time, and by the time I got to my room at night I was usually a bit too drunk to fathom out all the buttons, which meant I had to try to sleep with some of the lights on and the fire still blazing and the television still playing its 'Mr Cluckson, welcome' muzak.

This is my main beef with hotels. In countries with a smooth flow of electricity and no beheadings, they are all far too complicated. The check-in procedure is too lengthy and, after you've walked six miles to your room, you find the electronic key you've been given doesn't work, so you have to trudge back to reception, with your bags, to check in again. And then when you finally get to your room, it's like finding yourself at the controls of a Boeing jet liner and it's your job to land it. You just sit there thinking, 'But I don't know how any of this stuff works.'

Take the shower as a prime example. You can see what goes through the mind of the management when it is choosing an attachment and the controls. 'We are a good hotel and we must reflect that with a system that offers many jets and a sophisticated temperature-setting device.'

What this invariably means is that you turn it on and immediately get a jet of ice-cold water in your face. You know that you must turn the temperature up a bit, but the controls are located behind the jet of cold water, which, by the time you've found your spectacles to see which knob does what, has become hotter than molten lava. And your specs have steamed up and you're blind.

Until last weekend the only hotel I had ever encountered with a decent shower was in Red Deer, in Alberta. That's because there were so many holes in the ceiling I could just stand underneath one of them and wash my hair there. Although I almost certainly washed it in mouthwash because I was unable to read the microdot labelling used on miniature hotel bathroom products.

However, operating a hotel bathroom is nothing compared with the problems you encounter when you try to turn out the lights. There will come a point when you think you've cracked it. You've unplugged the lamp by the chair, drunkenly tripped over your suitcase, resorted to smashing the table lamp because it appeared to have no switch at all and then crawled back between the sheets thinking that you had only the bedside lamp to go.

But no. You've forgotten the wardrobe light, haven't you? And by the time you've figured that one out, dawn is breaking and you discover to your horror that the electric curtains that took four hours to close have been made from tracing paper.

Some hotels helpfully provide one big switch by the bed that turns everything off. Including power to all the electricity sockets. Which means that when you wake up in the morning your phone hasn't charged.

It has always made me wonder: what do people actually learn on hotel-management courses? Wear a tie. Stand up straight. And make sure the porn isn't identified on the bill. I'm sure all this is very important. But do they learn that there's no point providing guests with a television remote control if there are no instructions on how to use it?

All of which brings me to last weekend. Everyone in the country, it seemed, was going to a wedding in Winchester, which meant that every room in the city was booked. Apart from one at a hotel called The Winchester.

I arrived and my shoulders sagged. There was a wedding here too. The sort where all the men turn up in patterned satin waistcoats. Or a kilt, for no reason. The carpets were hideous, and the wallpaper looked as though it had been chosen from Osborne & Little's Liverpool Lottery Winner collection.

But the check-in procedure took four seconds, the electronic key worked – that's a first – and the mattress in the room was comfortable. What's more, there were instructions in the bathroom for the extremely simple shower controls, there were light switches by the bed that turned the lights off, the curtains were thick enough to stop shrapnel and, joy of joys, there was no temperature in the room. It wasn't warm and it wasn't chilly. That's another first.

I do not know who manages this hotel, but if you are running the Carlton in Cannes or London's Dorchester you should call them immediately and offer them a job.

15 May 2016

Sex is running riot on TV – and I fear *Countdown*'s next

A new period drama started on the television and, while I didn't watch it, I have seen all the coverage about how it was full of grunting Frenchmen playing Hide the Sausage and a pretty woman wandering about dreamily in a set of wet net curtains.

This seems to have annoyed large numbers of tweedy people who think that sex is a chore. They dismiss claims that it's natural by saying, 'So is defecating and menstruating, and we don't want to see that on the television either.'

Or do we? When I was growing up in the 1970s the BBC used to screen something called *Play for Today* in which there was some talking followed by a huge amount of sweaty sex. Then there was *Bouquet of Barbed Wire*, in which Susan Penhaligon found a variety of different reasons each week to remove her shirt. And on it went. Sex and nudity were so commonplace that I wouldn't have been surprised if Valerie Singleton had turned up on *Blue Peter* in a peephole bra. And nothing else.

At the cinema, things were even more free and easy. People queued round the block to see *Emmanuelle* and I wasn't even mildly shocked in *Young Winston* when a topless woman suddenly appeared in shot for absolutely no reason at all.

Nor did I bat an eyelid when, in the middle of *Battle of Britain*, Susannah York decided to slip out of her air force uniform for a moment and wander about in her stockings and suspenders.

In every bus stop and every lay-by, there was invariably a

large collection of mildly used pornographic magazines, and at the theatre, all the girls had their 1970s welcome mats on display all the time. The first time I saw Glenda Jackson wearing clothes, I was genuinely amazed. Helen Mirren too.

But then, one day, it all just stopped. We had *Dallas* and *Dynasty* and *EastEnders* and there wasn't even a whiff of rumpy-pumpy in any of them. We got so used so quickly to actors and actresses wearing clothes that we all ran around in a tizzy during *Baywatch* because Pamela Anderson nearly wasn't.

Paul Raymond was driven out of Soho, along with all the shops where you could buy a smutty VHS. And at the newspaper shop the *Daily Mail* decided that all nipples were revolting and must therefore be pixellated.

What happened is plain for all to see. Television audiences began to decline. Newspaper circulation figures fell off a cliff. *Nuts* shut. Theatres began to close. And all the while, sex on the internet was becoming more and more popular. I read the other day that one of the most visited sites in the world right now is *Pornhub*. That's why no one is going out to play, because they're all at home, playing with themselves.

Plainly, television executives have noticed this, which is why, all of a sudden, the nipple and the lady garden are back with a vengeance. We have *Game of Thrones*, which is just rampant candlelit lesbianism interspersed with some light murder. And *Orange Is the New Black* is much the same, only with different lighting. *Ray Donovan* is a favourite of mine and the second series opened with a lengthy sex scene, just to make sure fans stayed hooked.

House of Cards saw a threesome involving the president and the first lady. *Breaking Bad* had public masturbation. *Transparent* took it even further and, as a result, television is once again keeping people glued to the screens.

The only way mainstream television can keep up with this

festival of indecency is to join in, which explains why the BBC drama *Versailles* was so full of couples making the two-headed beast. There will be more of this kind of thing, I can assure you. I wouldn't be at all surprised if Rachel Riley doesn't do *Countdown* in the altogether fairly soon. Or is that just me?

The big question, however, is this: should we be alarmed? Is the rise and rise of sex on television a bad thing? Well, you may be surprised to find that, actually, I think it could be . . .

I'm not the sort of person who gets hot and bothered by the glimpse of an ankle and I have absolutely no problem with the sort of sex you saw in *Versailles* or even the *House of Cards* Kevin Spacey threesome. It's a bit awkward if you're watching with your kids, but these days we're told before any show starts how much swearing and hitting and flashing lights there will be, so no one can claim they were surprised by the sudden appearance of some breasts.

However, television is perhaps more competitive now than it has ever been. Which means that soon, normal sex won't be considered enough of a pull. So it'll have to become abnormal. And where will that end?

There's no point relying on censorship because that's impossible these days. It'll be governed only by public taste and decency, and that's a worry because, generally speaking, the public doesn't have much of that. Hear at the office water cooler that some beautiful young starlet is to be seen in the latest box set making love to a snake, and people will find an excuse to go home early for a gawp. Which means the next beautiful young starlet will be forced to make love to a goat, and so on.

We've seen this happen with violence. James Bond used to get by with a small pistol and a rudimentary knowledge of karate. Whereas now he gets tied to a chair naked and has his privates mashed to a pulp with a knotted rope.

In video games the action used to be cartoonish but players now are invited to stroll through an airport, armed to the teeth and shoot realistic-looking innocents. And that's the sort of thing that encourages fools to hop on a plane to Syria to try it out for real.

That's what will happen with sex. People will try out things they've seen on the screen, and that's a worry. Especially if you are a goat.

5 June 2016

At last, a folly to love from the EU do-gooders

In 2006 a Baltic mayor with an unpronounceable name helped persuade the EU to reward cities that have shown commitment to the ecological cause by creating the Green Capital Award. Each year the winner would be given a lump of money to further its clean-living endeavours with exciting new projects involving leaves and sunshine and ethnically diverse people smiling and holding hands. It all sounds too revolting for words.

But inevitably it caught on, and in 2015 Bristol became the first place in the UK to win the £7 million award. By the time the council had chipped in, the city's lunatics suddenly had access to more than £12 million that they could spend on all sorts of harebrained ideas and projects.

Immediately they decided to wire up a beech tree with a sound-and-light system that would be activated by falling nuts. I'm not sure I follow the logic of this idea because either the tree would be far away from people's houses, in which case no one would ever see the sound-and-light show. Or it would be in a residential area, in which case everyone would get a full-on Jean-Michel Jarre experience every time the tree decided to shed a bit of its fruit.

Neither option seems terribly sensible, but it was all academic in the end because it turns out that beech trees drop their nuts every two years. And 2015, for the tree selected for the sound-and-light show, was a year off. So that was £37,000 of our money up the Swanee.

And I'm afraid the lunacy didn't stop there: £49,000 went

on a solar-powered hot-air balloon, £3,800 was spent on pies for guests at the launch party and Sir Fiennes trousered five grand for turning up to tell everyone the Poles aren't as cold as they used to be. They even gave Aardman Animations £18,000 for the right to use something called 'Shaun the Sheep' in promotional material.

And they contributed towards a £49,200 system that shrouded one of the city's foot bridges in mist. Who thought that would be a good idea? 'I know. Let's drench everyone when they're walking to work.' The only reason they didn't come up with an exhibition on slavery to make people in the city feel guilty is that such a thing already exists. Of course it does.

However, they did make a video showing lots of volunteers doing good works. And we were told that a thousand children visited an exhibition on sustainability. Yes. On school trips. But they don't count because the children had no say in the matter.

As I watched them playing with the interactive displays, their faces etched with an urgent need to slip outside for a cigarette, and maybe a snog, I couldn't help feeling that the whole thing was just like the Millennium Dome. A power station for turning money into absolutely nothing at all. It was, I reckoned, exactly the sort of EU-inspired nonsense that will cause millions to vote 'leave' on 23 June.

However, there is one legacy I reckon makes the whole project worthwhile. It's an enormous pair of wicker whales that appear to be half submerged in a field. You can see only the head of one and the tail of the other and it's brilliant. Provided the whole thing isn't burned to a crisp by vandals, which is a very real possibility, it will live on for many years, bringing joy to people's lives.

And therein lies the problem with all the criticism of

Bristol's year as Europe's Green Capital. Yes, a lot of money was pissed away by idiots and communists who hate commercialism and shampoo and anything that makes things better and more comfortable. But the city did end up with wicker whales. And in the future it'll be grateful for them.

Today no one is building stuff for the sake of it. They daren't. Because they know that someone will pipe up and say, 'Do you know how many incubators the NHS could have bought for what you've spent?' This saddens me.

Every weekend people flock to Broadway Tower in the Cotswolds and stand in its shadow, oohing and ahhing and marvelling at its splendour. Many wonder why it was built, and the answer is simple. It was built by a rich woman who wanted to find out whether it could be seen from her house twenty-two miles away.

Britain and France are littered with other examples of this madness. We call them follies and we love them. There are castles that were built to look as though they'd fallen down hundreds of years previously, and Gothic temples and pyramids and rocks upended by Druids in Wiltshire, and in South Yorkshire a Tuscan pillar that was built by someone to celebrate the fact his best mate had got off a court-martial. Nobody said when it was finished, 'Yeah, and how many incubators would that have bought?' Mostly people wrote to its creator to thank him for the work.

I have thought often about mounting a replica Spitfire on a plinth on my farm, but I know that, if I do, the planners will tell me to take it down and the *Daily Mail* will say that I should have spent the money on something more productive and in the end it won't have been worth all the heartache.

That's why I'm in favour of ideas such as this EU Green Capital malarkey. Of course, because it's an eco-thing, it attracts madmen and unwashed women who will waste most of the money they're given, but occasionally they'll come up with something wonderful. Such as the wicker whales.

I have no idea how such things promote sustainability or cleaner living or even what relevance the whales have to a field in Bristol, but because they were built with eco-money by eco-people for an eco-future, nobody dares say that the £84,000 they cost could have been spent on a hospital. And the planners won't make them be dug up.

So the north has its angel and now the south has its whales. And that's why I shall vote to remain in the EU when the time comes.

12 June 2016

Come quietly, Tiddles, or it's jail for your owner

When I was growing up among the dark and satanic slag heaps of northern England, I well remember watching big flocks of golden plovers hopping about in the spoil, looking for tasty morsels. And in the family garden we would regularly see bullfinches and blue tits and chummy little wrens playing Tag with the sparrows.

One day, at dusk, a truly gigantic swarm of starlings arrived and spent a few moments painting extraordinary kaleidoscopic shapes in a sky that had been dyed a fabulous mix of purple and orange by the setting sun and the emissions from the mines and the power stations. You can forget herds of wildebeest and the Grand Canyon. That was, and remains, one of the most spectacular things I've ever seen.

At school I drew pictures of terns in my exercise books and I wrote projects on ospreys and peregrine falcons. I loved birds and I still do, even though I can't remember the last time I actually saw one.

These days I have a farm in the high, rolling hills of the Cotswolds. And sometimes I take a bottle of wine with me and sit at the highest point, on the still sharply defined earth banks of a Neolithic fort, thinking about, oh, just stuff.

It always makes me sad, though, because the only birds I see are the pheasants and partridges I reared and then failed to shoot last winter. Once, I saw a small flock of yellowhammers darting around in a hedgerow, and sometimes a gang of fieldfares will arrive in a tree to ravage it. But mostly the skies are as empty as they are on Mars.

I've planted acre upon acre of game crop and I've erected owl boxes and I've created wild, untended motorways for the insects and the voles to use. Because if you get the insects and the voles, you get the birds. Except you don't. Not any more. The fact is that in 1966 there were 210 million birds in the UK and now there are fewer than 166 million. That's a fall, in just fifty years, of 44 million. And that's huge.

Sometimes the RSPB raises this point, but then, because it has been hijacked by lunatics and communists, it always comes to a shoulder-saggingly political conclusion, blaming the empty skies on the motorcar, and people who eat meat, and fertilizer, and Margaret Thatcher.

Last week, however, we learned the awful truth. The extinction-level event that has reduced the dawn chorus to nothing more than a moment of quiet reflection is actually the domestic cat. Yup, your precious moggy has wreaked more havoc on the world's wildlife than the Exxon Valdez and the Torrey Canyon oil spills put together.

Let me give you some numbers. In America the number of birds killed by cats every year is – sit down for this – 3.7 billion. In the UK it's 55 million. And that's just birds. They also murder – and there's no other word for it – 220 million small creatures such as shrews and voles. Ever wondered why you never see hedgehogs any more? Well, for an answer, stare into the slitty, unblinking puddles of evil that masquerade as a cat's eyes.

I appreciate there are people who like their cats, but I have no idea why. They spend 80 per cent of the day asleep and the other 20 per cent ignoring you. Occasionally, one will leap on to the kitchen table and raise its tail so you can see its anus, and then, after you've given it some extremely expensive food, it will go outside to kill whatever it can get its claws on. For fun. *Tom and Jerry* wasn't a cartoon. It was a documentary.

Make absolutely no mistake about this. If you were six inches tall, your cat would amuse itself by tearing you to pieces, instead of doing what it does now, which is sit around, waiting for you to die of loneliness.

This is what cat owners must understand. That they are feeding and housing an animal that kills for a laugh. Which means they are giving house room to a psychopath. 'Oh, but he's so clean and he always disposes of his poos thoughtfully,' says Marjorie in her moggy's defence. Yes, Marjorie, but Fred West also disposed of his poos thoughtfully, and you wouldn't want him living in a basket in the kitchen, would you?

Cats also ruin furniture, give me asthma, wake me up in the night by fighting and clog up Instagram. And what do their owners get in return? Nothing. That's what. I asked my colleague James May last week why he has cats and he actually said, 'Because they don't care about me.' So what's the point, then? He might as well have an ant. Or a stick.

If I were in charge of everything, I'd announce the immediate introduction of a cat amnesty. Owners would be told they had twenty-four hours to hand their cat in to a police station, and anyone who failed to comply would have to go to prison.

Because we face a simple choice: cats or birds. And I'm sorry but that's like saying, 'Would you like to spend a fortnight in St Tropez this summer or would you rather fall into some farm machinery?'

However, it seems there is a third option. According to John Bradshaw, who somehow makes a living by being a cat behaviour expert at Bristol University, it may be possible to breed the murderer traits out of a cat.

He says there are only a dozen or so genes that differ between a domestic cat and the bigger, more jungly and more effective hunter variety and, if these could be studied more carefully, then boffins could get to work with their erasers and rub them out.

Yes, and after they've removed its killer instinct, maybe they could give it paws without vicious claws, and doe eyes, and perhaps a gene that makes it want to put its head out of the window when it's in a car, and fetch sticks and retrieve downed pheasants from the middle of a lake, and bark at burglars and love its owner to death. Because that, surely, would be the perfect pet.

19 June 2016

I'm going to hell in a handkerchief and no one cares

Yes. I'm going to ignore the elephant in the room. I'm going to pretend it isn't there, that there was no real news at all last week and no important resignations. And instead I shall write about hay fever.

Hay fever is one of those ailments that garner no real public sympathy. It's like insomnia. Tell someone you can't sleep and they'll say, immediately, 'Oh, I can. Head hits the pillow and I'm out like a light.' Which, as David Baddiel once pointed out, doesn't happen when someone says they're blind. You don't reply by saying, 'Ooh, I'm not. I can see colours and shapes and everything.'

Last week I was filming in Wales, in fields full of long grass, on what might fairly be termed a perfect summer's day. Except it wasn't perfect because of my allergies. My eyes were not so much bloodshot as actually bleeding. My nose was a tap. And I felt as though death might well be near. And all I got from the crew was an 'oh'. It was as though I'd told them I'd cut my finger.

It used to be worse when I was younger, but did the school care? No. Not even a small bit. In fact, it used to deliberately make everything worse by making me play cricket. I'd be forced – because I wasn't any good at it – to stand in the long grass, miles from what passed for the action, until I had actually sneezed out a lung. Occasionally the ball would come my way, scalding hot from re-entering the Earth's atmosphere, and from all over the pitch, people would order me loudly to catch it.

Which was impossible, because I was sneezing and blind and completely disabled. Usually the ball would cnnect with the end of my hopelessly outstretched middle finger, driving the entire digit into the palm of my hand, before falling, to a chorus of 'You useless prat', to the ground.

Later, much later, when I really should have been in hospital, they'd tie pads to my legs and give me a bat and make me stand in the middle of the pitch so a huge boy called Phil Lovell could throw at me what was, to all intents and purposes, a rock. And I wouldn't know it was coming until it hit me in the left testicle.

I would beg the teachers to let me off cricket, but they would have none of it. They would talk about the trenches and how people didn't moan about hay fever back then, and two days later send me back out to have the other testicle mashed to a pulp as well.

I was sent, eventually, to a clinic, where the doctors determined, by stabbing me in the arm about four hundred times, that I was allergic to grass and should avoid it where possible. Which is pretty tricky in a country where only 2 per cent of the land has been built on.

But it was an actual doctor's note. An official document that I could present to the teachers . . . who simply tore it up and told me to report to the cricket field immediately.

In the sixth form I simply refused to do it and they would punish me by giving me two hours of detention on a Saturday afternoon. They would actually punish me for being ill. Except, of course, it wasn't really a punishment, because sitting in a room with the windows shut to keep out the pollen reading a good book was, frankly, a lot better than having my fingers and my testicles broken.

Exams? Absolutely no concession was made at all back then. I sneezed so much on to one history paper that after two hours it looked as if I'd vomited on it. Eventually I was expelled, for a number of reasons, some of which involved my refusal to play cricket. Which means I was expelled, in part, for having hay fever.

Since then, of course, the world has changed. Teachers are no longer allowed to fondle their pupils. Police constables have been banned from clipping apple scrumpers round the ear, and victims are allowed to do pretty much what they want until they get 'closure'.

Yet hay fever is still treated as a mild and pathetic ailment that troubles only the weak and the feeble-minded. A friend of mine told the people who'd photographed him jumping a red light that he'd been sneezing at the time, but he still had to pay the fine. He was lying, of course, but they never even bothered to find out.

You could say your burqa slipped and they'd let you off. You could say you had premenstrual tension and they'd offer you counselling. But hay fever? No.

Last week, as I sneezed and retched my way round the hay fields of Wales, my cameraman, who is a genuinely decent old-school socialist, told me that drug companies have developed a cure but won't release it because they make more money from selling stuff that reduces the symptoms.

Yes, Ben, and there are aliens in the Nevada desert, the oil companies are suppressing an engine that runs on water and Mrs Thatcher was the devil. Your theory falls down, I'm afraid, because the one thing hay-fever sufferers know for a fact is that no pill or potion works. It should say on the bottle, in huge letters, 'This is totally useless.' Hay-fever alleviants either do nothing at all or send you to sleep, which is fine if you are a student but not fine if you are driving down the motorway.

There are injections you can have before the season begins,

and they too are a terrible con. Because when you go back to your doctor in July to tell him that you are still sneezing and crying every time you walk past a hay bale, he will say, 'Yes. But think how much worse it would have been if you hadn't given me £75.' And there's no arguing with that.

Some scientific research was being done to help sufferers, but that was a pan-European effort, and now, well, that's the elephant in the room, isn't it? And I'm not going there. I'm just waiting for the autumn, when it will be dark and cold and wet and we will have a prime minister we didn't elect. And everything will be better.

26 June 2016

Our only hope is a second vote – and a truly rotten PM

At work recently we had a vote and decided to invest a considerable sum of money in a new venture that within a week we could see was not going to work. We all sat around wailing and gnashing our teeth until someone had a brilliant idea. 'I know,' he said. 'Let's have another vote.' So we did and, as a result, financial ruin was averted. Phew.

Today lots of people – me included – are suggesting there should be a second vote on this whole Europe business, but we're told by people in suits that this is not possible. And when we ask why, they say, 'Because you just can't.'

Why not? Where in the constitution does it say we must abide by the result of a plebiscite, no matter how moronic that result might be? It doesn't say that. It doesn't say anything, in fact, because we don't really have a constitution in Britain. So we can do what happens to be sensible at any given moment. And what is sensible now surely is to hold a vote when everyone is equipped with the most powerful tool in the box: hindsight.

Of course this would infuriate millions of idiotic north of England coffin-dodgers who are prepared to bankrupt the country simply because they don't want to live next door to a 'darkie'. Many will write angry letters full of capital letters and underlining to their local newspapers. And there will be lots of discontent in various bingo halls, but who cares? They'll all be dead soon anyway.

It's also true to say that a second vote would make us look ridiculous on the world stage. But better to look silly for a short time than to live for ever in a dimly lit, poverty-stricken, festering nest of warts, mud and minority-bashing incidents on the bus home every evening.

The last time Europe was truly united the Romans were in charge, but then one day everyone decided they didn't like the wine and the roads and the baths and the smart uniforms any more and for the next five hundred years Britain endured the Dark Ages when everyone died at the age of twenty-seven, in hideous agony, having achieved absolutely nothing at all.

Then there was the Reformation, when a bunch of people decided they wanted to go it alone without Mr Pope. The thirty-year war that resulted killed up to 40 per cent of Germany's population.

It'll be the same thing all over again if we leave the EU. The Germans will grow tired of supporting the Greeks on their own and become Hitlerish again. The French will go on strike. Hadrian's Wall will have to be rebuilt and manned with armed guards. England will be plunged into a recession so deep that we will be forced to eat one another and then Vladimir Putin will arrive in a tank and there will be a war.

Yes, 17.4 million people voted to leave the EU, believing that they'd immediately get their job back from that bastard Latvian at No. 24 and that new and exciting trade deals would be done and that the NHS would get £350 million a week.

But now they have realized that, actually, all the money we save by not being in the EU will have to be spent policing the camps around London's St Pancras station that will need to be built to house the million Syrians who've been ushered on to a train in Paris. And that the fishing quotas won't change. And that going abroad on holiday will be too time-consuming at the airport and too expensive. And as a result many are ringing Jeremy Vine to say that, if they were given their time again, they'd vote to remain.

This is the problem. We could soon be in the situation where 80 per cent or 90 per cent of the population is lying in the street, covered in weeping sores, begging for a second referendum, and we won't be able to have one because a man in a suit says, 'You just can't.'

It's such a stupid state of affairs that even my hair is angry. I toss and turn at night, beating the pillow with impotent rage as I think how little humanity would have achieved if it had never been given the opportunity to change its mind. And how my kids are going to live miserable lives because our generation was too stubborn and too frightened of looking silly to say, 'Let's try that again.'

There is, as I see it, only one glimmer of hope. One chance that the day can be saved. And, tragically, it is called Tom Watson.

He is, as I write, still the Deputy Leader of the Labour Party. He is also very possibly the worst human being on the planet. I hate him on a cellular level. I dislike him so much that on long car journeys I often amuse myself by thinking up new and interesting ways of peeling off all his skin.

The hatred began when he started to persecute friends of mine in the world of newspapers and it was curdled with added venom when he initially refused to apologize after accusing an innocent man of being a rapist and kiddie fiddler. He is a terrible man but, given the tumult surrounding the Labour leadership, he does stand a chance of being the party leader by the time the country is faced with its next general election. Of course, Watson has suggested that he won't run for his party's leadership – but then that's what Michael Gove said.

And if Watson does become leader, all he needs to fix this Brexit mess is to say in his manifesto, 'If I am elected, I will hold another referendum on Britain's EU membership.'

He'd win by a landslide. Even I would vote for him. And

then in the referendum that followed, the young would actually get off their arses and go to the polling booth, millions would change their mind, we'd be back in the bosom of the EU, the uncertainty would end, the financial tap would be turned back on, the recession would be avoided, Scotland would hang around, there would be no famine and Putin's tanks would remain in their bunkers.

The only downside, of course, is that we'd end up with a horrible, horrible man as prime minister. But that, in my book, is a price worth paying.

3 July 2016

No bull, Miguel, you look nuts in that gold lamé

If you grow up in Spain, there are many sports to keep you fit and amused. Spanish football is about as good as it gets. Tennis is big too, thanks to Rafa Nadal. And for those in the north of the country, there's pelota, one of the most beautiful and exciting games I've ever seen.

Sadly, however, a young man called Victor Barrio decided that none of these things was quite his bag and that he wanted to be a bullfighter. It didn't go well. Because last weekend, in front of a good-natured summer crowd, and his pretty wife, he was stabbed in the aorta and died.

Needless to say, everyone is now running around waving their arms in the air and saying that no sport is worth the life of a participant and that bullfighting must be outlawed immediately. But that of course is nonsense. Almost everyone who takes part in horse riding is killed at some point, and it's the same story with the Isle of Man TT races, which have a higher rate of attrition than the Ebola virus. And no one is suggesting that these sports should be banned.

Then there's golf. On almost every course in the land, there's a dead fifty-five-year-old businessman in one of the bunkers, his heart a ruined bag of mush and his face etched with pain and regret. But again, no one is saying that golf should be outlawed. Well, I am. Not because it will eventually kill many of my friends, but because I don't like their trousers.

Bullfighting, however, is different. Yes, the trousers are pretty terrible, obviously, but actually it's safer than Formula One motor racing, which these days is more safe than sitting in a box full of eiderdown, and about as exciting. Until Bar-rio got gored, no participant in Spain had died for thirty years. Apart from the bulls, obviously.

We can't therefore ban it on safety grounds, and neither am I overly bothered about the animal-cruelty issues. I'm happy to poison a fly and watch it headbutt itself to death in a series of high-speed impacts against the French windows, so why should I get my knickers in a twist about a bull bleed-ing to death? However, I do think bullfighting should be stopped, because it is stupid.

Let me put it this way. If the concept of sport were to be invented next week, people would look at football and say: 'Yes. That's pretty good.' It's the same story with 100-metre races and rounders and the aforementioned pelota. But I'm fairly sure that if someone proposed bullfighting, everyone else would say, quizzically, 'Just run that past me again.'

It goes something like this. A 'matador' goes into a ring, where a four-year-old bull, which weighs getting on for a ton, is wondering what the hell it's doing there. The matador observes the bull's behaviour and character while attempt-ing to form an emotional bond with it.

Having failed to do this, because he's a man and the bull isn't, he summons a junior bullfighter, who arrives in the ring on a horse. The bull attacks the horse and tries to disembowel it. This makes several children in the audience cry. After the bull has failed to disembowel the horse, because it's wearing a funky padded hazmat suit, the junior bullfighter sticks a spear into the bull's neck, which makes it angry.

In the next stage, more junior bullfighters stick more spears into the bull's neck until most of its blood is on the outside of its skin and its neck muscles are so worn out it can barely hold its head up. And at this point the matador himself, the senior man, waves a red rag at it while doing a disco dance.

And then after a little while he stabs it with a sword and he's the winner.

Sometimes, he decides for no particular reason that he will not stick a sword into it and the bull is allowed to live out the rest of its days on a farm, with a gaggle of lady cows, until one day Lamborghini names a car after it.

Now. If you were to suggest that as a sport, everyone would say, 'Don't be an idiot,' and that would be that. Which is exactly what happens whenever someone suggests that it should be banned. They are told, firmly, that this will not be possible, and the debate is over.

The argument centres on the fact that bullfighting can trace its roots back to 2000 BC, when men would prove their manliness by fighting animals. Well, yes. But that's because in those days they needed some light relief from making bronze and they had no PlayStations. Today, if a young man wants to prove he has testicles the size of water melons, he can invite a girl to watch him play *Call of Duty*.

Which causes bullfighting enthusiasts to say that it's a tradition. And that makes me so angry that even my hair hurts. Because on that basis we could amuse ourselves by drowning women in a duck pond.

Britain's red telephone box is a tradition. It's a symbol of everything that made us great. But only a handful of lunatics minded when it was replaced with the iPhone. A policeman's tall helmet is a tradition. But it was phased out because it's not really practical in a terrorist shootout. And it's traditional for our soldiers to wear red. But they don't any more because it would be silly.

We have learned to let things go when they start to look ridiculous, and I'm afraid that Spain's bullfighting enthusiasts must do the same. If they want to impress girls by killing animals, then fine. It's not for me to stop them sneaking into the neighbours' garden and strangling a cat. And if they want to make some kind of sacrifice to amuse their God, again, it's not for me to interfere.

But I would point out that dressing up in a gold lamé suit and waving a red rag at a bull, on television, makes you look like an imbecile. Because the rest of the world has known for some time that bulls are colour-blind.

17 July 2016

Let Russia dope: I want to see the heroin hurdles

So it's been claimed by various people with stern faces that the Russian secret service has been using all sorts of devious methods to conceal the fact that hundreds of the country's athletes and sports people have been routinely testing positive for drugs. I think we are supposed to be surprised by this.

Well, I'm not. When I was a small boy I clearly remember wondering why half of Russia's women shot-putters appeared to be men. One, I seem to recall, had chest hair that went all the way down to her scrotum. Another, from somewhere behind the Iron Curtain, had plainly been taking something that had turned her into a tractor.

You had the pretty young woman from France and the game filly from Great Britain lobbing the discus forty yards, and then out would lumber Ivana Shrek, who'd throw it out of the stadium. And we all sat there thinking, 'Oooh. Isn't the Soviet Union scary and impressive?' Which I suppose was the point.

I assume that back then it was not possible to determine who'd taken what. But now it is – hence the alleged involvement of Russia's FSB. It's said that at the Sochi Winter Games laboratory staff passed tainted urine samples from athletes through a secret hole in a wall to agents, who somehow broke the tamper-proof seals and replaced them with urine that was as fresh and natural as Sophie Raworth's next fruit salad.

Investigators reckon that in the four years until 2015 there were 312 dodgy results covered up by Russia's sports ministry, which then said that the man mountains it was sending to toss the caber and the supercomputers who were turning up to play chess were able to become so brilliant because they'd been brought up on a healthy Russian diet of turnips and beetroot. And vodka.

Now of course there are calls for Russia to be banned from all Olympic competitions. And I get that. If I'd trained for twenty years to be the best pole vaulter in the world and then I was beaten by someone whose blood sample would trouble a Geiger counter, I'd be livid.

But I haven't trained for twenty years to be the best pole vaulter in the world. I'm just someone who quite likes to watch sport when I'm bored. And I must confess I find myself hoping Russia reacts to the proposed ban by setting up an alternative Olympic Games where anything goes.

That way, the athletes who've trained and done everything the old-fashioned way can play Dodge the Mosquito in Rio, which is all very lovely for those who enjoy watching people running about and jumping over stuff. While on cable TV the rest of us could watch – all the way from Moscow – Olympians on Drugs.

Come on. Who wouldn't want to watch a 400-metre race for people who'd just filled themselves up with heroin? Or a tennis match between two people who were suffering from massive paranoia? Stoned hurdling – that'd be good too. I think this would work especially well at the Winter Games, because I know from many years of experience that my skiing in the morning is timid and slow and rather boring. But after lunch, when I've had some wines, it becomes fluid and fast and thrilling. And then I have a crash and break a small bone. Drunk skiing would be a tremendous spectator sport.

It's the same story with motor racing. When I was young and completely irresponsible I hosted a grass-track banger event for friends, and anyone suspected of being in proper control of their vehicle was summoned to the pits and made to take a breathalyser test.

If it revealed they were under the limit, they were made to drink three pints of beer before they were allowed to rejoin the race. A similar idea would, I think, transform Formula One. 'Oh, look. It's Fernando Alonso and – ha-ha-ha – he's going the wrong way round the track.'

I could of course go on, matching various sports to various hilariously inappropriate intoxicants, but actually there's a serious point to be made here. Scientists have already developed genetically modified wheat that is more resistant to disease than the wheat that nature invented. So why should they not be allowed to genetically modify human beings?

Boffins have already worked out that by altering the CCR5 gene they could make someone incapable of catching HIV. Sickle cell anaemia, muscular dystrophy and certain types of blindness could be eradicated too.

Recently doctors announced that by using stem-cell technology they had effectively cured a teenager from Bristol of a rare blood disorder that had already killed his big brother.

Jesus enthusiasts, I know, have some issues with this sort of thing, and so do various tub-thumping politicians. Even some very wise people have pointed out that we've only had a complete map of human genes for thirteen years and it's too soon to start fiddling. They say more research must be done, and that brings me back to my Olympians on Drugs idea.

Because here we would have many fit young men and women who, because they want to be the best of the best of the best, would readily volunteer to become the first real-life Jason Bourne. They could be the guinea pigs.

Obviously, they'd have to be neutered in some way. Because if the genetic modification and drug combo didn't work and they became werewolves or Daleks or something, we wouldn't want them breeding and creating a master race that would wipe the rest of us out.

But what if it did work? What if science could turn even the most stupid person into a genius? What if it could make Captain Fat capable of running the hundred metres in six seconds? And what if there were no drawbacks?

So long as we all rush around, waving our arms in the air and accusing Russia of cheating, we're never going to know if they're on to something. Far better, I reckon, to shut up and let them get on with it.

24 July 2016

Sun, seeds and squirrels – it's hell in the parks police

At school we had a careers master who was on hand to help pupils choose what job they'd like after they left. And at no point did he say to me, 'Well, son, I should think you'll be able to make a pretty decent living by driving other people's cars too quickly round corners while shouting.'

In fact, he gave me the choice of being an estate agent, a bank clerk or an accountant – and then he gave me a two-hour detention for saying, 'I want to be a homosexual astronaut.'

Actually, I was lying. What I really wanted was to be a meteorological officer in the Sahara Desert. I'd file my report every morning, saying the day would be hot and sunny, and then I'd go back to sleep, knowing that, 98 per cent of the time, I'd be correct.

My son had an even better idea when he was asked at school what he'd like to do. He said he wanted to be A. A. Gill, but without the writing. In other words, he wanted to go to excellent restaurants and watch television, and then spend the rest of the day doing as he pleased.

Today, as I understand it, a huge number of young girls say that when they grow up what they'd like to do most is 'Be famous'. They read the sidebar of shame in the *Mail Online* and all they see is an endless parade of women 'jetting' in and out of Los Angeles International Airport and lying by the pool, earning a living simply by having breasts.

It's why there are queues round the block for the chance to warble your way through a Celine Dion song on *The X Factor*, and it's why every newsagent's is rammed with people frantically rubbing away at a scratchcard. Everyone wants to be Katie Price, or me, or Adrian Gill. To do something that doesn't apparently involve any actual work.

It is a noble dream. But it so very rarely works out . . .

I was in Liverpool last year, in the back of a taxi, moaning about how I didn't want to be there, doing whatever it is I was on my way to do. And in the gloom of a wet and cold November evening I went past a branch of PC World where I saw a young man in a purple shirt doing whatever it is that shop assistants in PC World do.

And in a moment his life flashed before my eyes. He'd work hard until he was made store manager and then, with some careful arse-licking, he might one day become a regional manager, which would enable him to attend the annual conference at a hotel in North Wales, where he'd get a bit drunk and accidentally insert himself in Janet, the regional manager for the north-east.

And that would be the highlight of his life. The moment that would bring half a smile to his greying lips as he lay on his deathbed many years in the future. I stopped moaning immediately and I haven't since.

PC World man is not alone. I look at Nicholas Witchell on the news, endlessly commentating on Prince George's new hairstyle and how the Duchess of Cornwall smiled at an old lady, and I think, 'Is that how you wanted your life to turn out? Really?'

It's the same story with people who chisel fat from London's sewers or those who sit at an air traffic control computer, or the man who comes to dust the plants in my office. If you'd said to any one of them when they were sixteen that this is what they'd be doing twenty years down the line, they'd have jumped in front of a train.

It's not a money thing I'm talking about. I have many

friends who work in the City, and they all have Range Rovers and stick-thin wives and adorable, clever children who attend agreeable, leafy schools where no one gets knifed. But all they do, all day, is watch ones and noughts float across a computer screen. And that's a terrible way of filling time between the two eternities.

All last week I was thinking about this, about what job would allow our children to spend their days doing not much of anything at all. And while sitting in Holland Park, in the sunshine, enjoying a morning cup of coffee, I cracked it. They should join the parks police.

The normal police are obviously no good because you have to spend all day talking gibberish while waiting for someone to throw a petrol bomb at your head. And you aren't allowed to climb ladders or rough up crims or do anything that is fun because there'd be too much paperwork afterwards.

The parks police, however, are different because parks, by and large, are used by people on Tinder dates and quite attractive women with dogs. Maybe you will occasionally have to ask someone to cycle more considerately and sometimes you will have to put a carelessly discarded sweet wrapper in a bin. But that's about it. They even give you a Volvo.

Think about it. Have you ever heard of a parks police shootout, or witnessed a parks police high-speed car chase? Has there ever been a criminal gang that has decided not to ram-raid the sweetshop by the boating lake in case it gets collared by a burly parks policeman or policewoman?

The parks police website says you may be asked to provide security at any concerts that are being staged in the park, which means you get free tickets and front-row viewing of something you'd want to see anyway. Also, it says you may be called upon to advise the public on dog chipping and cycle marking. But it adds that, if you see any crime that may involve running, you can call upon the actual police, who will do it for you.

This means you are free to spend your days sitting in your comfy Volvo, in pleasant surroundings, watching pretty women walking past with their dogs. It is then, quite literally, the perfect job for somebody who doesn't want one.

31 July 2016

Blow a billion quid – only fatties and idlers need apply

After the riots of 2011, which were so massive and so terrifying that I can't remember where they were or what they were about, or how much damage was done, the government decided that everyone would go back to an Enid Blyton-style state of contentedness if the nation's poor people were given £448 million.

On paper this looks a promising plan because if someone who is fat and unwashed is suddenly given a large lump of money it's likely he or she will immediately send their child to school instead of letting them do burgling and drugs.

And a child who's read Milton and Chaucer is statistically less likely to throw a brick through a shop window than a child who hasn't. There's no actual proof of this, obviously, but we know it to be so.

The trouble is that, having decided to narrow the gap between Waynetta Slob and Roman Abramovich, the government faced a bit of a problem. Because it couldn't just load £448 million into a van and drive round council estates in the north of England throwing bundles of it at anyone in a tracksuit. Ministers needed a system so they could work out who was deserving of the money and who was not.

And they decided that this responsibility should be handed over to local authorities, which, again, sounds good on paper. You ask a government minister where all the poor people live in Bolton and he won't have a clue. But people on the borough council will.

There is a problem, however, with this scheme in practice,

and it's this: by and large, the people who work for borough councils are just traffic wardens who got lucky.

Think about it. No one grows up dreaming of the day when they can work for the local council. It's what you do when the pox doctor says he doesn't want a clerk any more.

Have you met someone who works for a local council? No. Strike that. It's a silly question, because of course you haven't. You only see them in the town hall, behind a glass partition, below a sign saying, 'I am useless at my job. I know that. But if you remind me, you will be prosecuted for verbal assault.'

Certainly, I wouldn't trust the deputy assistant to the equalities officer on a council to manage a village hall tombola, let alone the distribution of hundreds of millions of pounds. But that's exactly what the government decided to do . . .

After a little while the government started to ask if the councils were happy to have been sent a large amount of money. And it turned out, amazingly, that they were. Thrilled, in fact. Overjoyed.

They sent reports to London saying the scheme had been a huge success. And they released figures showing that 90 per cent of about 117,000 families selected to benefit from the handouts had turned their lives around and become model citizens. They really did. They said that 90 per cent had been cured of their sloth and their violent tendencies and had turned over a new leaf.

And what's more, they argued that, having invested £448 million in the scheme, the government had saved £1.2 billion, thanks to a reduction in the cost of policing and providing truant officers and benefits, and so on.

Back in Whitehall, the government believed them. It really and genuinely thought that £448 million had solved the nation's great divide. It also believed, amazingly, that it had got a threefold return on its investment almost instantaneously. So, figuring that the more it handed out, the more it would save, it decided to give the councils £900 million to share among a whopping 400,000 families. With a net that wide, even Elton John was likely to get a knock on the door asking if he'd like a bit of extra cash.

The way this whole enterprise was being described, you'd imagine the police in places such as Barnsley and Preston were shutting up the stations at night because there was simply nothing to do any more. Naturally, when I read about it, I saw in my mind classrooms full of rosy-cheeked children, all with their hands up, eager to answer the teacher's question. And, outside, parents in well-cut jeans talking about the lovely little bar they'd found in Val d'Isère last year.

However, and this will come as a surprise to no one at all, it seems councils may have exaggerated the benefits of having a money-distribution van. Because a report released last week found that the scheme had no impact. The people who wrote it actually used those words. It had 'no impact'. As in: none. Diddly-squat. Zilch.

Nearly half the families who took part in the scheme were still claiming benefits a year and a half later. And you find the same percentage among similar families who did not take part. Truancy levels were no different either. And neither were the numbers of those being cautioned or convicted of a criminal offence. This means the government has in effect thrown away more than £1.3 billion.

It makes my shoulders sag, because surely by now people with a modicum of intelligence must know that social engineering just doesn't work. Give everyone in the country a quid and by next week two people will be multimillionaires and everyone else will have nothing. That's just a fact.

Give 400,000 jobless fatties nearly a billion quid and by

next week all of it will be in the hands of Allied Breweries, Ladbrokes and Pablo Escobar. You can't change that.

We've watched countless leaders in countless countries attempt to level the playing field. And they've all failed. The only reason Jeremy Corbyn's supporters haven't realized this is because, mostly, they haven't grown up yet. And they haven't been to Cuba. Certainly, they haven't realized that some people are born to be rich and some are born to be poor.

Trying to do something about this is as impossible as deciding that life would be fairer if everyone were good-looking. Yes. But some of us aren't. And there's nothing that can be done to change that.

So, Mrs May. Here's a tip. The next time there are riots, don't spray anyone with money. Spray them instead with a water cannon.

23 October 2016

Pipe down and come with me on a tour of Trump's Britain

Almost all my friends are bleeding-heart liberals. They weep when they see pictures of those poor Syrian children having their backs waxed to make them look younger. They host fundraising evenings to buy padded bras for people with transgender issues and they are utterly bewildered and devastated by the Brexit vote.

They cannot understand why we are having to leave the EU, because everyone they ever meet, in every pastry shop and at every dinner party and on the touchline of every school sports pitch, wanted to remain. I've tried mentioning Barnsley, but to them it's the pretty little Cotswold village they pass through on the way to Babington House. 'Liz Hurley used to live there,' they say, wondering why my eyes are rolling.

Of course, they are completely stunned by the Donald Trump thing, because the Americans they know seem so sensible. 'I was with Gwyneth only last night, trying out some of her new smoothies, and she's such a lovely girl . . .' Then they wander off to talk to Gary Lineker.

He's their new messiah. He started off by preaching about the awfulness of Brexit, moved through the iniquities of immigration and is now in full Bible-thumping mode on Trump. In Gary's mind, everyone's a racist or a sexist or a bully or a homophobe, and his disciples are to be found applauding wildly. My friends love him.

They can't understand the US election result, because they all go to America a lot and to them the place always seems so reasonable. They stay at the Mercer in New York and Shutters on the Beach in Santa Monica, California. And they've all partied with Sean Penn and Jay-Z and Bruce, all of whom were behind Hillary Clinton. And yet, somehow, she lost.

Naturally, my mates have decided that everyone who lives between the Mercer and Shutters is stupid because they either voted for Trump or they didn't vote at all. And now they are all wondering out loud whether democracy has had its time. If I were to suggest that people with low IQs should be given less of a say in who runs a country than those in Mensa, most would nod sagely and say pensively, 'It may have to come to that, because it's ridiculous that my cleaning lady has the same influence in an election as me.'

Yes, but this would mean that, for the rest of time, our leaders would continue to be cut-out'n'repeat clones of Mr Blair and Mrs Clinton and Mr Cameron. And they'd continue to push for gay rights and transgender traffic lights and cycle lanes and anti-bullying campaigns and tougher rules on hate crimes and more immigration and lower speed limits and healthier polar bears. And they'd be warmly hugged by everyone they met for their tireless campaign to make saying 'period' a crime.

But I'll let you into a little secret. All the words I cannot use any more in this newspaper. All those jokes no one can say any more on television. All those phrases that are no longer socially acceptable in Notting Hill and the Home Counties. Well, up north, you will hear all of them, all the time. Political correctness simply does not exist in a Doncaster pub. Because there's no time to worry about the correct word for 'cross-dresser' when you haven't got any money.

In parts of America there are people who spend all day in the cold, freezing half to death in a queue for the food bank.

Many have no warm clothes or teeth and, forgive my language, but exactly how much of a shit do you think they give about transgender issues or the effing polar bears?

And it's not just America. In the parts of Britain that my friends see only from their Range Rover windows as they drive to Scotland for a bit of shooting, there are towns and villages that are full of young people who have nothing to do all day but mate. 'Dims breeding dims,' is what my grand-father used to say.

Every time there's an election, a politician comes on the television they've half-inched from the social to say he will make life better for the underprivileged. So they vote for him and then find out later that his idea of 'underprivileged' is actually someone who wants to dress up in a frock.

Yes, my heart bleeds for those who are bullied because of their sex or their looks or their sexual orientation. Yes, it bleeds for the dispossessed of Syria and the victims of female genital mutilation in Egypt. But it only bleeds because I've got a ton of money and two houses. If I had an empty larder and a rash and a terrible hacking cough, I assure you of this: I wouldn't care a bit.

Trump talked a lot of nonsense in his campaign, and I think, if I was to meet him, I'd dislike him on a cellular level. However, he maintained throughout that politicians had let the poor down. Ker-ching. He said they would always let the poor down. Ker-ching again. And the only thing that could provide them with jobs and money was business. Big ker-ching. They liked the sound of that and said to themselves, 'Yup. The future's bright. The future's orange.'

It was the same story here with Brexit. Poor people in the north of England were given a chance to poke the liberal elite of London in the eye. And they took it.

And it's going to get worse. Because the more we continue

to ram political correctness and cycle lanes and environmentalism down everyone's throats, the more they'll think, 'Oh why don't you sod off, you southern poofs.'

We will end up with extremism. A lunatic party will sweep into office on a tide of resentfulness. We will have our own Trump in Number Ten.

Happily, however, I have a solution. The Palace of Westminster is to be closed for essential refurbishments. This means MPs will have to meet somewhere else, and I reckon they should all go to Hartlepool. Because after a few years in this former steel town they might start to understand that in the big scheme of things Eddie Izzard's right to wear a pink beret is not that important.

13 November 2016

O Adrian, who will make me laugh now?

In 1981 there was a big working-men's pub in Earls Court, and on Cheltenham Gold Cup day it was crammed because, unusually for the times, the race was being shown on a television above the bar.

The whole place was a seething cauldron of braying Irish labourers and sloshing Guinness and cheap cigarette smoke until, with two furlongs to go, the door burst open and a lunatic dashed in. He leapt on to the bar, turned the television off and then ran out again. Welcome, everyone, to the man who would become my closest friend: A. A. Gill.

He was living back then in a dog basket in Kensington, dealing drugs to pay for his colossal thirst and hanging out with a group of very posh heroin addicts who spent their days forgetting to go to the funerals of their flatmates and friends. That he didn't croak then, in a puddle of his own urine and vomit, is a miracle.

But he has now. He died last weekend, leaving us with a body of work that beggars belief. It beggars belief partly because he didn't start writing until he was thirty-eight but mostly because of his profound dyslexia. He'd have had a better chance of getting his letters in the right order if he'd lobbed a tin of alphabet soup into a ceiling fan. He'd often text me to say where we were having lunch and I'd have to use a Turing decoder to work out what the bloody hell he meant. 'Twersy', for instance, was 'the Wolseley'.

The way Adrian dealt with this was a lesson to all sufferers today. History was his favourite subject at school, but he always got a bad mark so he asked his teacher why. You're one of the best in class, said the teacher, but you've got a problem with your writing. Adrian decided angrily that he didn't have the problem; the teacher did. And he vowed ever afterwards to make it someone else's problem, not his own.

Adrian struggled, too, with reading. It would take him half an hour to read the inscription on a statue or a war memorial, which is something he did a lot, and yet somehow he knew everything about everything.

Why do the lampposts on the Mall have ships on them? Who invented chewing gum? How do the pirates off Somalia operate? All of that – and all of everything else – somehow was in his head. 'Polymath' doesn't even begin to cover it. He was Wikipedia with a cravat.

But his real gift, as we all know, because he was the cornerstone of all our Sunday mornings, was not just delivering the facts. It was making them come alive. Once, when I was away, he wrote my motoring column and said his TVR sounded like two lesbians in a bucket. It remains the best description yet of the noise a V8 makes at tickover. And it wasn't even his specialist subject.

He also said that an Aston Martin sounded like Tom Jones bending over to pick up the soap in a Strangeways shower. And more recently, my new television show is '*Top Gear* in witness protection'. No one, and I do mean no one, could phrase-make like him.

And lines such as this didn't come to him after hours of pacing up and down and sucking on the end of a Biro. They were a constant soundtrack to his life. We were flying once to Blackpool, at night, in a helicopter. And after a long period of zooming over nothing but inky blackness we passed over the sodium-orange glow of a town. 'What's that?' Adrian said to the pilot. A check on the map revealed it to be

Preston. Adrian looked at it quizzically for a moment. 'What's the point of that?' he asked.

Later he met a Tory Cabinet minister who blustered on and on about how important it was for people to get on their bikes and make something of their lives: start a business, perhaps. 'That's what I did when I was young,' said Adrian enthusiastically. The Tory went into a back-slapping, that's-the-ticket routine, which was cut short when Adrian said, 'Yeah. I was a drug dealer.'

Over the years, Adrian stopped the drugs and the booze and even the cigarettes by becoming addicted to other stuff. Mostly this involved buying trousers. I think he bought a new pair most days. And another cravat. And a cardigan or two. And perhaps another stupid suit, lined this time with all the flags of Siena's *contrade*.

Which brings us on to the man. He was unfathomable, really. Because he was a screamingly camp straight man, an un-Christian believer and a potty-mouthed poet. 'C∗∗∗' was pretty much his favourite word.

It's been reported that he was upset and bitter about being denied expensive treatment for the cancer that killed him. But he wasn't. He accepted it. Because he was a terrible old leftie who thought like a Tory. Or it might have been the other way round. I never really knew.

Occasionally, when we wrote pieces together, we'd plan them so I'd have one opinion and he'd have another. But as often as not he'd get to where we were going and he'd change his mind. We went to Midland in Texas, which I knew he'd think was a hellhole, and he loved it. So I took him to France, which he had always loathed, and he decided as soon as we arrived that he didn't.

Before he died we were planning to write a piece together about whether Italians were more interested in food or cars.

If it had happened, I just know he'd have said the Fiat 500 was way more important than some silly bits of fish in a tomato sauce. (Which it is, by the way.)

It sounds as if he was a contrarian, but he actually wasn't. He just had opinions, and sometimes they'd change and sometimes they wouldn't, and sometimes they'd contradict one another. And he really, really, didn't care if you agreed with him or not.

Nor did he have an off button. If he thought your new sofa was ghastly, he'd tell you. And if you'd put on a bit of weight, he'd bring it up. Once an artist proudly showed him their work and he said, 'That's amazing. How long have you been painting with your feet?'

I'd watch people sometimes, spooling up for an argument with him, and I'd sit there thinking, 'Oh, no. Don't poke the beast. Don't poke it.' But they usually did, and then he'd eviscerate them, because he was faster than they were, and funnier and cleverer.

It's been said that Adrian and I were very close, and we were. But the truth is, he was close to thousands and thousands of people. If you walked down any street in what he called London – nothing with an 'E' or an 'N' in the postcode – you'd have to stop every twenty feet so he could embrace someone coming the other way. In every restaurant it would take him twenty minutes to get to his table because of all the hugs and wide-eyed 'daaaaaahlings' he'd have to do on the way. It seemed sometimes that he knew everyone.

Three days before he died he had Hillary Clinton's former security adviser, James Rubin, on one side of his hospital bed, reading him bits from the *Guardian*, and Rebekah Brooks on the other. Then in came the designer Tom Ford to talk spectacles.

He had thousands and thousands of friends because, deep down, he was kind, warm-hearted and extremely loyal. But by far and away his greatest gift was his ability to make people laugh. Me especially. When we broke our golf virginity together in Cheshire, I damn nearly hacked up my own spleen. When he decided it would be quicker to kick the ball round the course, I honestly thought, 'If I don't breathe in soon, I'm going to die.'

It was the same story when he accidentally reversed an Abrams main battle tank into an ornamental lake in the middle of Baghdad, or on shoots when we'd spend all day trying to land birds on each other's head. Or when I opened the paper and saw the restaurant he'd reviewed had been given no stars. 'Oh, this is going to be good . . .' I'd think. And it always, always was.

Yes, he was brilliant at writing serious stories about serious issues. And he was brilliant also at picking apart a television programme or telling you why it's a good idea to put nutmeg on cauliflower cheese (which it isn't). But he was at his absolute best when he was being funny.

Towards the end, he and I were sitting around in Whitby with the comedian Jimmy Carr. Adrian announced he'd just started to watch the *Westworld* series on the television.

'Ooh,' said Jimmy. 'That's a bit ambitious – it's a ten-parter.'

It's the last time I heard Adrian burst out laughing. And that's what I'll miss most of all. Well, that, and every other bit of him.

18 December 2016

For a healthier, happier you, just live like it's 1617

Doubtless you have awoken this morning full of steely-eyed resolve to become a new person in 2017 – fitter, healthier, thinner and less full of drink and smoke. But it won't work. It never does. Because being healthy and fit and sober is boring.

So allow me to suggest a new resolution. A resolution that is easy to do, and that will cause you to live a longer and happier and more interesting life. Get rid of all your stuff.

We shall start – as you did a few minutes ago – with your coffee machine. It drives you mad, doesn't it, because every time you ask it to do what it was designed to do, it says that it needs water, or beans, or some kind of decalcifying procedure, which means you have to spend the next half an hour shouting at your family because the instruction book isn't in the drawer where instruction books are supposed to be kept. And when you do find it, it's full of badly drawn diagrams that make no sense.

Of course, you may have a much simpler Nespresso machine that produces delicious coffee without much palaver at all. Yes, but is there anything on God's green Earth that generates so much unnecessary waste? One day we will all drown in discarded Clooney capsules.

And have you tried to buy replacements? You are asked if you have an account with Nespresso, by which it means a facility that allows it to sell your personal details to other luxury-good suppliers. And if you do, you can simply put your purchases on account, which takes exactly five minutes longer than paying by credit card.

So if you want a happy and less stressful life in 2017, put your coffee machine in the bin and go back to a kettle. And then throw your wi-fi equipment away as well.

Think about it. No more rummaging around in a cupboard you can't quite reach, trying to read the microdot on the back of the box that is your code. No more turning it off and then on again. No more frustration when the film you've selected starts to freeze. No more children glued to their phones throughout every meal.

Naturally, you will also be cut off from the world, but is that such a bad thing? I had a very happy Christmas precisely because, without a functioning wi-fi, I was blissfully unaware that every single celebrity in the world had died.

Next, you should throw away everything that needs a charger. Because imagine that. Going on holiday with a suitcase full of books and clothes rather than wires.

And do you need two cars? Yes. Definitely. There was that time in June when you had to be at your parents' and your wife or husband had to take the kids to Alton Towers. You couldn't have done that with just one set of wheels in the drive. But for the rest of the time they are just sitting outside, depreciating, costing a fortune in insurance and developing faults.

It's the same story with your complicated driverless lawn-mower and your octopus pool cleaner and your motorized pepper grinder. You imagined that such things would make your life easier, but instead you have to spend every spare moment shouting at them because they've gone wrong.

As you may have heard, I recently lost a bet with my colleagues on the television show we make, and as a result they blew up my house. This meant I had to get planning permission to build a new one, and on paper it all looks jolly enormous.

However, because it will take three or four years to finish,

I've renovated a very small cottage and moved into that. It's so small I can run a bath with one hand and clean the Aga with the other. And I'm sitting here now, with my laptop wedged between the dishwasher and the wood-burning stove, thinking, 'Why did I buy a dishwasher?' And more importantly, 'Why do I need anything bigger or more complicated than this?'

The water comes – quite slowly, I admit – from the stream at the bottom of the garden, I'm warmed by logs I forage from the woods, there are no dimmer switches to break and no loos that shoot jets of water into my bottom, and if I want to close the curtains I'll have to buy some first. At the moment, I have gaffer-taped blankets over the windows, and that seems to work fine.

The furniture – and there isn't much – was scavenged from my mother's lockup, and I must confess it's quite nice sitting here, surrounded by memories from my childhood, knowing that, because it was all made from wood by warty peasants in the seventeenth century, none of it will ever snap.

In fact, up here in the sticks I have only two pieces of twenty-first-century engineering: a Range Rover, which has broken down, and a quad bike, which has also broken down, mainly because some kids from the village filled the petrol tank with what I hope is water but which I fear, having siphoned it out, is more likely to be urine. Because that's what I'd have done.

This means that if I want to go to the village for supplies, I must walk. And as I am allergic to this kind of thing I went outside the back door this morning with my gun and shot a partridge. Tonight it will be supper. Along with some vegetables that I bought before Christmas at Daylesford with the £215 I've now saved by eschewing all form of modern living.

Later this week, of course, I shall have to go back to London, to my hi-tech flat, where I shall spend a few days trying to turn the thermostatically controlled windows off. It'll be the sad end of my new year's resolution to spend the rest of my life in the seventeenth century.

Although, as I near the end of this column, I realize that my trip back to the misery of modern living may have to begin a bit sooner. Because if I print this out and put it in the post, it won't arrive at *The Sunday Times* until Tuesday. Damn.

1 January 2017

My body's a write-off in waiting, so why have all these repairs?

If you have chosen to do the dry January thing, you will have realized by now that every single drink that doesn't contain alcohol is either full of enough sugar to cause your heart to explode or so dreary that you'd rather die of dehydration.

If you've gone out at all, you'll have stood at the bar for an hour thinking, 'I don't want a Coca-Cola, I've had enough elderflower cordial to have left an impact on Britain's hedgerows, I hate water, and coffee will keep me awake all night.' Then, much to the exasperation of everyone who was queuing behind you, you'll have given up and gone home.

Where your friends won't have called in, because why would they? They don't want to sit around with someone who's being sanctimonious and boring and who, by 10 p.m., would be finding none of what they have to say either funny or interesting.

And what's the upside? Yes. You'll have proved to yourself that you are in control of your own destiny and that you have a backbone. And you may even have lost an inch from your turkeyed-up waistline. But by 4 February, after you've let your hair down again, you'll be back to where you started.

Plus. How do you know, as the long evenings crawl by in a cold, damp blur of films you've already seen, box sets that don't make sense and endless trips to the fridge to see if there's a cold chicken that you didn't notice the last time, that you aren't on the verge of a burst aneurysm or a heart attack? Or that one of your cells hasn't just decided to become cancerous?

In short, how do you know that you're not going through a friendless, month-long hell for no reason?

That's why before I started dry January I decided to make sure I wasn't already booked in for an appointment with the Reaper. So I went for a medical. There was a bit of running on a treadmill and quite a lot of lying in a hot, noisy tube, but mostly it involved the doctor manually checking my eyes, hearing, skin and prostate by putting his whole head in my bottom and having a look around.

It's really not fair. Women check themselves for cancer by playing with their breasts, which is a lovely thing to do. Whereas men have to allow another man to ferret about in their exhaust pipe. Which is not lovely at all.

But with crossed eyes and a slight sense of shame and regret I was told that, apart from a fat liver and some mildly bunged-up arteries, I'm likely to be around for a little while yet. So I went home, bought some elderflower cordial and poured the Château Léoube down the sink.

And then I decided that, rather than concentrate only on my liver, I'd sort everything else out as well. So, with my bottom still smarting from the medical, I went to the dentist, who hurt me even more, using various *Marathon Man* prongs and some jets of cold air. This enforced pain revealed that I needed three root canals, two fillings, four crowns and a wisdom-tooth removal.

Later that day, as I chewed idly on a piece of nicotine gum, trying to figure out whether 'searing' was a good enough adjective to describe the agony that lay ahead, a tooth that had been identified earlier as healthy broke in half. Which meant an emergency recall to the White Angel and the news that, actually, I needed four root canals, two fillings, five crowns and a wisdom-tooth removal.

And a new nose. The blood vessel that's gone wonky on

the top-left side is only a small thing at the moment but, if I fail to get it treated, I'll end up with a port-wine stain as big as a medium-sized town, which would be at odds with my newly thin liver and my sound mouth.

So I went to see a man in Harley Street, who shot me – six times – in the face with a space laser. Apparently, it's the same sort of treatment ladies use to keep their gardens in check, and I'll tell you this: if I were a woman, it'd look like a 1970s welcome mat down there because, oh my God, it hurt. And I've to go back five more times before the blood vessel is dead.

Which will be tricky because I need to find time to do something about my numb thigh, my painful left shin, my gut and what I thought was a wart but isn't on my right index finger.

I was also intrigued by a policy currently being pursued by my colleagues Richard Hammond and James May, who have both decided to become vegetarian.

At first I thought this was for health reasons, and I was intrigued. But as they are sporting identical beards at the moment and have bought identical motorcycles, maybe the vegetablist thing is just some kind of weird bonding. Whatever. I have chosen not to go down that road.

It's for the same reason that I've decided not to accompany three friends on their annual trip to a clinic in Germany next week. They speak of the dried toast and the gruel and the misery, but they also talk – quite a lot – about the communal showers and the amount of all-male nakedness, and I'm not sure that's my thing.

Besides, with the teeth and the liver and the nose and the finger and the thigh and the arteries, I have quite enough on my plate already. So much, in fact, that I'm beginning to wonder whether what I'm actually doing is trying to shore up one of those clifftop houses.

At great expense I'm putting in new foundations and building tidal barriers and inserting sturdy new props, but the sea is coming and it is going to win and, one day – no matter what I do – I'll wake up at the bottom of the cliff and it'll be cold and black and endless.

Would it be better, I wonder, to abandon the policy of raging at the setting of the sun and embrace it? Over a nice plate of cholesterol and a bottle of Château Minuty?

15 January 2017

Sure, you'll get by on £85,000 a day – but the family won't

It seems that Diego Costa, a charismatic and brilliant foot-baller who scores many goals for Chelsea, has been offered nearly £600,000 a week to sign with a club in China.

This raises an interesting question. How much would I have to be paid to pack a suitcase and start a new life in Beijing? And I think the answer is, 'There isn't enough money in the entire world.'

I once saw half a dog in China. From its nose to about three-quarters of the way down its ribcage, it was completely normal, with sticky-up ears and a doggy face, but at some point in its life it had obviously been run over by a steam-roller, which meant that its back end, its tail and its hind legs had been converted into what looked like a weird rug.

It was going about its business as though nothing was wrong, scavenging in bins for food and using its front legs to pull its wafer-thin rear end around.

I'm not saying all dogs are like this in China, but the mere fact that this poor creature had had the time to come to terms with its significant disability meant that over a period of several months or even years no one had had the presence of mind to put it out of its misery. They'd seen it, noted it and then moved on.

We are told that China is a technological powerhouse and that it is home to the brainiest and best-funded scientists in the world, but none of them had seen the half-a-dog and thought, 'Hmmm. Tonight I shall fit its back end with a set of steerable wheels.'

That's what would have happened in Britain, and we'd have seen the results in a tear-jerking film on *Blue Peter*.

There are other things in China that are odd. For example, on my most recent trip I ordered sushi and was presented a few minutes later with a fish that was still alive.

It was flapping around on the plate, which would have been fine, except that one whole side of it had been carved into thin slivers that were still attached. The waiter explained that I should simply tear the strips off, one at a time, and eat them.

Well, now, look. I appreciate that sushi should be as fresh as possible, but I feel fairly sure that, if the fish had been killed in the kitchen before it was carved up, my taste buds wouldn't have been able to tell the difference. Nothing's going to decompose noticeably in sixty seconds.

Other things. Well, pop socks are seen as some kind of fashion highlight, the smog is bad, the traffic is worse and the weather is nuts. The first time I went to Beijing it was a hundred degrees – and pouring with rain.

Plus, I wouldn't be able to go to the cinema because I wouldn't understand what was going on. And there wouldn't be enough leg room.

And I wouldn't be able to tell the time because after two days the second hand would have fallen off my new Rolex, indicating that it wasn't really a Rolex at all.

Most important of all, though, I'd get home every night and sit in my sumptuously appointed apartment all alone, trying to make my television work and then giving up because it wasn't really a proper Sony. My bank balance would be swelling at the rate of £85,000 a day, but I'd have no one to spend it on. Because that's the next thing you have to think about when you are offered a big-money deal to move to the other side of the world: your family.

You'd have work to keep you occupied, and therefore a reason for getting up in the morning. But your wife? Your children? It's fairly safe to assume that, if they tagged along, they'd be so bored they'd be sniffing glue by week two, just for something to do.

And it's not just China. It's everywhere. If you were offered £30 million a year to move to Los Angeles, where the fishes are dead before you eat them and there are patrols to remove halved dogs from your line of sight, you'd be off in a flash. But what would your family do while you were lunching at the Ivy in LA with your new colleagues?

In your mind they'd be invited round for tea and buns by Cameron Diaz and they'd spend all day at the beach, sharing ice creams with George Clooney. But that wouldn't happen. They'd know no one, they'd have nothing to do and, as a result, they'd all be alcoholics and drug addicts by the middle of March.

There are many places in the world that I truly love. The south of France is right up there. I'm always overcome by a tidal wave of joy when I land at Nice Airport. I think it is completely impossible to be unhappy if you are in St Tropez ... unless you actually have to live there.

Because how many games of boules can you play? How many bits of raw cauliflower can you eat at Le Club 55? And how long would it be before you gave up pretending that you weren't looking at breasts on the beach and just gawped openly like a lunatic?

I'm not a lunatic, so I'm not going to pretend that money is the root of all evil and that you'd be happier with nothing more than an orange and a piece of string.

But we must face facts and accept that, while money enables you to do all sorts of stuff, it is no good on its own; you need something else as well. You need your friends. And the fact is: they're here.

Unfortunately, from Chelsea Football Club's point of view, Diego Costa's friends are not here. They are in Brazil, which is where he was born. So from his point of view London and Beijing are exactly the same. Neither is home. So either will do.

22 January 2017

Our inner ape is released in a most inconvenient way

Disturbing news from the public lavatories of China. To prevent people from using too much lavatory paper or, worse, stealing the whole roll, the authorities in one of Beijing's parks have installed a system that dispenses just seventy-five centimetres of paper at a time.

It works, rather distressingly, on facial recognition. So when you've finished your business you are asked to remove all of your facial furniture – hat, sunglasses, smog mask, and so on – and then, after a photograph is taken, you get your paper. Nine minutes must elapse before the software allows the same person to receive more.

I'm not sure that's long enough. I can easily while away half an hour on the loo if I have access to Instagram and Twitter and the *Mail Online*'s sidebar of shame but, on the face of it, China's efforts to remind people of their responsibilities while visiting a lavatory are understandable.

I work in an office that's staffed by extremely bright, university-educated twenty-somethings. They can sort out complicated customs forms, manage James May's constant demands for more beef Hula Hoops and arrange filming schedules at the drop of a hat, on the other side of the world.

You'd imagine, then, that they could manage a simple trip to the loo without any problems. But no. Every time I go in there, it's as though it has been used to house Bobby Sands for a year. And it was the same story at a firm of top lawyers that I visited the other day. The visual evidence suggested that all the partners were suffering from a bout of dysentery.

I used to go every summer to a school sports day, and it was middle-class heaven. You'd have Jeremy Paxman lying in the long grass by the river, watching the punts go by, and you'd have Niall Ferguson holding court on important issues of the day. People had their pinkies raised and their hampers arranged just so.

Everyone was always on their absolute best behaviour. They would never, for instance, say they were going to the lavatory. They'd either slip away quietly or ask to be excused for a moment. But when they got into the portable loo and closed the door, they all turned into cavemen.

It was possible even sixty years ago to drop a bomb from 20,000 feet in the sky and hit a target on the ground. But somehow, people in public conveniences can't even hit the target when they're sitting on it. And never mind seventy-five centimetres of paper. Everyone at those sports days used all of it and then left it lying on the floor, before re-emerging to pour Paxman another glass of Whispering Angel.

At festivals, things are even more out of hand because everyone has to face the problem of doing their number twos and vomiting simultaneously. This gives them the opportunity to miss at both ends. And all of it makes me wonder . . .

When you go to the lavatory in someone's house, it's always immaculate. There are amusing hunting-scene cartoons on the walls and some tastefully framed school photographs. There's a candle, of course, to mask any unpleasant odours, the lavatory paper is often folded into a neat V at the end, or it's in a little box tied up with a ribbon, and there's some soap made from the tears of actual angels.

If a Martian were forced to guess what goes on in such a room, he'd say it was used for heart transplants. We are all like this at home: fastidious, clean, tidy. And we are all like this when we are out in public. We behave ourselves. We don't shoplift, we don't push homeless people over for fun and we don't set fire to municipal flower displays on round-abouts, no matter how much we hate them.

We are able to keep ourselves in check because we know we are being watched. And now we hear that drones will soon replace what some newspapers still refer to as 'bobbies on the beat'.

This means we will know for sure that, if we decide to abandon our clothes and run naked through the park, the moment will definitely be witnessed. And I fear this may cause the freedom streak that lives in us all to become squeezed to breaking point.

My grandmother, in her later years, would often spend a whole day sitting in her local dress shop laughing openly at anyone who came out of the changing room. 'Oh no,' she'd say, 'that's terrible.' Or she would sweep into a room full of pompous women having tea while their husbands were at the lodge, and push a cream cake into someone's face.

I dream of being able to do that sort of thing and I'm sure you do too. Every time you walk past some neatly stacked tins of beans at your supermarket, you must occasionally feel a need to push them over. And when you are presented with someone's new baby, there's always a piece of you that says, 'Go on. Say it's a bit ugly.'

But we never do any of this. We can't. We don't like to be judged. And that's why, when we are finally given a moment of absolute privacy in a public lavatory, we revert to being what we actually are. Apes.

We know we are not being watched. We know we can get away with doing whatever comes into our heads. And that's why so many bright, normal, sensible people suddenly feel the need to leave a right mess.

I worry what will happen in China now the authorities are

using what they say is 'science and technology to control behaviour' in the public loos. I fear it won't be good. People have to let off steam somewhere and, if they are forced to behave while having a poo, the country could slide into anarchy, which would almost certainly precipitate a nuclear war.

26 March 2017

Moove over, refugees. Militant vegans have claustrophobic cows to save

Not long ago, after being accused of abusing its powers, the RSPCA decided it would stop bringing trumped-up prosecutions against children who fail to clean out their rabbit hutches properly and concentrate instead on the real villains.

There are plenty of targets, it seems. Last year one woman was successfully prosecuted for cutting the heads off her two pet snakes with a pair of scissors. And that's only right and proper, because while they may only be snakes, you have to be fairly weird to think, 'Right. I need to kill them, so I shall go through my sewing kit to find the right weapon.' Certainly, it would only be a matter of time before a person like this were pushing babies into a waste disposal unit.

Then there was a man who kept a golden eagle in his kitchen, and two brothers convicted of headbutting their bulldog. Why would you do that? Bulldogs have already had their snouts headbutted into a concertina by the cruelty of deranged selective breeding. So all of them already look as if they've run into a wall while travelling at a thousand miles an hour.

I applaud the RSPCA for its new stance. It's sensible to leave averagely lazy pet owners alone and go after the people who are plainly mad, and possibly quite dangerous.

However, there are other animal welfare enthusiasts who it appears are not quite so sensible. That brings us to a pro-vegan organization called Animal Equality, which believes that fish can be sad, that an egg is an abortion and that milk is murder. I don't doubt that some of its supporters spend their evenings sending dog poo to scientists who make beagles smoke pipes.

Last week it released photographs and video of some cows living in sheltered accommodation on a farm in Dorset. It pointed out that the hutches in which the animals took cover when it was raining were too small and that many had open sores on their backs from trying to get inside. And it said that Marks & Spencer, which prides itself on the ethical nature of the food it sells, is still selling milk from the farm in question. M&S? S&M, more like.

The law – there's a law for everything these days, it seems – says that cows can be kept in individual hutches only until they are eight weeks old, after which they must be allowed to stand in the rain in a field doing absolutely nothing until they die of boredom. And there seems little doubt that the cows in the pictures are more than eight weeks old.

However, M&S says it dispatched a team of experts immediately and that, after an investigation and assurances from the farmer, it will continue to buy his milk. The farmer says spot audits have been done and all were passed. Dorset Council's trading standards people have also paid a visit and did not detect any breaches. So the farmer, the council and M&S say everything's fine, but the animal rights people still argue it isn't. And the photographic evidence appears to back them up.

Hmmm. Who knows? Dairy farming is a tricky business these days. You need a gigantic herd to make more than £2.75 a year, and one tiny blip in the weather or one punctured tyre on a milk tanker can wipe out any profit in an instant. So maybe for a short while cows that were more than eight weeks old were kept in hutches that were a bit on the tight side.

Maybe, then, the book should be thrown at Farmer Giles. Maybe he should be imprisoned and fined so heavily he is forced to sell his farm to property developers. Or maybe, instead, we should seek out the lawmakers who decided how much space a veal calf needs to be happy and ask them, 'What were you thinking of, you imbeciles?'

Near where I live in the countryside there are fields that, at this time of year, fill up with tin boxes that are, in some cases, no more than fourteen feet long. They are called 'caravans', and whole families sleep and eat in them for weeks at a time.

Others are even less fortunate and have to live in a plastic triangle with nothing to protect them from the elements other than a jammed zip and a small stove that they use to keep warm and heat what they call 'food'. Often this amounts to nothing more than a thin gruel with some beans in it. And do we have legislation to prevent this kind of cruelty? No. We do not.

You could argue that people are not forced to live in these 'caravans' and plastic triangles, but that's not so. If they'd had a decent education and had earned more money, you can be sure they'd rent a villa in St Tropez instead.

And anyway, what about the people who live in the refugee camps of Jordan or South Sudan? They are trudging through a mind-numbing existence of acute hunger, disease and devastating loss and they don't even have the privilege of being milked twice a day. No one comes with clean bedding every morning. No one mucks them out. No one supplies food or clean water or shelter when it's cold.

Occasionally, a big-hearted volunteer will arrive with a few sacks of grain and a bagful of aspirin, but these visits are few and far between. Because, I'm sorry to say, most people are too busy hiding in the bushes in Dorset, filming cows that may or may not be too large for the sturdy and clean accommodation with which they've been provided.

I'd like to close with a message to the friends and supporters of Animal Equality. Why don't you go to a small coastal village in Africa one day and tell the people there that the fish they've just hauled from the sea are sad as a result? And let's see how far you get.

1 April 2017

Oi, Fatty! Join me in a little act of rudeness and we'll make Britain normal again

Now that we have Mr Trump in the White House, and Mrs Hitler on course to take France out of the EU through a hole in the fence made by the elderly folk of northern England, many people are wondering what has gone wrong with the world.

Well, for an answer we should look no further than an announcement made during the FA Cup semi-finals at Wembley last weekend. The gist of it was: if you are offended by someone's behaviour, you can text the person's seat number to God knows who and he or she will be given the full United Airlines treatment as security men hurl him bodily from the stadium.

This worried me greatly because I know that over the years I have caused a great deal of offence to a great many people: vegetablists, socialists, the French, the Americans, short people, fat people, bicyclists, football referees, public sector workers, the Koreans, people who drive Peugeots, people who are left-handed, people who wear stupid shoes, traffic wardens, Highways England traffic officers . . . The list is endless, and so there was a good chance my seat number would be texted to the thought police, and shortly afterwards I'd end up in a skip with a loose tooth.

Causing offence has somehow become the nation's number-one crime. Which means that if you live in the public eye your number-one rule must be: grin and be medium.

The result of this on television is Matt Baker, who hosts *The One Show* and *Countryfile*. He would host everything else if they could clone him in some way, because Matt is the sort of man you'd want your daughter to marry. Matt has never looked at pornography on the internet or put a stickleback down a waste disposal unit. Matt has great teeth and a range of jumpers that are lovely. Also, he speaks with one of the regional accents that we find cute (not Birmingham) and, I bet, writes long and brilliant thank-you letters.

On *Newsnight* we see that the acerbic Jeremy Paxman has gone and in his stead there's a small, bald man who smiles a lot. At home the small, bald man wears weird clothes, but at work he wears a suit and an open-necked shirt and is polite to his interviewees, all of whom wear burqas and turbans, so they don't offend anyone who's watching.

And it's not just on television. You may not be noisy any more when leaving a pub, in case you cause offence to the neighbours. You may not smoke within half a mile of a child. You may not roll your eyes at the post office counter girl, no matter how stupid she has been, because abuse of staff will not be tolerated.

Only last week we were told in an Oxford University newsletter that, if you avoided eye contact with someone, you could be guilty of racism. But that's OK, because these days everything is racist, except all the stuff that is sexist as well.

All this makes life virtually impossible for politicians. Because if they don't establish eye contact with Emily Maitlis when they are being interviewed, they are being racist, and if they do, they are being misogynistic bastards.

And things are even worse when it comes to answering an actual question. Last weekend Jeremy Corbyn, who leads the Labour Party, was asked if he'd drop a bomb on the head of the man who runs ISIS. Well, that's impossible for the old goat, because if he says no, he will offend the *Daily Mail*, and if he says yes, he will offend everyone in ISIS.

It's the same for the Tories. When asked about the NHS, they can't say, 'We really should shut the bloody thing down,' because that will cause offence. So they have to pull a serious face and make noises until the reporter is bored, or reports them for being racist.

This means no politician can say what he or she is thinking. And neither can they tell the truth. They know, without a shadow of doubt, that badgers transmit tuberculosis to cattle. But if you say, 'Do badgers transmit tuberculosis to cattle?', I guarantee that not a single one will say yes.

At home we know this. We know, as they waffle on while staring at the bridge of the reporter's nose so as not to be thought either racist or sexist, that they are lying, that they are spinning a yarn designed to keep Paul Dacre and Gary Lineker and the Twitter hordes off their back, and we are fed up with it.

Nigel Farage, by contrast, offended vast swathes of the population with his red-telephone-box, Morris Minor, Love Thy Neighbour vision of Britain. But people liked him because they could see he was talking from the heart. And it was the same story with Trump. And it's the same story with that mad Frenchwoman whose name I can't be bothered to spellcheck.

Sensible, centrist politicians must start taking note. They've got to stop trying to please everyone, which is impossible, and say what they think. And we can help them by agreeing not to be offended quite so easily.

We can start at the FA Cup final next month. When the announcer comes on the loudspeakers asking you to report anyone who's being offensive, report him to the number on the screens. Because unless we clamp down on this sort of nonsense, we are going to see the rise of a new Hitler.

30 April 2017

A licence to cull could be a lifeline for Prince Philip – and Mrs Tiggy-Winkle

Most people seem to agree that after nearly seventy years of pretending to be interested in tribal dancing and civic arts centres the Duke of Edinburgh is entitled to put his feet up and enjoy what little time he has left.

Hmmm. At present my diary is a hilarious collection of parties I'll have to cancel because I'll be out of the country, flights I'll miss because I'm too hung over, scripting days that will get forgotten and newspaper deadlines that won't be met.

And in among it all there's the horror of next Sunday. I get back from Croatia late on Saturday night, and the next thing I must do is get to a filming location in Berkshire by 7 a.m. on Monday. This means I have a whole day with nothing to do, nowhere to be and nobody to see. It frightens me.

Because when you get into bed at night knowing that you have done nothing that day apart from looking in the fridge every half-hour to see if there are any cold sausages that you didn't spot last time, you know you have wasted what is a significant portion of your life. You have drained the world's resources and given nothing back. You've been a human sponge. A wastrel.

This is what will happen to Prince Philip. When he doesn't have to get up and put on a suit so he can listen to stuttering bores who've set up a jam festival, he will lie in bed thinking, 'What's the point of getting up at all?'

Eventually, at about ten, he will start to think about having a small whisky, and at ten past he will succumb. After a short while, the combination of alcohol and inactivity will be fatal and he will die.

The facts bear this out. Studies have found that people who work beyond the age of sixty-five tend to die about 10 per cent later than those who put their feet up. Except if you're German, in which case it's the other way around. This is bad news for Mrs Queen, who is from that neck of the woods. But good for Philip, who, as we know, is Greek.

Actually, I'm only guessing that it's good news for the Greeks. No one knows for sure what happens there, because the concept of 'stopping work' doesn't apply in a country where no one ever really starts.

Whatever, it's bad news for you and me because it means that, if we retire when we are sixty-five, we get about ten minutes before the Grim Reaper comes up the drive in his beige people-carrier.

The only way to deal with the problem is to retire from your normal job and then keep busy in some other way. Not exercising, obviously, because there's nothing as tragic as an old wrinkly person in an Ali G outfit dragging their arthritis round the park. And not golf. Everyone dies on the golf course. And not bridge, which is just blackjack for the incontinent.

No. It needs to be something with a point, and that brings me neatly on to what's happening in the small village of Burton Fleming in East Yorkshire. A couple of years ago terrible floods drowned every hedgehog in the region, and now a seventy-two-year-old called Kate Mercer has decided that she and her friends from the village hall should do something about it.

Taking advice from a genial-looking seventy-eight-year-old hedgehog enthusiast in the next county, she has transformed the village, drilling holes in fences, installing little ladders in ponds and erecting feeding stations. Her work has been described as 'the best thing that's ever happened' to the community.

I was, at this point, going to say that beating Hitler was probably even better, but the truth is, I quite like the idea of old people staging a hedgehog reintroduction. It's gentle and everyone wins, because hedgehogs are like ice cream and David Attenborough and Rome. Everyone likes them.

Put it like this. When I drive past a road sign saying, 'Thank you for driving slowly through our village,' I always think, 'But I didn't.' However, if there were a sign saying, 'Please slow down for our hedgehogs,' I'd crawl along at 2mph, straining my eyes like the tail gunner in a Halifax.

Cars, however, are only one of the threats that hedgehogs face in these difficult times. Another is habitat loss. Replace your lawn with decking and you are robbing Spiny Norman of his insect-rich feeding ground. Put up a fence and you are imprisoning him.

And then there's Tyson Fury, who, to strengthen his gypsy credentials, said recently that he'd eaten a hedgehog. He's unusual, though. Most travellers these days prefer a party seven of Kentucky Fried Chicken.

That still leaves us with the badger, though. This is the real menace. When he's not marauding about the place, knocking over walls and killing cows with his arsenal of vindictive diseases, he likes to eat as many hedgehogs as possible.

One of the main prerequisites, in fact, for turning your village into a hedgehog-friendly zone like Burton Fleming is that the area is not infested with an army of Brian May's flea-ridden mates.

Which brings me neatly back to Prince Philip. When he stops walking around with his hands behind his back later this year, he could very easily keep his mind fresh and his body active by joining a hedgehog reintroduction scheme near one of his castles.

Obviously, I can't see him drilling holes in a fence or erecting a small ladder. Nor can I see him running a bring-and-buy stall in Sandringham's village hall. However, I can see him doing his bit by pouring himself a nice glass of red and sitting at his bedroom window with a brace of Purdeys, waiting for a badger to heave into view.

7 May 2017

If Farron really wants votes, he must deal with our most grievous malaise: culottes

So if Labour wins the general election, Jeremy Corbyn will reintroduce the Deltic railway locomotive, put Mungo Jerry back in the charts and make rich people in the south buy everyone in the north of England a brazier so they can be warm when they are picketing someone else's place of work.

Meanwhile, the Liberal Democrat, who is called Timmy, says that if he wins a Commons majority he will lower the voting age to six and take us out of Europe by not taking us out at all.

This has annoyed the Green Party, which thought of these things first, so it's gone further by saying that, if it wins 325 more seats than it got last time around, it will increase the number of bottle banks, issue free tampons to the poor and make prostitutes cheaper.

That leaves us with the strong and stable Conservative Party, which may look as though it's being run by the steering committee from Carshalton golf club but says that, despite appearances, it will provide strong and stable leadership to create a strong and stable country where the strong are stable and the stable are strong.

Don't you find all this a bit depressing? I mean, here they all are, all these parties, with the chance to say and promise whatever they like. And all they can come up with is more bottle banks and something about British Rail. Seriously. Is that the limit of their imagination?

What we want is someone with vision. Someone who really does want to make life better for as many people as possible. Someone who understands that the most important thing facing the nation right now is not the NHS or Brexit but the average-speed camera.

That's what we want to hear from a party. 'If we are elected, we will immediately remove all speed cameras. And restrict bicycles to children's playgrounds, which is where they belong. Oh, and women will no longer be allowed to wear culottes.' That would get our attention.

And how quickly would you vote for someone who said they'd introduce profiling at airport security so that people who are very obviously not terrorists – because, for example, they are very obviously Andrew Lloyd Webber – would be allowed to board the aircraft without being irradiated and sexually molested first?

If you are standing for election, you have a clean piece of paper. You can fling whatever you like into the mix and see if it sticks. So why not say you will introduce the death penalty for people who drop litter?

Maybe people would be appalled by that, in which case you'd lose. But maybe they wouldn't. Maybe they'd like to see the carcass of a fly-tipper hanging upside down from a lamp-post. I know I would.

I think it'd also be a good idea to imprison anyone who's called *The Jeremy Vine Show*, or written something on the *Mail Online*'s message boards. And while we are on the subject of prison, why not say that inmates will be locked up in an unheated cell and will only be able to survive if they become adept at sucking moisture from the moss on the walls?

I'm on a roll now. So how about preventing newsreaders from saying, 'The following report contains flash photography'? We know already. And freeing advertisers from the need to employ a shorthand speaker who has to read out the terms and conditions and caveats and complex financial implications extremely quickly at the end of every radio commercial?

Gillette would be forced to stop selling razors in packaging so robust you need dynamite to get through it; newspapers (this bit may be edited out) would not be allowed to put supplements in polythene bags; and foreign aid and intelligence-sharing would be denied to any country that refused to adopt the British plug.

At the moment you have the Labour Party saying it'd spend an extra £37 billion on the NHS and the Tories thumbing their noses a day later and saying they'd spend £38 billion. And we all roll our eyes, because we know this sort of stuff is important, like getting your tax return done on time and flossing regularly, but what really bothers you is that your wi-fi router keeps breaking down. That's what you really want the government to do. Something about that.

You have Corbyn dribbling on about how he'll introduce forty-two more bank holidays and Theresa May saying she'll stop foreigners joining her golf club, and then you have *Question Time*, where all these things are discussed as though they are gravely important. Which they're not. Not when your husband has died and his bank account's been frozen and you don't know what probate means and you have to get a bus that's full of diseases to go to Citizens Advice, which is shut because the staff are on a two-day 'equality in the workplace' course in Harpenden.

So you have to go back at the end of the week and you're cross that you've been made to wait so you shout at the young woman behind the counter and she calls the security guard because abuse of staff is not tolerated, so you're back on the bus, which now smells of sick, and you still don't know what probate means and what you're supposed to do with the endless forms that keep slithering through your letterbox.

A person such as this is going to vote for any party that says it will encourage customers to abuse counter staff. Especially if it goes on to say that all workplace courses will be banned.

21 May 2017

Um . . . let me break the ice, Mrs May. Have you ever been to a lap-dancing club?

As you may know, Donald Trump has been on a tour of various places the folks back home have heard of: Saudi Arabia, Israel, the Vatican and, of course, Sicily, which was made famous by *The Godfather*.

Naturally, his progress has been mocked mercilessly by most intelligent people. Many thought he would get Palestine muddled up with Palmyra and that in Rome he'd have referred to the Pope as Mr Hanks. But I reckoned he'd do OK because these meetings, really, are just a chance for two people to do small talk – and Americans are good at that. They speak to one another at the urinals. They're open and interested.

Mr Trump will have breezed into the Saudi royal palace and said, 'Hey, Mr King. Nice hat.' And they'll have talked about hats for a while, and how much gold leaf you can get away with on a chair, and then they'll have called in the photographers and signed the arms deal and promised to stay in touch.

Look at it this way: after you've shared a lift with an American, he will get out and say, 'Good to know you.' Whereas we'll say, 'Good to meet you.' Because we understand that, after a minute or two in someone's company, we don't know them. Knowing someone, if you're British, takes years.

I was speaking about this with Richard Hammond the other day. He is famously useless at passing the time with a stranger, so I said, 'You just have to be interested in other people.' To which he replied, 'But that's it, you see – I'm not.'

This is why, if you meet Hammond, he will just stand there looking at you.

My problem is subtly different. I never know when to switch from small talk to something more meaty. Knowing when to change from the weather to body fluids is second nature for an American, but for me it's like knowing when to move in for the first kiss. And I'm completely useless at that as well.

Once, I dropped a girl back at her flat just as Hazel O'Connor's 'Will You?' came on the radio. She reclined her seat and said, 'Oh, I love this song' and yet I continued to sit there, talking about how warm it was for the time of year, until the song finished and she said a rather puzzled goodnight.

This is why I'm hopeless at drinks parties. I recently made the mistake of sitting down and talking to a stranger, which meant I was stuck. I couldn't get up and walk off, and neither could they. We didn't know each other well enough to talk about genital warts or politics or anything like that, so we just went round and round the politeness bush.

I once met Nelson Mandela and, for two days, I sweated buckets about what I'd say to break the ice. Being British, I have only two fallback positions – school fees and property prices – and neither seemed appropriate. So in a panic I opened with, 'So, Mr Mandela. Have you ever been to a lap-dancing club?'

This meant I spent the next hour sweating and stuttering through the wreckage of our meeting, knowing that I'd committed a social faux pas and that, if I'd been there to sign an arms deal, it would have fallen through. Yet the truth is that 'Have you ever been to a lap-dancing club?' is a bloody good opener. It bypasses the need for small talk completely. Which has to be a good idea.

A couple of weeks ago we needed to hire a pretty young woman for the film we were making. And because we were in Croatia, it didn't take long to find one. She arrived, as Hammond and I were waiting for the clouds to be the right shape, and didn't bother with an introduction or any of that unnecessary nonsense. She simply squatted down and said, 'When I got the text asking me to do this, I was at doctor's with a pipe up – how you say – my back ass.'

There was a pause, which Hammond broke by saying, 'I got nothing.' And the truth is, I had nothing either. I was in a state of shock. But pretty soon we were talking about polyps and colon cancer and why the French insist on ingesting everything medicinal up their anuses, and this was far better than sitting there talking about property prices and school fees and how nippy it was for early May.

Actually, Hammond did bring the conversation on to the unseasonable coldness, but she was having none of it. 'I know,' she said, flattening her T-shirt over her breasts. 'Look.'

This Eastern European directness probably explains why Croatia's roads are in such an impeccable state of repair. Their guy simply turns up at the EU and says, 'Give us some money immediately because we want to make our infrastructure better,' and walks out five minutes later with a cheque.

Whereas the Britisher arrives and spends an hour talking about the speed of the train he's used, and the weather, and how Marlborough is probably better than Heathfield because property prices are lower in Wiltshire, and soon he's forgotten what he went there for. That's why Croatia is on the up and up and we are heading for the 1950s. Because we're imprisoned by our own good manners.

They cause problems in other ways too. Because if you spend an hour swapping conversational amuse-bouches with someone, you never really work out whether you like them or not. Which means ending up with an address book full of charlatans and bores.

And that brings me on to a clever test dreamed up by a friend. She makes a point, whenever she's introduced to a new person, of using the C-word straightaway. If they shy away like a frightened horse, she knows they will have nothing in common and moves on.

It's a better filter than sniffing one another's bottoms for half an hour and learning nothing more than what the weather is like on their side of town.

28 May 2017

Honestly, ladies, I do sympathize with you about the menopause – men get it too

It's fairly safe to say that most men don't really understand anything about the menopause. Except that we can't make jokes about it. It's profound and important and life-changing. It causes hot women to become hot in other ways. It makes them behave strangely. In parts of Europe it causes brain surgeons and rocket scientists to come home from work one day and decide to spend the rest of their lives in shapeless black dresses, cleaning the front step with an old scrubbing brush and sobbing.

Here bright, clever women who've been in love with their husband for twenty years suddenly decide they'd like to stab him in the back with a pair of scissors. And then go shoplifting. Many become obsessed for no obvious reason with keeping fit, and some discreet research last week revealed that more than you might think try their hand at a spot of afternoon lesbianism.

Men recognize these symptoms because when we say to our wives, 'Why are you trying to strangle me with a flex?' they use a very loud voice to reply, 'Because I'm going through the menopause, you hopeless bastard.'

What causes these behavioural abnormalities isn't clear, because it's only spoken about behind conspiratorial hands, in whispers, and never when there's a man round the table. As a result, we only know that something is going on in the ovaries, or is it the womb? Whatever, we know it's called 'the change' for a reason. Even if we are a bit blurry about what's changing. What we do know, as I said at the outset, is that we have to sympathize or die.

I've always been good at that. When I was a reporter on a local newspaper I'd often spend mornings in the magistrates' court where a succession of weeping middle-aged women of previously good character were wheeled out to be fined £10 for helping themselves to a bar of soap at the chemist's. It was then my job to put their name in the newspaper. Which naturally was a punishment a thousand times worse than the fine.

The trouble is that sometimes I'd pop to the lavatory and miss a case. Which meant that ten women would be publicly humiliated and one, because of my bladder, got off with a light raid on the contents of her purse. I reckoned this was unfair and raised it with my editor. 'Either we cover them all, or we stop covering them altogether.' This resulted in me being switched to cover parish council meetings.

A few months later the wonderful Lady Isobel Barnett, a regular contestant on *What's My Line?* and a woman I admired greatly, appeared in the newspapers having been convicted of stealing items worth 87p from her grocer. Just four days later, she electrocuted herself in the bath.

Everyone was saddened by that because we all knew that she was menopausal at the time of the crime. And we all thought she should have been treated with more dignity and kindness.

Which brings me on to the male equivalent of the menopause. It's called the midlife crisis and for some reason anyone who goes through it is always labelled as pathetic. And you can put your eyebrows down now, please, because I'm being serious.

When a man who has spent twenty years being the perfect husband and father suddenly gets a tattoo and a Harley-Davidson he is mocked and ostracized by his friends and family. How is that fair? We don't mock women of fifty for losing their decent waist, so why can they mock men for suddenly deciding after years of sedentary box-set living to get one?

A man doesn't decide when he gets to sixty that he wants to spend the next few years on the pull. It's not rational. It's not sensible. He doesn't want a pair of tight white trousers; they're uncomfortable. And he doesn't want a motorcycle either, because he thinks they're silly and dangerous. And yet, led by a peculiar drive from deep within his underpants, he suddenly decides to buy both things. And for some reason we find this tragic.

A boss who's spent all his working life treating his secretaries with good manners and kindness is suddenly consumed with a need to take one to a Premier Inn one Thursday afternoon for a spot of rumpy-pumpy. He's read books. He's travelled. He's run a business. He's wise. And yet now he's become stupid. That cannot be something coming from the head. It must be biological.

Cod psychology tells us that he's spent all his life being a lion and that soon he will be no good at it. His teeth will fall out, his testes will turn into sultanas and he will be left to ruminate on what could have been. If only he'd got the Harley and the tighty-whitey jeans.

There was a picture of Sean Connery last week, and it was a shock. Last time we saw him, in *The Rock*, he was old, for sure, but there aren't many women who would have kicked him out of bed. Now, though, he looks decrepit. And we know there must have been a moment when the lights went out. We all know that moment is coming and we want to cram our lives with as much as possible before it goes all dark and doddery.

That sounds like a reasonable thesis, but my point is that it doesn't happen consciously. Any more than Lady Isobel was acting consciously when she half-inched that can of tuna and tub of cream.

We must accept that the menopause and the midlife crisis are the same thing. And that they will come to us all in varying degrees at some point. And then, when we've accepted that, we must look at the middle-aged mad people who are campaigning for our votes in the coming election and think: 'Really? Wouldn't we be better off with someone who's thirty?' Anyway, the point is that we respect the menopause.

4 June 2017

BA lands in the brown stuff over a power cut. Next we'll blame it for turbulence

And in other news last week, a group of jumper enthusiasts called Skytrax left their Thermos flasks and B&Q folding chairs at the end of the runway at Heathrow and announced through their swollen adenoids they're thinking of taking away British Airways' coveted four-star status.

If the binocular boys from the plane-spotting community go ahead with their threat, BA will be ranked in the tables alongside the national carriers of Burma, Ethiopia and Uzbekistan.

Apparently, this has something to do with the fact that the seats in economy are now suitable only for the sort of people you see in an L. S. Lowry painting, and the food served back there would be rejected by most dogs. Well, I can't comment on that because I haven't turned right on a plane for years.

I suspect mostly, though, the main reason BA is facing a downgrade to junk status is that at the start of the half-term break it suffered a global computer crash that caused its fleet to become stuck in a giant game of Musical Statues. Many people's holidays were ruined, thousands of business meetings had to be cancelled and there was chaos. I saw it first hand. Angry-looking Heathrow security people were barring the doors, and there was much wailing and gnashing of teeth from those who were being inconvenienced. And then more wailing and gnashing when I was waved through after flashing my BA gold card.

Naturally enough, the trade unions say the global crash happened because BA recently outsourced its entire computer setup to a small industrial unit at 4b Queen Victoria

Way, Calcutta. Whereas BA says it was because of an electricity surge.

I'm not sure quite what's meant by this. Does the power supply suddenly come in a big lump? Do all your lightbulbs start to glow very brightly and does your washing machine swell up to the size of a chest freezer?

I thought it all sounded a bit far-fetched. Until I went to my little cottage in the country last weekend. Seemingly, there'd been what news reporters who want jobs on American television call a power 'outage', caused, according to Scottish and Southern Electricity, by 'trees coming into contact with our network'. A snappy line, that.

Now, in the olden days, when we had three-day weeks and I had to watch *Top of the Pops* on a small black-and-white TV powered by the battery from my dad's Ford Cortina, the power would start flowing again after a while and everything that had gone off would start to work once more.

Not any more. The power 'cut', as I shall call it, because I already have a job with a US broadcaster, had caused all the digital sensors that govern our lives to become confused, and as a result I was cast back into the fourteenth century.

Obviously, the wi-fi had gone. Even at the best of times, wi-fi routers are less reliable than an Austin Allegro, so after a power cut they sit there flashing their meaningless lights as you say to a man on the other end of the phone that you've already turned it off and on again. Three times.

No matter, I thought: I can do without my Instagram fix for one evening and catch up on a box set instead. Nope. The television could provide me with only terrestrial stations, which at four in the afternoon meant a selection of shows featuring men with silly moustaches going round auction houses with some uncomfortable-looking old people who thought that after they had sold their chintzy teapot they would have enough in the bank for a world cruise.

Quickly, I became stupefied by this, so I decided to have a shower. At first things went well. I was able to get a good lather going in my barnet, but then the water just stopped. Unlike your water, mine is pumped from a stream at the bottom of the garden and into a purification plant that is located in what is officially the dustiest, dirtiest barn in the world.

And that is where I found myself, squelching through guano and decomposing rodents, to find out what had gone wrong. And when I finally found the circuit board, I couldn't see it because of all the soap in my eyes, so I fumbled about with all the switches and levers until the dust and the dirt had mixed with the shampoo to turn my entire hair into a massive breeze block.

Unable to hold my head up properly, I stumbled back through the lake of pigeon crap to the cottage, where I used a hammer to free my head from the concrete. And there I sat, with rubble in my hair, watching another man with another moustache explaining to an old dear that her teapot had fetched £2.75 and she wouldn't be going on a cruise.

Now, this is a small house in the Cotswolds and it was plunged into the Middle Ages because – in English – some branches had been blown by the wind into power cables. So it's entirely plausible BA was crippled by some kind of disruption to its power supply.

I like BA, as a rule. I like being welcomed on board by a homosexual in grey flannel trousers. I like the soothing, confident tones of its pilots. And I really like Terminal 5, especially the check-in facilities for gold-card members.

That one of the windmills it is undoubtedly forced to use to offset its carbon emissions had a hissy fit and wrecked all its computers is just plain bad luck. And that's no reason to give it the same rating as an airline where you get beaten up, or where you get slapped for not putting your seatbelt on (that happened to me recently), or where you have about as much chance of surviving the flight as a prisoner in one of General Augusto Pinochet's detention centres.

11 June 2017

You young people were jolly naughty on 8 June. Go to your rooms with no vote

So that's two elections on the trot that have been messed up by Britain's young people. They couldn't be bothered to vote in the European Union referendum and we ended up with Brexit. And then, having realized the error of their ways, they decided they would vote for that arse Jeremy Corbyn in the general election, so now we've ended up with a hung parliament. Which won't be able to deal with the mess their bone-idleness created in the first place.

Frankly, I'd smack their bottoms and send them all to their rooms for the day, and then I'd raise the voting age to forty-six. Actually, I'd go further. I'd make people sit an IQ test before being allowed to cast a vote, because I'm sorry, but anyone who plumped for Corbyn is so daft they really need to be on medication.

Britain's national debt is more than £1.7 trillion and it's growing at the rate of almost £1 billion a week. Which is about £100,000 a minute. And the weird-beard Islingtonite thinks that this can be tackled by making Starbucks pay a bit more tax. He's deluded and should be in prison. The problem is he has a soft voice and kind eyes and he sounds genuine when he says that if Sir Elton John and Lord Bamford would only pay a little bit more to the government each week, it would end all poverty, hunger, crime, terrorism and war. I'm sitting there screaming, 'The man collects manhole covers. He's a lunatic.' But young and stupid people are turning to their fat friends and saying, 'Well, that makes sense.' In a northern accent.

We see this problem not just in Britain but all round the world. In America the people elected a man who has nylon hair because he said he'd build a wall along the border with Mexico. In France they elected a man who married his teacher because he has a nice face. In Russia they fawn over a president – who has at some point in his life at the KGB pushed another man's eyes into the back of his head – because he wants to reinstate the Soviet Union. And so it goes on.

In Canada they were offered a choice between a normal politician and a two-year-old. And they decided to give the toddler a chance because he has a huge tattoo of a weird raven on his left arm.

It's not hard to see what's going on. People are bored with politicians and politics and they want something new. Anything. Just so long as it doesn't sound like Tony Blair or David Cameron or any of the others.

At one point in the run-up to the election Theresa May took her campaign to Plymouth, or it may have been Portsmouth – somewhere with a lot of ships, anyway. There she was quizzed on camera by someone from the local newspaper, and she answered all his questions with the conviction and sincerity of a regional radio DJ. You could see she didn't mean a single word she was saying. She therefore said a lot of words without saying anything at all. And people are bored with that.

Remember Ed Miliband? The one who lost an election after he failed to eat a bacon sandwich? He'd plainly been told by his spin doctors that the news crew that had been sent to interview him would use only one soundbite and that, no matter how tricky or varied the questions might be, he should just say the same thing over and over again. So he did. And then, when the whole unedited interview ended up on *You-Tube*, we could see him sitting there, repeating himself like a Dalek.

Blair was an actor, so he made a much better fist of looking as if he knew what he was talking about. But he wasn't a very good actor, which is why we all knew there were no weapons of mass destruction in Iraq. We could see it in his eyes. But still the politicians keep on believing that a smile, a soundbite and a nice suit are all that's needed to keep them in a job. Well, they aren't. Not any more.

There's talk, as I write, that May won't be able to keep her job, but, seriously, when you look at the replacements whose names are being bandied about: Philip Hammond, David Davis, the other one? They're like milk bottles. It's impossible to say which you prefer.

Which is why we are drawn to the weirdos, the odd ones out. There's a theory in America that presidential elections are always won by the candidate you'd most like to have over for a barbecue on a Sunday afternoon. That's why John F. Kennedy beat Richard Nixon and Ronald Reagan beat Jimmy Carter, and it's why Donald Trump beat Hillary Clinton.

I think there's a kernel of truth in that in Britain too. It's probably why we have a hung parliament, because who would you prefer to have over for Sunday lunch, a woman who goes on walking holidays or a man who collects manhole covers? The answer is: 'Er . . .'

This is what the Conservative Party must understand in the coming months. If it gets rid of May – and it should, really, because she's a dead duck – it must remember that in Britain there are millions and millions of people who are stupid or young or both. And who thus won't really grasp the complexities of Brexit and austerity, and so on.

That doesn't matter. Any Conservative is going to make a better job of pulling us out of Europe and balancing the books than Corbyn would. That's the main goal. To keep him at bay. So the Tories must choose someone who's odd and funny and different from all the others. Someone who the voters would like to have over for a few beers on a sunny Sunday afternoon.

The only problem with this idea is that there's only one name from all of the three hundred or so contenders that springs to mind. It's Boris Johnson. Which means we've had it.

18 June 2017

Wish you were being drizzled on: last week's sun ruined my Riviera holiday

Well, as weeks go, that really should have been as close to perfect as it's possible to imagine. It began with a giant party in Siena at one of those houses that I thought only really existed in advertisements for Cinzano. Even Kate Moss was there.

Then I pottered up the Riviera to stay with friends in Portofino before heading on down, for no particular reason, to St Tropez. After that I did a bit of summer glacier skiing in Les Deux Alpes and then drove a Bugatti into Turin for a bowl of kidneys and much too much wine.

There wasn't a single view on the entire trip that was anything less than magical. There wasn't one person I met whom I didn't like. There was no unpleasantness of any kind. And yet the whole thing was spoiled just a tiny bit by constant reports that Britain was basking under the sort of summer skies it hasn't seen for more than forty years.

'Bugger,' I thought, when I consulted my Instagram feed every morning and saw everyone I knew at home frolicking about in ponds. And lots of shots of hot dogs. 'Bugger and blast.'

The weather on my trip was cloudless. The skies were constantly blue. And the thermometer was hovering in what those of us who can remember the summer of 1976 call 'the mid-eighties'. But it's hard to enjoy weather such as this when you know that the people back home are enjoying it too. I suspect I'm not alone in this.

When we come back from a holiday, radiating wellness,

we like people to say, 'Ooh, have you been away?' We don't want to come back, after spending thousands of pounds, to find that they are browner than we are.

This troubles me. God enthusiasts are forever telling us that the human being is fundamentally good and charitable and kind. But how can this be so if we are saddened to hear that other people are enjoying a bit of luck with the weather?

I wonder. Do very rich people resent those who win the lottery and become very rich themselves? Were we all a bit happy last week to hear Boris Becker has money troubles? And do we rejoice silently when the *Mail Online* brings news of a former supermodel's cellulite?

I recently ran into some people at an airport who said they were friendly with a chap I'd been at school with. Back then he was captain of everything, had a triangular torso and always went off with the girl I'd spent all night dazzling with my wit. 'How is he?' I asked. 'He's fat,' they said. 'How fat?' I asked with a hint of glee in my voice. 'Well, he weighs eighteen stone,' they said. And I'm sorry but that made me happy for a month.

All of which brings me to a new residential development not far from where I live in west London. Designed to be a place where thrusting City boys can spend evenings watching pornography and eating takeaway food, it's 'That'll do' architecture at its most uninspiring.

But last week it became a lifeboat. The City of London Corporation has done some kind of deal with the developer and ended up with sixty-eight flats that can be used, for ever, by those who lost everything in the Grenfell Tower blaze.

On the face of it, this is perfect. Those poor families have a brand-new place to call home and it's just a spit away from where their children go to school. The developer has apparently sold the flats at cost, but you can be assured that its next application to put up a ho-hum block will be passed very quickly by planners. So it's happy too. And Kensington and Chelsea Council is delighted because it's a one-fell-swoop solution to a problem that two weeks ago seemed insurmountable. So that's all lovely.

Or is it? Because in the past few months, people have been moving into that development. I see their expensive light fittings and curtains as I drive by. They've obviously coughed up God knows how many millions to live in a place that they thought would be filled with peace and quiet. And now it turns out they're going to be sharing it with people – many of whom have been refugees twice – from the other side of the tracks. Yup, the American Psycho will be living cheek by jowl with Mohamed from Somalia.

One day soon, and I can pretty much guarantee this, one of the City boys will complain. He'll say he doesn't like his new neighbour's cooking smells or that he found a used hypodermic needle on the landing. And when he does, he is going to have about twenty-five tons of brown stuff emptied on his head for being a callous, Tory-voting, selfish, thoughtless, heartless man-bastard.

We will all nod, of course, and gnash our teeth and say, 'Yes. He is all of those things.' But actually he's only doing exactly what I did as I sat in a harbour café in Portofino and read that Britain had just enjoyed its hottest summer's day since whenever the last one was.

The fact is that the God enthusiasts are wrong. Human beings are not fundamentally nice. We are fundamentally horrible. Put a video of a cat having a nice snooze on *YouTube* and no one will watch it. Put up a video of a cat falling off a washing machine and it'll get 8 trillion views.

The Grenfell Tower fire brought out the best in us. We rallied round and donated our trousers. It's the same story when we hear about children drowning in the Mediterranean or dying of starvation in Africa. We buy the charity records and we pull the right faces.

But then we go back to our ordinary, bitter lives, where we resent the success, the wealth, the beauty or even the good fortune of others.

Don't agree? Well, just remember that when you read earlier about my week in Italy and France, you thought – and don't deny it – 'You lucky sod.'

25 June 2017

School's out of touch – kids must learn to wire a plug and embrace nepotism

My elder daughter has written a funny book and I'm very proud. It's called *Can I Speak to Someone in Charge?* and it's a bit like the old television series *Grumpy Old Men*. Except it's a book and it's written by a grumpy young woman.

Young people today tend not to express themselves in print. They communicate on the Dark Web, where no grown-up can go, or they use their breasts as a placard on a march. It's unusual, therefore, to hear from a young person who's used ink and paper to let us know what her generation is thinking.

And what she's thinking is that she's cross. She's cross with Topshop for labelling all its clothes the wrong sizes, cross with internet trolls and cross with boys for thinking periods might attract bears (her words, not mine). She's cross with those who get between her and her Prosecco, and she's cross with all food. Mostly, though, she's cross about school.

As I'm her father, I found this particular chapter extremely hard to read, because I simply had no idea how unhappy she'd been as a boarder, how alien it all was to her, and how cruel. Mostly she explains that it was a complete and utter waste of time. I fear she may have a point.

Round about now, thousands of children will be leaving school for good, fairly confident they've learned all they need to know and are ready for whatever the world may throw their way. But as Emily points out, she had no idea about the difference between a credit card and a debit card, and while she was pretty well versed in the periodic table and what inferences can be drawn from the gap in the Wife of Bath's teeth, she had no clue what council tax was.

I've long held the belief that schools exist now solely to maintain their position in the league tables. Children are just meat. They're taught how to pass exams in the easiest possible subjects so that, when they do well, other parents will send their young fresh meat to that school, rather than to a rival establishment.

To maintain the illusion that it's all for the benefit of the children and not just about league tables, kids are told they have no time for frivolous pastimes such as reading newspapers or socializing because they must get to university, for which they will need four A*s. And a disabled parent, in a council house. University is held aloft as the be all and end all. The portal through which you must pass if you want to avoid a front-of-house career in fast food.

But that simply isn't true. I employ quite a few young people these days and, I'm sorry, but an upper second from Exeter is always going to be trumped by a spot of nepotism. If I know your mum and dad, you stand a pretty good chance. If I don't, you're just another name on a mile-high stack of CVs.

It may well be that you were a tremendous student. And that you did your coursework diligently while maintaining a neat haircut. But what do you think an employer wants: a kid who knows about Newton's Third Law, or a kid who can use pay-by-phone parking without calling his mum for help?

You'd be staggered how gumption-free some school-leavers are. Average-speed cameras, passport application forms, where water comes from – all this stuff is beyond half of them. We even had one come to work for us the other day who believed to be true something they'd found on Wikipedia.

When I asked them to phone the person we were researching to find out the truth from the horse's mouth, they looked at me as though I'd asked them to communicate with smoke signals. 'Talk to him?' they stammered.

They mock old people such as us for not being able to use Facebook or get a TV to work properly. But they can't boil an egg or use a saw or wire a plug. And they have not even the vaguest inkling what is meant by the word 'patience'.

When we grew up we had *Marine Boy* on a Thursday and then had to wait until the following Thursday to watch the next episode. Today, television is immediate. And it's the same with dating. I used to have to chat up a girl by walking up to her and saying, 'Have you seen Thin Lizzy? I have.' Now you just swipe right. Or left. Or whatever it is.

Then there's cooking. We actually had to chop stuff up before making it hot, whereas Emily, as she points out in her book, left school with no idea how to do this, and consequently relied on food that comes with an instruction manual. And that made her fat.

As a result of this 'I want it now' mentality, they can't understand why, after a day in work, they are still junior researchers. 'Why am I not managing director?' they wail, after they've been in the job for a week.

School could rectify this by teaching patience instead of maths, which, as Jeremy Corbyn has proved with his spending plans, is not something you need if you want to get on in life. I'd also force kids to gamble, so they can see how easy it is to lose, and take out a loan, so they get a grasp of the problems of paying it back. I'd show them farmyard animals mating and make them perform complex tasks while drunk.

Could they be tested in any of this stuff? No, not really. Which is why I'd abolish all exams past the age of eleven. Exams ruin childhood and exist only as a yardstick for universities, which aren't important either.

The result would be a country full of young people who have

no idea about tectonic shift or algebra but who are worldly-wise enough to cook chicken properly, cross the road without using Google and see Corbyn for the dangerous fool he really is.

2 July 2017

Centuries of male suffering inflicted by Croatian ragamuffins and French fops

As we all know, the world is in a bit of a pickle at the moment, so you'd expect Parliament to be a hive of important activity as members scuttle about discussing Brexit, the latest North Korean missile test, the lawlessness of Libya and how many tower blocks in Britain are basically great big tinderboxes.

Strangely, however, they seem to be mostly bothered about the recent announcement that ties would no longer be compulsory in the House. This has plainly irked a transport minister called John Somethingorother, who stood up last week and said, 'I ought to say as a matter of courtesy that I will not be taking interventions from any member who is not wearing a tie, on whichever side of the House that member may sit.'

At this point I'd have filled a paper aeroplane with the contents of my nose and aimed it at his head, but no one thought to do that, so on he went. 'I believe in generosity . . . and I will provide a tie . . . for anyone who is sartorially challenged or inadequate.'

Did he think people would find this funny? Because it wasn't. I've seen more amusing stuff in an instruction manual. But he ploughed on regardless, explaining that women could be exempt as he wouldn't expect them 'to dress in my tie, their own or anyone else's'.

There are people with dogs without a job, sitting on the pavement outside my local supermarket, who are capable of being more relevant and amusing than this.

But, staggeringly, his observations seem to have struck a

chord, because a new MP called Eddie Hughes leapt to his feet and said – hold on to your sides, everyone – 'I bought this suit at the weekend specifically to wear when making my first speech in this chamber, and although obviously I will be wearing exactly the same suit for the rest of the week' – punchline on its way – 'at least for today I'm looking my best.'

What a bonehead. Seriously. He's campaigned for months. He's won his election. He's now the member of parliament for somewhere awful in the Midlands and this is his big moment. And that's the best he can come up with.

That night, I bet, he will have called his wife and said excitedly, 'Were you watching, darling? Did you see me? It's in Hansard and everything. I told them about my new suit and how I'd be wearing it all week.' And she, if she had any gumption, will have thought, with a world-weary sigh and a pitying glance at her children, 'Maybe I should think more seriously about starting that affair with my gym instructor.'

Half the problem is that these two men have managed to get hot under their collars precisely because both of them were wearing ties. And ties are stupid. No. Don't argue. Because they are. They serve no purpose.

I've done some checking and it seems that the idea of the tie came about in the seventeenth century when some Croatian mercenaries turned up in France wearing knotted handkerchiefs around their necks.

Instead of saying, 'Thank God you're here. We need all the help we can get to fight these pesky Protestants', the French – because they are French – said, 'Wow. Cool neckwear, boys.' And immediately rushed off to create what became known as the cravat.

Later it became fashionable for rich young Englishmen to do a grand tour of Europe so that they could become even more boring at dinner parties by talking about art and music. And to let everyone know they'd been away, they started wearing idiotic stuff round their necks to make them look more French.

Because they were not only boring, but bored, they started to invent new ways of tying up this neckwear. And there were various publications, all of which were edited by Dylan Jones Esq., which helped them learn how to look more preposterous.

So when you put on a tie today, what you are actually saying is: 'I'm a bore. I'm vain. And I want to be French. Oh, and it doesn't matter that I have a piece of silk dangling round my neck because obviously I don't work on the shop floor so it's unlikely I'll be garrotted by a piece of heavy machinery.'

I made a vow on the day I left school that I would never again wear a tie and, with the exception of Margaret Thatcher's funeral and a couple of television appearances, I haven't. I'm not sure I can remember how to tie one any more. I also, between the months of April and November, rarely wear socks.

This means my performance in the day is vastly improved, partly because I don't have to waste time in front of a mirror every morning trying to make my tie the right length. And partly because I'm never too hot. I'm relaxed. So relaxed that today I spilled some noodles down the front of my shirt.

If I were to turn up for a discussion in the Houses of Parliament looking like this, the Tory MPs – whose wives, even as we speak, are texting their gym instructors – would huff and puff and suggest I wasn't capable of thinking straight.

But that's the thing. I am. And what I see these days is a world run by tech giants who slob into work wearing jeans and a T-shirt, Kim Jong-un, who wears a boiler suit, and various rock stars who put on whatever doesn't smell too bad.

Nobody says to Mr Bonio, 'I'm sorry but we aren't interested in what you have to say because you aren't wearing a tie.' And no one has yet asked Mr Edge to take off his hat.

Whereas whenever a man in a tie comes on the television, we always turn it off because we know he's not being funny or interesting in any way.

9 July 2017

Clarkson on the horror of modern stag dos

Boating enthusiasts on the Norfolk Broads – or UKIP, as they're known these days – have taken to the internet to express their dismay about how the peace and tranquillity of this enormous bog is being ruined by the rowdy behaviour of visitors. 'Some of them may even be foreign,' no one has said specifically. But you can bet it's what many were thinking.

Stag weekends seem to be the main cause for concern, and when I read that my eyes started to roll with despair. Yes. No one likes to share so much as a postcode with a bunch of boorish drunks celebrating the forthcoming nuptials of a mate. But these things are a part of the fabric of society, so we just have to accept that from time to time a night out in the pub is going to be spoiled by some sick and a bit of broken furniture. 'Twas ever thus.

However, if you actually examine the complaints from Captain Farage and his mates, it looks as though they may have a point. One says he recently witnessed a stag do where all the participants got drunk and then started throwing one another into the water. So far, so normal – back in your box, Boaty McBoatface. But then he goes on to say they stripped the groom naked, in front of everyone, waxed him – that's weird – and, after throwing him into the water too, took out their penises and urinated on him.

I'm sorry, but that's disgusting. I thought a stag night was something that involved a group of friends. Which raises a question. What sort of friends would decide to urinate on their host? I once urinated on someone who tried to get a selfie while I was standing at a motorway service station's urinals. But I've never peed on a friend and never would.

It turns out, however, that this is far from an isolated incident. Recently, a plane had to make an unscheduled landing at Gatwick after someone on a stag party thought it would be hilarious to set fire to the groom. So he did. He looked at his mate, someone he'd presumably known for years, and he thought, 'I think it would be for the best if he were to be married while sporting some third-degree burns.' So he set fire to his hair.

It gets worse. Several years ago, various people on a stag party on a blazing-hot day in Bournemouth decided that the bridegroom and his best man should be cooked. So they staked them out in the sun using handcuffs, stripped them naked and covered them in flour, eggs and tomato sauce. I find that odd. Because I've been drunk many times, but I've never looked at Jimmy Carr, who's a friend, and thought, 'You know what? He'd be lovely on a bed of fresh pasta.'

I'll be honest. I'm not really a fan of stag nights. I find the whole idea of all-male company extremely distressing. All that cigar-infused nonsense about snooker cues, speedboats, business deals and hookers that men feel compelled to talk about when left to their own devices makes me nauseous.

Things are even worse when you sprinkle a bit of forced jollity into the mix. Taking off a man's clothes and chaining him to a set of traffic lights could possibly, if you are twenty, be mildly amusing if it's spontaneous. But feeling obliged to do it? Nah. That's just rubbish.

That said, there was one occasion I was on a stag night and was hauled out of my dining chair to hold down the groom while other chaps shaved off his pubic hair. It seemed to me to be a terrible thing to do and I was very unamused about being forced to join in. Until they got his boxers down and we noticed the poor man had quite the smallest penis we'd ever seen. The embarrassed silence was eventually broken by someone saying, 'You can't get married with that.'

Mostly, though, the stag nights I went on in the 1980s and 1990s were reasonably calm affairs. I think I once played football with a bin bag on the Fulham Road. And I seem to recall that in an Indian restaurant someone once threw a nan into the ceiling fan. I fear it may have been me. But that's it. No one ever got driven to London Zoo and fed to the lions or strapped to the live-fire targets on Salisbury Plain.

Today, things are very different. Now, a stag night is as often as not a stag weekend. You get to the airport, drink a hundred pints, get on the plane, drink a hundred more pints, say something offensive to the stewardess, get off the plane, say something racist to the immigration officer and then spend a thousand pounds drinking more pints until it's time to experiment with some drugs your mate's bought. And then, when you wake up from the coma, you find Instagram is rammed full of pictures of your naked and freshly tattooed arse with a chicken sticking out of it.

Strippers are now compulsory. And give me strength on that one because what face exactly are you supposed to pull while some enormous Romanian woman pushes her pudendum into your mate's sunburned forehead?

I blame *The Hangover*. It was a brilliant film. I laughed a lot at nearly all of it. Unfortunately, for a whole generation, it was more than that. It was a new minimum standard. Anything less than an angry Chinese person in the boot, some amateur dentistry and a stolen police car and you haven't given the groom the send-off he deserves.

Hmmm. I'm not sure. I think – and I'm going to have the backing of the Norfolk Broads boating community on this

one – that, more than anything else in modern society, someone needs to press the stag-night reset button and go back to
the days when you drank a bit too much port on the night
before the wedding. And then went to bed.

16 July 2017

Living to 125 is a doddle: you simply get the government to make dying illegal

As we know, because Lily Allen keeps telling us, the Conservative Party wrapped Grenfell Tower in petrol-soaked rags and then set it alight on purpose so that as many poor people as possible would burn to death. And now comes news that the evil blue bastards are deliberately starving the NHS of cash so that the maximum number of elderly people die too soon and in a puddle of their own urine.

To try to understand the reasoning behind these latest accusations, I turned to the *BMJ* – formerly the *British Medical Journal* – which says that in 2015 there was a blip and a lot of people in the UK did die. But that last year almost everyone stayed alive. And that, as a result, the life expectancy for people in Britain continues its inexorable rise.

Somehow, though, Channel 4 and the *Guardian* managed to look at the same figures as the *BMJ* and come to a completely different conclusion. They ran headlines saying our life expectancy had stalled. Whereas the BBC – which perhaps had other things on its mind, such as where to go for lunch – recently said that it had actually fallen back and that soon everyone will die when they are two.

Many reports quoted a chap called Sir Michael Marmot, who said the trend for longer lives had pretty much stopped; he blamed this on Tory austerity measures. 'They are deliberately killing your mum and dad,' he implied, 'so that Starbucks can pay less tax.'

Naturally, I assumed Sir Marmot was in some way related to Lily Allen, but it turns out the two are simply joined at the hip politically. He is director of University College London's Institute of Health Equity (me neither), having once been an adviser to Gordon Brown.

According to the *Guardian*, he is held in high regard, but I can't see why, because the man says he is surprised by the figures and had expected us to keep living longer lives. What? For ever? You expected everyone to live in the future to be what? A hundred? Two hundred? A million?

The fact is that we no longer send every young man in the land to fight the Germans in a Belgian field. That's helped. We are also getting on top of HIV and many sorts of cancer, which is good news too. But by surviving AIDS and the big C and the Germans, we have now been driven into the arms of dementia.

Doubtless, Sir Marmot sees the day when science gets on top of that – and I do as well – but afterwards who knows what terribleness might be lurking in the shadows? We might die because our eyes fall out or we spontaneously combust.

And what's life going to be like in Sir Marmot's world when everyone is living to be a thousand or more? How will everyone be housed? How will they be fed? And who will change their sheets?

Then you've got the most important question of them all. Yes, I'd like to live for ever, but only if I had the physical attributes of an eighteen-year-old, not if I were sitting there with no teeth, no bladder control and fingers like burst sausages.

This, then, is what Sir Marmot should worry about. How to stop the able-bodied dying before their time. Because if you eliminate death in younger people, you naturally raise the average age at which we croak. Let me put it this way: eighteen-year-olds falling off motorcycles play havoc with the statistics.

There's a simple solution right there. Ban the motorcycle.

I bet Sir Marmot is making a note on that as we speak. And we can't have forty-year-olds catching lung cancer, so we'd better ban the sale of tobacco too, and alcohol, while we are at it. Because no good can ever come of that pesky and debilitating toxin.

Already, there is a great deal of health and safety in the workplace. In our office we have to jump through hoops like police dogs at a Horse of the Year Show intermission before we can get insurance to film anything. But even though we have to assess the risk of a giant meteor landing on someone's head, Richard Hammond still manages to put himself in hospital every time he tries to drive anywhere. And that has to stop too, which means health and safety must be tightened up still further.

Then we have the roads. At present the annual cull amounts to about 1,700 people, some of whom are children or fools who use children's toys to cycle to work. Drastic measures must be taken here, because if we can keep this lot alive until they are 127, the figures will look tremendous. That means more average-speed cameras, lower speed limits, a ban on cars on roads used by cyclists and a new type of tarmac made from feathers.

Maybe we could take a leaf out of the book they use in southern France, where they routinely live to be 112. This would mean encouraging people to sit in a plastic chair at the side of the road in a grandad shirt eating foie gras all day.

Then, after we've pulled down all the flammable tower blocks, banned cheese, tomatoes, milk, cream, butter and anything else the *Daily Mail* says gives us cancer, shut down every KFC and Maccy D in the land, set up boot camps on the coast where we all do star jumps to keep fit and locked up anyone who may be a murderer, things will improve still further. Though I think that maybe it'd be best if the government simply made it illegal to die before you are 125.

Threatening to lock up your children if you fall into some farm machinery or allow yourself to be tied to a bungee rope by a man who's plainly been smoking weed would be a very good way of keeping us alive.

Or, if you don't fancy living in a walking-pace world of flower-arranging and poetry, you could just accept that we have to die at some point or the world won't work.

23 July 2017

When I went to hospital, I was at death's door. But a far, far worse fate awaited me

In all my adult life I've never been ill. Oh, I'm sure my children have found me in a white-faced heap on the kitchen floor from time to time, and they must have heard me calling for God on the porcelain telephone, but they've never seen me in bed, whimpering and pleading for soup.

I've led an idiotic life filled with smoking and danger and germs but, despite this, I've never taken a sick day. I've never had an antibiotic. I've never had food poisoning. I've never broken a bone, and I sure as hell have never spent a night in hospital.

I'd always hoped that when the luck ran out I'd catch something exotic, something that would cause a doctor to harrumph, reach for his textbooks and then pull together a panel of great medical minds from all over the world to discuss in wonderment what might be done. About the chap with a supernumerary penis growing out of his forehead.

But no. Instead I got a pneumonia, which is what my mum said I'd catch if I went outside without a vest. It's pathetic.

I was on holiday in Mallorca when I started to feel ill. And after three nights spent spasming in my bed I thought I ought to go and see the doc.

He sent me for tests at the hospital, where I was put into a plastic dress with a slit up the back and told by a man in what looked like a swimming hat that I'd have to be admitted for at least a week.

'Impossible,' I snorted. 'I have to go to New York on Tuesday and I've my columns to write; then on Friday . . .'

'A healthy person's CRP should be five,' said Mark Spitz. 'Yours is 337.'

I had no idea at the time what a CRP was – it turns out to be something your body makes more of when you have an infection – but 337 sounded a lot.

'If you don't do as I say,' he added, 'you will die.'

I did understand that.

I'm sure many of you will have found yourself in hospital, not having planned to be there. But for me it was a new experience. And a weird one. Because I was in a room with nothing on the walls except wallpaper, and most of that was coming off. And I was in there for an hour, on my own, with absolutely nothing to do. The boredom was so bad I thought often about killing myself.

But then an army of nurses arrived to wire me up to a drip, which meant for the following hour I was effectively fastened to the wall. If only I'd thought to be travelling with a baseball glove and a ball when I was captured, I could have managed more easily but, stupidly, I'd left them at the villa.

I pushed the help button on my emergency panel and a nurse arrived. 'I'm very bored,' I said. 'And I can't find the remote control for my television.' It turned out that these had to be rented at €30, or £27, a day. I'd have paid €3,000. But luckily, I didn't, because all there was to watch was golf. In Spanish. So I summoned the nurse again and asked if she could get me a rock hammer and a big poster of Raquel Welch.

Much, much later, the head honcho arrived. I knew he was the head honcho because I have seen Jed Mercurio's medical dramas, so I know that head honchos in hospitals swoosh into the room followed by a team of fawning assistants.

'Do you smoke?' he asked.

I said yes.

'Good,' he replied. 'That keeps me in work.'

He then stroked my knee tenderly and left. And that was that. Consultation over.

In the night I was shaken awake by a nurse, who was furious because I had been sleeping in such a way that the drip wasn't working. Addressing me with the tone, accent and volume that a Vietnamese bar owner would have used on a GI who was attempting to leave without paying, she yelled for two minutes, hurt my elbow and then left.

I was grateful for these moments, because here's the thing. My right lung was more than half full of mucus. I was running one hell of a fever. I had almost no breath at all and even less energy, but all I could think was: 'I am dying of boredom here. Literally dying.'

Then my girlfriend arrived. To say she was going for lunch with friends on a superyacht. But very sweetly she did say she'd stop off in Palma to pick up some essentials for me. After I'd spent four more hours watching my wallpaper fall off, she came back with a beautifully soft black leather bomber jacket.

Normally, when I'm bored, I smoke. Or drink. But both those things were out of the question. I just had my drugs. Thousands of them. There was one that caused lightning bolts to ricochet around in my toes and one that would apparently ruin my stomach and loads more I didn't understand, but there was one that was – and remains – the highlight of my day. I was hooked.

It's called Fluimucil Forte, and its purpose is revolting. It's designed to dislodge the phlegm and the gunk in my lung and bring it up in the sort of dark, meaty globules we haven't seen since Mrs Thatcher shut down the mines. But holy sweet Jesus. It's a taste sensation.

You can forget the joy of a cold Coke on a hot day, or an

early-evening sip of Château Léoube. This was in a class of its own. And pretty soon I was telling the nurses I'd spilled it and could I have another?

Then my heart sang even more because my son arrived. After I'd spoken to him at some length about my new wonder drug, he got up and flew back to London.

This is the problem with hospitals. People who stay in them become institutionalized and incapable of speaking about anything other than what nurse brought what drug at what time. Boredom turns them into bores.

And when they get out, as I have, and there is nothing to do for two whole months apart from get better, things are even worse, because all I can talk about is my illness. And, as my dad used to say, 'A bore is a person who, when asked how they are, tells you.'

13 August 2017

My foolproof recipe to kick the fags – chewing gum and a hideous chest infection

Whenever you are interviewed by a medical-or life-insurance person, they always begin by asking if you smoke. You can tell them you like to spend your free time wrestling tigers while driving a burning motorcycle, and that despite your massive heroin addiction you work in the underwater explosives business, and they won't care. Just so long as you have pink lungs.

It's much the same story at people's houses. Ask your hostess after dinner if it would be all right if you fondled yourself, and she'll say, 'Yes, of course,' and politely look the other way while you get on with it. But ask if it would be all right to smoke and there will be a lot of flapping and huffing, and pretty soon you'll be puffing away in the back garden, in the rain.

Smoking among adults is now more antisocial than murder but, apart from one brief pause a while ago, that's never stopped me. I've smoked nearly 630,000 fags over the past forty-three years and, aside from the very first, there hasn't been a single one that I didn't enjoy.

But then, as you may have heard, I got pneumonia while I was on holiday, and I was told, by everyone, that I had to stop. Immediately. I had no choice at the time because the blood poisoning was so bad and I was so racked with the resultant rigors that I couldn't work a cigarette lighter. Also, I was fastened to the wall of my hospital room by an intravenous drip. And I couldn't really breathe.

So a week went by with no smoking. And then my daughter came to look after me as I recovered, and she's very fierce so I didn't smoke for that week either. And then after another week I came back to London, where an insurance company needed to know whether I was fit enough to return to work.

This meant going to a hospital in west London and passing my credit card through the reader until it melted. In return, I was made to empty my lungs into a tube and then empty them some more. And then keep breathing out until I could feel the hairs on my head being sucked into my skull.

Then I had to run up some stairs, and afterwards the doctor was horrified. I had 96 per cent of the lung capacity you would expect in someone my age. And I could breathe out harder and for longer than a non-smoking forty-year-old. Plus, after I'd run up the stairs, my blood was more oxygenated than it had been when I was sitting in a chair. Which is impossible, apparently.

In short, getting on for three-quarters of a million fags have not harmed me in any way. I have quite literally defied medical science.

And yet, for reasons that are not entirely clear, I decided that, having done three weeks without smoking, I might as well keep going, so now it's been a month. I've pushed it. I've got drunk. I've stayed up late. I've been to bars with smokers and sat outside in a cloud of their exhalations. And, so far, I haven't cracked.

I've been tempted, of course, usually when every single person I meet says, 'Ooh, have you thought about giving up drinking as well?' No. Why in the name of all that's holy would I want to do that?

Then there are those who think that because I'm not smoking I should take up running, or cross-country skiing. I was invited this weekend to the south coast so I could go swimming. Swimming? In the English Channel? I'm off the fags, for Christ's sake. I haven't gone mad. Swimming in British waters is something you should consider only if your Spit-fire's been shot down.

What people who smoke don't realize – and what people who don't smoke realize even less – is that nicotine's a fiend. Giving it up is really hard. It requires constant attention, and you can't be distracted by changing your life in any other way.

But there are a few handy hints I can pass on. You could move to Australia, where smoking is just about impossible. But that would mean living in Australia, which would be a bit dreary. So stay here and go to the cinema a lot. Or shopping centres. And go to bed early.

The next handy hint I can pass on is Nicorette four milli-gram 'original flavour' gum. At £18 a pack it's more expensive than smoking gold, and it causes you to hiccup sometimes, but it delivers the nicotine and that keeps you on an even keel. Because of it, I've murdered only three people in the past two days, and one of those was an Uber driver so that doesn't really count.

What's more, I spend so much time chewing gum, I can't eat and, as a result, since I gave up, I've lost a stone. True fact, that.

Some say that vaping is the answer, but I'm not sure. Partly this is because that steamy stuff makes me cough until my lungs are hanging out of my mouth, and partly it's because people with vapes look like complete idiots.

The main trick, however, is to try to find a friend who's prepared to give up at the same time. I spent the latter stages of my holiday with a woman who'd been forced by bronchitis to quit, and having her around, in the same boat, was a genu-ine source of strength.

Mainly, though, it's willpower. And to help with that, never say that you're giving up for good, only for the week, or the morning, or whatever seems manageable. And then, when that time is up, and you've coped and you haven't stabbed anyone, think of another time frame that seems achievable.

And when it all gets too much, which it will, try to imagine how much damage each puff is doing. Which, of course, is my biggest problem, because tests have shown I'm going through all the pain and the misery for absolutely no reason. I may as well have given up sandwiches.

27 August 2017

Grab your hippie-hemp bag, the little shop of package-free horrors is open

Often, when I tell the young woman on the supermarket till that I do in fact need a couple of bags to carry my shopping home, I get the sort of contemptuous look that leaves me in no doubt that I alone am responsible for the flooding in Houston and the plight of that idiotic polar bear we saw on the BBC last week trying to eat a walrus.

I know I've been bad. I know I should have turned up with a reusable bag made from hemp or mud, and that the oil used to make the plastic for my new, use-once-and-chuck-away carrier bag would have been better employed in the engine of my Range Rover, or in Alan Sugar's hair. I know all that.

But I don't shop like normal people. I drive around until I see a parking space and then I go to whatever stores happen to be near it. You go out to get washing powder and you come home with washing powder. Me? I never know what I'm going to come home with. It could be a new shirt or a stone otter or a Lamborghini. And I can't possibly be expected to carry around a selection of hippie-hemp organic bags to cope with such a wide range of possibilities.

I hate waste as much as anyone else. And I especially hate wasteful packaging. I hope there is a special place in hell's sewerage system reserved for the people at Gillette, whose products are sold in such robust packaging that to get at the razor itself you need an axe and two hand grenades.

The other day I found a parking space near Tottenham Court Road in central London, so I went into a computer shop and bought a memory stick thing. It was the size of a woodlouse but it came in a plastic display cabinet that was about 2 foot across. That made me angry.

And that's why my eye was caught last week by the antics of a former Manchester United footballer called Richard Eckersley. Actually, let's be clear on this point. Although Eckersley did grace the subs' bench at Man U on a few occasions, he later joined Burnley and spent most of the time being loaned to clubs such as Plymouth Argyle before ending up in defence at the powerhouse of international football – Toronto FC. Both of the Canadian team's supporters remember well how he helped them to a big win over the Vancouver Whitecaps.

Anyway, Eckythump is now back in Britain and has opened a shop in Devon where nothing at all is packaged. This fills my heart with joy, and I hope one day a nearby parking space is free as I drive by so I can pop in and buy some of his, er . . . well, that's where the problems start.

Mr Eebygum and his lovely wife, Nicola, are plainly very environmentally aware and wish to tread lightly.

They have called their business Earth.Food.Love. And as far as I can see, all of what they sell is expensive, revolting or pointless.

There's toothpaste, for instance, that isn't packaged. I'm not entirely sure how that works. And then there are bamboo toothbrushes, which Mr Eebygum seems to like a lot. He tells us they're made by a German company that says, 'We all need water . . . to live.' Crikey. These eco-boys are sharp. Until the manufacturer goes on to say that 'Every living being arises from a drop of water.' Really? I thought it was sperm.

Naturally, you can buy reusable sanitary towels that come from a community project in India and reusable sandwich wraps that are made by the inmates at a Scottish prison.

And then we get to the food, and I'm afraid there's nothing

here for me at all. It's beans, pulses, nuts, seeds, grains and various other things I wouldn't even put in a budgerigar's mouth. Apparently, the shop's most popular feature is its 'grind-your-own nut butter machine'. Honestly. You couldn't be more right on unless you were serving delicate pieces of Diane Abbott wrapped in old copies of the *Guardian*.

Now, I'm not daft. I know that there are many people who enjoy eating the same food as their pets. I stayed with a friend last week whose seventeen-year-old son is very thin. And when you looked in her cupboards you could see why. There was nothing in there a boy human would think about eating unless he was trapped in a desert cave and the only alternative was his arm.

The trouble is that mothers such as this, and lunatics in Islington and Mr Eckythump, are so earnest that even when they have a sensible idea, normal people, who drive cars and eat sausages and don't buy organic carrots because they're too hard to peel, put their fingers in their ears and hum.

A shop where nothing is sold with packaging is a brilliant idea. But not when it only sells stuff that appeals to cyclists and squirrels. I would love to buy Frosties without a packet, and Vesta curries and butter. Smokers, I'm sure, would love to buy cigarettes loose rather than in a box covered in pictures of someone's diseased throat. And much as I adore Nespresso coffee and the elegance of the machines that make it, I do despair at the sheer amount of effort and money and energy that's gone into making and transporting those capsules.

There's another thing too. Because there's so much packaging in our lives our wheelie bins fill more quickly. Now that might not be too much of an issue for you, but the drive to my cottage in the country is half a mile long.

So, as I'm dragging the bin full of used coffee capsules

over the cattle grids, which is not easy, in the rain and the wind, I have sometimes entertained the idea of taking one of those Nespresso machines and ramming it up George Clooney's behind.

3 September 2017

While CND was blowing up red balloons, nukes were keeping us healthy and safe

You and I both know that Kim Jong-un is not going to launch a nuclear attack any time soon. And that even if he did, his much talked-about KN-08 missile would wobble about in the sky for a few minutes and then crash into the sea. Or not take off at all.

We also know that, while Donald Trump may be a bit bonkers, he isn't going to launch the first strike. Nor will he retaliate if Kim makes the first move. Because why bomb someone who, in all probability, has just bombed himself?

This is why we can all get up in the morning and go to work. It's why we are not stockpiling food or making water filters from our central-heating boilers. And it's why the government is not digging out the old Protect and Survive public information films to tell us about how our lives will be spared if we take the bedroom door off its hinges and prop it up against the kitchen table.

The hand-wringing liberals, though, see things differently. They reckon that Trump's tiny little index finger will soon be used to fire one of America's 450 Minuteman III nukes at Pyongyang and that the only way to stop him is through the anti-nuclear movement.

For those of you who are too young to remember, in the 1970s and 1980s the anti-nuclear movement was a hilarious collection of former communists and IRA sympathizers who reckoned that if they could get Britain to abandon its nuclear weapons it'd be easier for the Soviets to take control.

As is always the way with the left, the whole movement

eventually splintered into a million factions such as the Judean People's Front of Nuclear Disarmament and the Judean Popular People's Front of European Disarmament, and then eventually everyone drifted off to become anti-capitalism, anti-G8 eco-warriors instead.

History tells us that the Cold War was eventually ended by Ronald Reagan's Hollywood-trained straight face as he outlined the 'Star Wars' defence system, a system he knew the Russians couldn't copy because it didn't and couldn't actually exist. And Mikhail Gorbachev's foolishness in believing it might. But according to the weird beards, the Berlin Wall was brought down by a bunch of women who in 1981 went to Newbury and chained themselves to a fence.

These are not to be confused with those who protested about the Newbury bypass by living in trees and digging tunnels like badgers. Impersonating animals and birds was never going to stop a government. But there are those who think that some light bondage did actually do the trick.

And because of this, they reckon that Kim, Trump and the various leaders in Pakistan, India and Iran could be brought to heel if only enough people would walk slowly down Whitehall with a Jo Malone candle.

Furthermore, it would cause all the world's terrorists to give up their fight with the infidel and stop scouring Aldermaston's wheelie bins for the ingredients to make a dirty bomb.

I wish them well, partly because the Campaign for Nuclear Disarmament – CND – and the ideals of the protest movement generated some excellent music: '99 Red Balloons' and 'Morning Dew' spring immediately to mind. I even liked the badge. And, my God, I'd rather listen to some weeping hippies droning on about strontium-90 than this turgid and never-ending debate about Brexit.

But mostly I wish them well because the anti-nuclear movement is such a fantastically amusing idea.

Because you can't campaign for the abolition of something that exists. It's like calling for an end to weather, or dogs. The nuclear bomb was invented and, unless someone comes up with a *Men in Black*-style memory-wiper stick, it'll never go away.

I agree, of course, that if a terrorist were to atomize London, it'd be hard for Theresa May to retaliate, because what co-ordinates would be fed to the subs? A house just north of Manchester? A block of flats in West Bromwich? Nukes work only as a deterrent against governments. Specifically, governments that are being run by people whose extended families would get irradiated by the return blow.

However, saying that we shouldn't have a nuclear arsenal because it will protect us from only a certain type of enemy is like saying you won't take medical precautions when travelling in the tropics because they protect you from only a certain kind of disease. Better, in my book, to cover some of the bases than none at all.

Which brings us on to the new darling of the hand-wringing liberals, the manhole-cover enthusiast and aspiring vegan Jeremy Corbyn. It's possible, or even likely, that he will be our next prime minister, and this is seen as a good thing by the Guardianistas because he's a man of peace. He even has a beard to prove the point. And yet he's on record as saying he would use nuclear weapons.

The only reason the liberals love him is that he qualified this by saying he'd be 'extremely cautious' about it. As opposed to what? That he'd do it on a whim? Or for a bet while pissed at a party?

The fact is that no single invention has saved more lives than the nuclear bomb. Without it, Russia and America would have started fighting in about 1958 and in all probability would still be at it now.

And nuclear power means millions of tons of carbon dioxide are not in the upper atmosphere making hurricanes more powerful, but still in the ground.

So I think we should encourage the people at CND, but only if someone else starts up an organization that champions the peace and clean energy that nuclear tech has brought to the world.

10 September 2017

Nab him, grab him, stop that pigeon – and let the homeless eat him now

As we know, there are a great many mad people in the south-western bit of the country. They claim often that a black panther is living on Exmoor and that, if you paint a picture, it'll be better if you are standing on a ley line.

And now the people of Exeter are saying that homeless people, many of whom may be from Poland, are roaming the streets at night eating pigeons. There are fears this could get out of hand with a local police community support officer saying, 'Now we're eating pigeons, now we're killing sea-gulls. It escalates.'

One resident said she saw two men pounce on a pigeon and put it in a sack and in the space of twenty minutes they'd captured fourteen of them. This has made the Royal Society for the Protection of Birds very angry, with a spokesman describing the incident as 'horrible'.

'Unlikely' is nearer the mark, though. I knew a man once who wore a suit, played a lot of golf and had never had so much as a parking ticket. But one day, while walking to work over Waterloo Bridge, he remembered being told that you can never kick a pigeon, because it has a housefly-like ability to get out of the way before your foot arrives. And for rea-sons that haunted him for the rest of his life, he decided to put the theory to the test.

So, in front of all the other suited-and-booted Margaret Thatcher enthusiasts, he took an almighty swing at the bird strutting about in his path and – wallop – it sailed six feet into the air and crashed back down to Earth, stone dead. This proved, much to his embarrassment, that you can kick a pigeon to death.

I had a similar moment in northern Spain about ten years ago. I was out and about in the packed streets of San Sebastián when I noticed a listless pigeon sitting on a windowsill. 'I'll put that out of its misery,' I thought, and tried to break its neck. But the manoeuvre went wrong and its head came off, which caused the body to fall to the floor, where, much to the horror of the many onlookers, it flapped about for several minutes before it decided there was no point any more and lay still.

The weird thing is that this was Spain, where stabbing cows and throwing donkeys off tower blocks is basically like Swingball. And yet they were horrified that I'd pulled a pigeon's head off.

I think the problem is that we learn from an early age that pigeons are clever. That you can take one to Berlin and it is able to find its way back to its loft in Peterborough.

The Nazis certainly thought this way. Heinrich Himmler was a pigeon enthusiast and made plans for birds to be used to convey messages from agents ahead of an invasion of Britain.

And when authorities here got wind of this, instead of saying, 'Oh, don't be stupid. Why would you use a bird to convey a message when you have a radio?', they decided the south coast should be patrolled by falcons. And in the Scilly Isles, it really was. That really did happen. It was the Battle of Britain, with feathers.

That legacy lives on in the way people react when pigeons are being harmed. But the thing is that salmon can also home and no one minds when Jeremy Paxman hauls one of those from a river and clubs it to death. Or when a little old lady buys a tin of its flesh and feeds it to her cat.

The fact is, though, that unlike salmon, pigeons are a menace. In towns their muck ruins buildings and in the countryside they can do more damage to crops than an army of drunken students with an alien fixation and a garden roller. If you shoot a pigeon – which is harder than kicking one, I assure you – and you open it up, you'll find more grain in its stomach than in the silos at Hovis.

Which brings us back to the issues in Exeter. If you are fit and sober and you have a gun, it is only just possible to kill a fit pigeon. So I'm suspicious of the story that these homeless drunks are able, in the space of twenty minutes, to get fourteen live birds into a sack. (I feel a game show coming on here.)

Let's just say, though, that they are able, through the fog of strong cider, to catch pigeons, and if things escalate, seagulls. So what? Yes, under the Wildlife and Countryside Act of 1981 it's illegal to kill, injure or take any wild bird, but this was drawn up to stop people stealing ospreys and ptarmigans.

Let's not forget, shall we, that Ken Livingstone, darling of the left and therefore an RSPB poster boy, ejected all the people selling grain to tourists in the pigeon-infested Trafalgar Square and when Wilbur and Myrtle continued to show up with birdseed they'd bought from a Chelsea ladies' health food shop he introduced a Harris hawk to the area. Which is the Messerschmitt of the skies.

He'd be the first to say that homeless people should be encouraged to eat pigeons, and I'd go further. Right now, the hedgerows on my farm are teeming with succulent blackberries and the few trees that haven't been ruined by deer and squirrels are laden with all kinds of delicious fruit.

If a homeless person were to spend a day in the woods with some Rambo traps and a bit of cunning, he would end up with a feast that even Henry VIII would call 'a bit extravagant'.

The problem is, if he killed a deer for some venison and a squirrel for seasoning, he'd have the whole country calling for his blood. And that's ridiculous. We need to lose our dewy-eyed Disney sentimentality and accept that homeless people eating pigeons they've caught is better for them, better for our windowsills and better for the coffers at the NHS than encouraging them instead to eat takeaway pizza and Double Decker chocolate bars they've half-inched from the local corner shop.

17 September 2017

Some terrace chants are mean, but Manchester United fans are just bigging up their new hero

This year Manchester United signed a footballer called Romelu Lukaku. And it seems he's been doing very well, scoring so many goals that adoring fans sing songs in the stands about the magnitude of his member. However, they've now been asked to stop doing this by anti-racist campaigners, who say that it's racial stereotyping.

I was a bit confused about this, because Mr Lukaku is Belgian and I was unaware that Belgians are notorious for having oversized genitals.

Undeterred, the do-gooders go on to point out that any racist chant that is threatening, abusive or insulting to a person is against the law.

And again I'm confused, because never in all human history has a man felt abused, threatened or insulted by someone saying, 'My word, old chap, that's one hell of a sausage you've got down there.'

I can't speak for Mr Lukaku, who has urged supporters to 'move on' and #RespectEachOther, but I can tell you that if I were at work and 80,000 people were singing loudly about how my penis was two foot long, I'd feel pretty damn good.

There was a time when racism in football was monstrous. People would turn up at games with sackfuls of bananas that they would throw at black players, and the chants would boggle the mind of anyone born after 1990. But by and large it's gone now. It's not so much 'kick' racism out of football as 'keep' racism out of football.

I'm a season-ticket holder at Chelsea, and every other week-end Stamford Bridge is like a super-condensed rainbow nation. The pitch is full of people from all over the world, and the stands are crammed with every conceivable skin tone: black, brown, white and even orange when we are playing Manchester City and half of Cheshire is in town.

And yet there are signs everywhere urging us to say no to racism. Which is a bit like having a sign in *Tatler*'s office urging staff to say no to state-school kids. It's stupid. I never think, 'Oh, no. Don't pass the ball to Eden Hazard. He's Belgian and he'll trip over his organ.' I just see eleven men in Chelsea colours. So does everyone else, as far as I can tell.

Last week we played Nottingham Forest, and their supporters suddenly started to sing, to the tune of 'Guantanamera', 'You're a shit, Jimmy Savile.' I turned to my son, who is an expert on football crowd mentality, and asked who they were singing about.

'Oh,' he said, 'it'll be a Chelsea supporter who's come to the game with his grandson.'

Before I'd even had time to pull the appropriate face, they'd changed tack and were singing, 'You're on the register.'

Imagine that. You save up all month to take your grandson to watch his beloved Chelsea team play football. You pull on a tracksuit to keep out the autumnal chill, and maybe you tousle the lad's hair after your team has scored one of its goals. And what do you get in return? Several thousand people pointing at you and calling you a paedophile. And that's somehow fine.

All of which brings me naturally to a tapestry that is held in the vaults of a museum in Bristol. More than 250 big-hearted volunteers took about twenty years to complete this remarkable 267-foot work. Prince Charles put in the final stitch in 2000.

Called the *New World Tapestry*, it was created to commemorate Britain's colonial exploits between 1583 and 1642.
Many were hoping it would be put on display in a few years
to commemorate the four hundredth anniversary of the
Mayflower's voyage.

But that now seems unlikely, because a Native American
lady has decided that one of the scenes in the tapestry, which
shows local people laughing as they set fire to white settlers,
is racist.

The principal artist, Tom Mor, described these accusations as 'rubbish', saying, 'It's reality – we slaughtered the
Native Americans and they slaughtered us.'

I fear, however, that this argument will fall on deaf ears,
because it's a fact that we stole their land and gave them nothing in return, apart from medicine, food, electricity, phones
and Las Vegas. Anyone who says otherwise is a racist. And,
yes, that would include John Wayne and anyone else who
starred in a cowboy film.

It's the same with Horatio Nelson. I couldn't follow the
story closely because my eyes had rolled into the top of my
head in despair, but someone apparently said the admiral
was a racist too and that he should be removed from Trafalgar Square.

Meanwhile, in Canada, the image of William Lyon Mac-
kenzie King is to be removed from the $50 banknote. He
was the country's longest-serving prime minister and by the
standards of the early twentieth century he was extremely
liberal, but his diaries reveal that he used contemporary racial
epithets, so that is that. He will be replaced with another
former prime minister.

It is entirely possible that the anti-slavery campaigners Thomas Clarkson and William Wilberforce also used
words that would be deemed inappropriate today, so what

should we do about that? Tear down the statues erected in their honour? Strip naked and burn effigies of them in the streets?

Actually, don't answer that.

24 September 2017

Terrorists have put half the world out of bounds, and bedbugs patrol the rest of it

With a new super-strain of drug-resistant malaria rampaging through Southeast Asia, various Notting Hill people called Arabella are having to think twice about taking their holidays next year in Cambodia.

This is causing them all sorts of grief, because obviously they can't go to the Middle East either – that's where footballers go to get papped for either wearing or not wearing a wedding ring – and North Africa is out because, although the beaches are swept quite often, it's usually with machine-gun fire.

North America? Nope, because who's to say that by next summer Mr Kim won't have turned the entire continent into the sort of post-apocalyptic wasteland you thought only existed in Hollywood's box of CGI tricks? And South America is a no-no as well because, in all the ways that matter to Arabella, it's just the same as Notting Hill. And that's before we get to the Caribbean, which so far as I can tell isn't there any more.

The world is all a big worry at the moment, but the truth is that if you come back from your holidays with a bullet hole in your arm or without one of your ears because you were kidnapped while trying to score a gram of coke in Bolivia, you do at least have a dinner party anecdote.

And you really shouldn't worry about malaria either, because, as I've said before, the only Westerners who catch it are those with orange faces who need to explain to the *Daily Mail* why they have a sniffly nose and mad eyes, so they get their spokesman to say they caught, er, malaria while digging a well for villagers in Rwanda.

I've travelled the world quite a lot, and only once did I catch something unpleasant. I'd been in Cuba filming for a couple of weeks, and a few days after I got back I was lying in bed wondering why I seemed to have so many new freckles on my arm. On both arms in fact. And my legs. And between them.

I had a bit of a poke about, squeezing one of them to see if it was perhaps cancer, and immediately I wished it had been, because the skin broke and out popped what can only be described as an animal of some kind. A spider? A crab? An alien? It was hard to be sure because it ran off before I'd had a chance to examine it more closely.

What I did examine was the next freckle along and, sure enough, when I squeezed that, another animal leapt out and scuttled away. And I had hundreds of freckles. Maybe even a thousand.

I went to see the doctor, who asked if I was feeling ill. I was. Lousy, in fact. 'Well, that's not surprising,' she said, lifting her head from my nether regions and turning off her Davy lamp, 'because you have lice. That's where the word "lousy" comes from.'

Now, I'm sorry, but coming back from an exotic foreign trip with an exotic foreign disease is quite cool, but coming back from Cuba in the 1990s, when pretty much every single woman under the age of thirty is basically a prostitute, that's not cool at all. 'That's disgusting,' said all my friends.

But it wasn't as disgusting as what happened next. The doctor had given me some cream to rub into all the affected areas, saying that after forty-eight hours all the lice would have left my body and died. Sadly for the next person into the cubicle, the forty-eight hours was up when I was in one of the lavatories at Kuala Lumpur Airport, on my way to Australia.

I pulled down my shreddies to see if any had fallen out, and it was like a horror film. There were hundreds and hundreds of dead lice, all of which I swept on to the floor before leaving.

You might imagine that illness and problems of this nature are all part of life when you are travelling to weird parts of the world, but last week I came back from a two-day trip to the part of France that is full of people who miss Terry Wogan and I had an itchy right nipple.

Further investigation revealed that I'd been bitten by a bedbug, which I thought was a harmless cartoon character designed to make young children feel all snuggly and safe when you tuck them up at night.

Well, it's not. My nipple looks as though it's exploded, and because it itches enough to make scratching impossible to resist, I find people are looking at me in restaurants as though I may be practising for some kind of weird transgender pole-dancing routine.

It turns out bedbugs are extremely common in even the most expensive hotels, and there is much advice on the internet about how you can minimize your chances of being bitten. One reputable site suggests that before putting your clothes, suitcase, or yourself on to the bed you should peel back the sheets very carefully and check for bugs using the torch you're bound to have in your hand luggage, because everyone does.

Next, you must remove the sheets and scrape the mattress, using a credit card to peer under the buttons, before switching your investigations to the headboard. This is the most terrible game of Hide and Seek ever, and it gets worse, because you also need to check the stand on to which you will place your suitcase later, and the bathroom.

Now, excuse me, but if you are on holiday, you are not going to be inclined to do a four-hour *CSI* search of your room looking for something that, in the worst case, is going to make you a bit itchy for a day or two.

Far better to accept that, when you go away, there's a chance that you will catch something either irritating or nasty. Or that you will be shot, kidnapped, irradiated or blown into the sea and drowned. It's what travel agents mean when they describe a holiday as exciting: that you may come home in a box.

1 October 2017

The best art criticism is done not with words but with craft knife and spray can

As we know, the French have always been very open about sex. Thirty years ago, while we Brits were sitting in a hotel room watching a porn film that had been edited so heavily it was nothing more than a forty-minute close-up of a sweaty man's face going up and down, Johnny Frenchman could sit down after a hard day on strike and watch full-on sex on terrestrial television.

Well, I say 'full-on sex', but most French films of this period usually had quite a lot of meaningless preamble. By which I mean we had half an hour of a man sitting outside a restaurant in Paris, stirring coffee and staring wistfully into the middle distance while smoking a Gitane. Then he'd ask the waiter if the ham was happy, and it would cut to a naked woman with armpits like Monty Don's shrubbery writhing around in a bed. After which it would cut back to the man at the restaurant, who was now standing up, saying at the top of his voice, 'What is the meaning of this table?' Then there'd be some sex.

It was the same story on the beach. Frenchwomen were wearing nothing but a few inches of dental floss while we were still hopping up and down behind a windbreak as we tried to get our flab into an all-in-one romper suit.

Today a French infant can marry his primary-school teacher and go on to be president, and it's not uncommon for a man to arrive home at the end of the day and say to his wife, 'Sorry I'm late, darling. I stopped off at a hotel with my mistress for a couple of hours.'

Naturally, French art is just porn. A recent example was a video promoting an art exhibition that showed various naked people writhing around on the floor biting one another. It was all very odd until the camera pulled back and we saw they were spelling out 'Sade'.

Now a panel of French art experts – can you imagine how little they find funny? – has decided that a thirty-ton sculpture by a Dutch art collective the name of which I can't be bothered to remember should be exhibited in the Tuileries Gardens as a centrepiece of this month's Paris contemporary art fair.

To the casual eye it looks like a collection of shipping containers held together with oddly angled beams. But if you study it for more than about one second, it's very obvious that it's a man – how can I put this in a family newspaper? – hanging out of the back of a dog.

Now you may think this is the sort of thing the French show on Pierre Bleu at five in the afternoon, but it seems not. The people who run the gardens where the gigantic *One Man and His Dog* sculpture was to have been displayed have said *non*.

Naturally, they've said *non* not only because it would be inappropriate to have a forty-foot sculpture of animal sex in the middle of the city but because they think it might be vandalized.

This would not be a first. A few years ago an American artist was asked to make a modern-day Christmas tree sculpture, which was then mounted in Place Vendôme.

That all sounds very jolly and festive, but anyone who's even walked past a sex shop would tell you that the sculpture was nothing more than an enormous gentleman's sex toy. I believe the term is 'butt plug'. I also believe the sub-editors will take that reference out.

Anyway, it was vandalized, and so, at the Palace of Versailles, was a huge hollow tube that at one end flared out into the shape of – there's no other way of saying this – a lady part.

There are those who say that this vandalism is the work of right-wing religious nutcases, but that seems unlikely, because no right-wing religious nutcases have vandalized Brigitte Bardot's breasts. No. I think it's more likely these things were vandalized by people who like art.

People in France have lived with sex and general disgustingness for decades, so why should they suddenly decide now that it's time to make merry with the spray cans? Aren't the culprits more likely to be people who think, 'No. I'm sorry. But filling the beautiful gardens at Versailles with a massive metal tube, no matter what shape it is at the end, is just not on'?

Things in Britain are a bit more tricky, because sex here died when Robin Askwith hung up his Y-fronts and Barbara Windsor put her bosoms away. We don't do metal vaginas or bestiality sculptures in Hyde Park, so our art fans have no excuse to become vandals. Which is a pity.

Last week a contemporary art fair opened in Regent's Park in London, and I don't doubt for a moment that true connoisseurs were appalled by the collection of cardboard boxes that had been fastened somehow to a wall, or the enormous lollies that were to be found outside, stuck into the lawn. And that's before we get to the skeleton draped over a chair.

Unfortunately, the whole place was full of visitors wandering around scratching their chins and using lines on one another that they'd picked up from watching the Pierce Brosnan remake of *The Thomas Crown Affair*.

Some of them were actually shelling out because, like pretty much everyone in Britain, they have walls, and walls need to be covered with stuff.

Something must be done about that. It's tricky enough for normal people to buy art, because we don't know what's good and what's tosh. We therefore need people who do know to become a bit more French and smash stuff up before we have a chance to make fools of ourselves.

And come home from an art fair with a boot full of empty cereal packets.

8 October 2017

Oh blow, our star role in a hurricane epic has gone with the wind

It can't be much fun being a weather forecaster in Britain because there's almost always nothing to do. You spend all day looking at isobars and algorithms and they always say the same thing: tomorrow will be grey and boring with a slight chance of rain.

You look from time to time at weather forecasters in other parts of the world and you are green with envy because they have hurricanes and cyclones and tornados and temperature extremes that can shatter or melt steel. Whereas all you ever have is another minor low trundling across the Atlantic, which means that tomorrow it will be fifty-seven degrees and drizzling. Same as it was yesterday and the day before that.

You dream of the day when something interesting happens because then you will be promoted from the tail end of the news to who knows? The lead item? You may even be sent out of the studio to stand in the weather you've forecast. You'll be an actual reporter, with messed-up hair and maybe even a bulletproof vest with 'Press' on it.

Which brings us on to Hurricane Ophelia. It started to form a couple of weeks ago several hundred miles south-west of the Azores. This was on approximately the same latitude as Morocco and that's way further north than the zone where hurricanes usually gird their loins. Because it was so far north the sea temperature wasn't particularly warm, so it took longer than usual to develop its eye and that familiar circular cloud pattern. But eventually it was up to strength and off it set . . .

Doubtless the forecasters in Britain sat at their desks,

looking at it with their chins in their hands, thinking about how their colleagues in the Caribbean and Florida were going to get all the action – again. They'd be the ones standing in front of huge, crashing waves while pointing at advertising hoardings as they tumbled down the streets.

But then something odd happened. Instead of heading west, Ophelia began to move north-east. This had happened before. In 2012 Hurricane Nadine did the same thing, but then became trapped by a combination of witchcraft and who knows what and just sat there for nearly a month – the fourth-longest-lasting Atlantic hurricane in recorded history.

Weather reporters went off to ground zero dressed up like Kate Adie.

Everyone expected Ophelia to do the same thing, but it didn't. It broke free and set a course directly for the British Isles. Well, you can imagine how exciting that must have been for our forecasters. 'We have five days,' one of them will have said, 'before it hits.'

In my mind, whooping alarms will have sounded and someone will have leapt to his feet and ordered no one in particular to 'secure the perimeter'. The weather services computer room will have looked like the bridge of a nuclear submarine at Defcon 1. Or is it 5? I never know which way round that goes.

Britain was going to get a hurricane, and every weather reporter went into the television station's war room and half-inched every bit of combat kit they could find. They were going to be the lead item and they wanted to look good when Armageddon arrived.

They also wanted to be at ground zero, which they'd worked out would be on the west coast of Ireland. So off they went, dressed up like Kate Adie, and every half an hour they'd film updates for the rolling news channels.

Sadly, they weren't getting quite what they'd wanted because the Irish, being Irish, had decided that, instead of boarding up their windows and stocking up on bottles of water, they'd be better off at the pub. Some had even decided to go for a swim. So we were treated to the ridiculous spectacle of someone dressed like they were off to the South Pole reporting on scenes of intense jollity.

In a desperate attempt to make the locals frightened, a flock of birds was photographed flying overhead. 'Look,' screamed the reporters. 'You've seen *2012*, that disaster movie with John Cusack. The birds knew the end of the world was coming in that. And they know something's up here too.'

Warnings were issued that wind speeds would hit 75mph, but then someone decided 75mph didn't sound that bad. So it was converted to 120kph and that sounded much better. Meanwhile, an amber warning was issued that, said the man in the anorak and storm boots, meant lives were in danger. Millions would be mangled. The UK and Ireland would be wiped out. This would be an extinction-level event.

But then disaster struck. As the hurricane began to near Ireland it decided to become a storm. And then a stiff breeze. But there was no way they'd admit to this because then they'd have to go home and return to looking at isobars. So they stuck it out, desperately finding narrow passageways that would amplify the wind and make their hair look messier, and puddles in which to stand while reporting.

Five hundred hacks raced to the scene of a fallen tree in Dublin. And Instagram was rammed with shots of upended wheelie bins. Three people died. And the roof of a school came off. 'And it's heading your way, London.'

Well, we waited and, at three in the afternoon, it looked as if the warnings were all going to come true. The sky went the weirdest colour I'd ever seen, a phenomenon caused, we were told, by Stiff Breeze Ophelia whipping up Saharan dust and smoke from forest fires in Portugal.

By four it was horror film-tastic. And strangely warm. And still. Too still. At any moment I expected a howling burst of energy to rip the Chiswick flyover from its mountings and send fire engines high into the ionosphere. But by five the sun came out again and that was that.

I'd like to say it was the biggest anticlimax in modern recorded history, but that accolade still rests with the Great Storm of October 1987. Which was not quite severe enough to wake anyone up.

22 October 2017

Wine bore's red? Wide-awake white? No, I'll take the vino in-betweeno

Right, then. That's it. British summertime is over and for the next five months it will be constantly dark and cold and foggy. There will be steamed-up windows and runny noses too. So it's time to put away the Pimm's and break out the Bovril. Or is it?

Next weekend the nation will gather round various bon-fires, oohing and aahing at all the fireworks. We will be in our duffle coats, and our children will have pink cheeks and sparklers, and we'll be wondering how on earth it's possible for the smoke to blow into our eyes no matter which side of the fire we choose to stand.

Naturally, our host will provide liquid refreshment, which will be either warm brown beer made by a brewery with a silly name, or mulled wine. Both of which will be disgust-ing, so I have a suggestion. If you are thinking of hosting a bonfire party, do what I'd do: serve only rosé wine. With lots of ice.

Some people find my love of lady petrol rather weird. And when I point out that Noel Gallagher has similar views, they look quizzical and say, 'Well, he must be weird too.' But we are not alone, because the world is divided into two distinct camps. Those who have realized that rosé is the only drink worth drinking. And a tiny number who haven't. Yet.

There was a time when you'd only drink rosé when you were staying with friends at their villa in the south of France, in August. You wouldn't dream of buying it in England, in November, because, well, you are a man and you have your own tankard in the pub and you wouldn't be seen dead drinking pink. But not any more.

Waitrose and Marks & Spencer say rosé sales have recently leapt by more than 100 per cent, and it's easy to see why. If you drink white wine with your supper, it will turn to sugar in your stomach and at three in the morning you will sit bolt upright in bed as though John Travolta had just pumped your heart full of neat adrenaline.

If, on the other hand, you choose to drink red, your face will be in the bouillabaisse by eight in the evening and you'll snore all through the main. Rosé, meanwhile, steers a neat course through the two extremes, getting you nicely tipsy without waking you up in the night or putting you to sleep during the starter.

And there's more: if you drink rosé, everyone will know you know nothing about wine. This is a good thing because anyone who does know something about wine is incapable of keeping this knowledge to themselves.

This is a problem for me at the moment because recently I was given a case of something called Château Cheval Blanc that was made in 1985. I'm told this is an excellent wine and should be shared only with those who'll truly appreciate it. Which would mean inviting that sort of person round to my house, and that's not something I'm prepared to do. In case they appreciate it out loud.

Mind you, things are worse in restaurants, because nothing – and I do mean nothing – causes my blood to boil quite so quickly as some pompous arse in red trousers sitting at the head of the table poring over the wine list for half an hour and then wasting another half an hour discussing his knowledge and brilliance with the sommelier.

And that's only the start, because when the red-trousered arse has finally decided what heavy red he'd like and the sommelier has congratulated him on his 'excellent choice', there's that whole swirling and examining against the light and sloshing procedure to be endured. I know he thinks that everyone round the table is sitting there, with faces like raisins, thinking, 'What a cultured fellow this man must be' – but we are not. We are all sitting there thinking, 'What an insufferable show-off.'

How would he feel if he climbed into the passenger seat of my car and I sat there in silence for an hour listening to the engine and blipping the throttle occasionally? He'd think I'd taken leave of my senses. Almost certainly he'd say that a car is just a car and ask if I wouldn't mind setting off sometime this week. Well, quite.

To express his displeasure at a restaurant full of wine snobs, my dad, upon being asked to taste the wine, once took off his jacket, rolled up his sleeve and dipped his elbow into the glass before saying to the wine waiter in a loud voice, 'Mmmm, yes. That's delicious.'

Rosé gets round all that nonsense. You don't have to let it breathe. You don't have to swirl it around or smell its cork. And if you comment on its quality, or how it's 'opened up nicely', people are going to laugh at you. I'm not saying all rosé is lovely. It isn't. If it cost you £1.99 from the petrol station and it's the colour of Ribena and the bottle has a screw top, it'll make you go cross-eyed every time you take a sip. But if it's a Château Minuty or a Whispering Angel or, best of all, a Château Léoube, you can cut the top of the bottle off with a sword and get cracking immediately because it will be tremendous.

I'm really not alone in this view. I took two bottles of Léoube to a friend's dinner party the other night and before we'd even sat down it had all gone. No one there was drinking anything else. And yet here's the strangest thing. Most restaurant wine lists have eight hundred pages of wine that's red or white, and then a Post-it note on the back listing the two they have that are pink. British Airways doesn't serve rosé at all. Not even in the lounge.

I think that's why it's no longer the world's favourite airline. Because it doesn't serve the world's favourite wine.

29 October 2017

Guy Fawkes was an amateur. You should have seen me and my friends blow up Hull

I was once invited to spend Bonfire Night at a party near Hull. We were young back then – and poor – so everyone turned up with a party seven of Worthington E and a small box of Standard Fireworks. The sort that fizzes momentarily in a flowerbed and amuses no one at all.

It was decided, therefore, that, rather than set them off individually, we would meld them together to create the mother of all Fireworks. The biggest rocket to be developed in Britain since Blue Streak. A bomb so big that it would make seismograph needles wobble as far away as Buenos Aires.

The powder and the effects from each small firework were emptied on to the kitchen table; duct tape and a collection of cardboard boxes and tubes were found and shaped. A broom handle was sourced from beneath the host's stairs. And eventually six burly men were summoned to carry the monster we had created out to the back garden.

Everyone was invited outside to watch this thing strut its stuff in the crisp night sky. The blue touchpaper was lit and then . . . whoooooosh. Up it went. And then up some more. Soon it was out of sight. Moments passed. And then we waited a moment while some more moments slid slowly by. And then, after a long moment, someone suggested we should all go back inside, because, plainly, it hadn't worked and it was too cold . . . And as everyone turned to do just that, Hull blew up.

I've seen an Abrams M1A1 main battle tank unleash hell in a live-fire exercise, and I've worked with James Bond's special-effects people. So I've experienced some fairly loud bangs, but nothing has compared to the explosion we created that night. Roof tiles were dislodged. Chimneys were bent. Windows were shattered. And for a moment, through the hole we'd punched in the atmosphere, we may have caught a glimpse of Guy Fawkes himself sitting up there in the heavens with a puzzled look on his face.

The poor man must be constantly puzzled, because he and his mates were pretty useless. One wrote a letter to a parliamentarian, urging him to stay away from the Palace of Westminster on 5 November. This was passed to the authorities, which searched the cellars and found Guy guarding the gunpowder.

His co-conspirators, meanwhile, had ridden north to start their Catholic rebellion, but they still had a fair bit of gunpowder with them and it caught fire, which meant some were smouldering gently when they were arrested.

They probably thought things couldn't get worse. But they did, because the men were stretched on the rack, hanged until nearly dead and then let down and made to watch as they were castrated. After that they were disembowelled and cut into four pieces and their heads were put on spikes.

Fawkes was facing a similar fate but was lucky because he jumped, breaking his neck. So, while they still chopped him into quarters, he didn't feel a thing.

It can't have been much fun, though, lying there, paralysed and ready to be cut up, knowing that your plot had failed and that the hated Protestants had won. He must have had a very real feeling that he'd be forgotten in a week . . . But no. To commemorate his failure, his effigy was burnt on 5 November for centuries. Then the Chinese firework corporations moved in, and now the date is marked by doctors having to work overtime to deal with burns victims.

As legacies go, that's fairly weird, but Christmas is weirder still. We gather to celebrate the possible birth date of someone who may or may not have lived by giving one another electronic goods. And then there's Easter, when we stop work to celebrate the death of the man who may or may not have lived by eating eggs made from chocolate. I'm absolutely certain that if Jesus really did mooch about in the Middle East two thousand years ago, spreading his message of goodwill, and if he really did rise again to sit with God in the clouds, he's going to be pretty pissed off to see the biggest beneficiaries of his endeavours are Nintendo and Cadbury.

However, the weirdest legacy of all is what a few fancy-dress enthusiasts celebrated last weekend: Halloween.

I thought it was some American thing, like Thanksgiving, when they all get together and eat turkey to thank the Native Americans for dying in such great numbers. But no. Halloween started on this side of the Pond, possibly in Scotland, where people would gather at the end of the harvest to give thanks.

And yet somehow it's become an excuse for young women to put on no clothes and go out after work on the pull. And for parents to send their children into the street to practise the art of extortion on frail old ladies.

There's a ghosts-and-ghouls element in the mix as well, and it's hard to see what this has to do with Mrs McTavish and a bag of root vegetables. So I did a bit of checking, and it seems Celts celebrated Samhain, as they called it before the Christians came along and renamed it All-Hallows Eve, by communing with the dead. And the ghostly night in the graveyard was the afterparty to the rather nicer bring-and-buy festival at the village hall.

This obviously excited America's marketing departments, which said, 'Yes, we have a small gap here between the end of the summer holiday and Thanksgiving. Let's slot in a new thing where people can paint their faces with fake blood and go out vandalizing, and we can sell them plastic turnips and make a film about a man who won't die.

'And then let's export it to Englandland, so they can have two weekends on the trot when no one gets any bloody sleep.'

5 November 2017

Injured at school, the Famous Five go in search of a no-win no-fee lawyer

The Famous Five enthusiast who is now running Ofsted announced last week that children should be encouraged to run about until they are exhausted and explore caves, even if there's a chance that they'll be captured by smugglers and tied up.

Amanda Spielman said nursery schools that do not allow kids to be tied up by burly men in caves could actually be harming children's development and has called for climbing frames not to be removed from playgrounds so that they can understand what it feels like to break an arm.

Because we are broadly the same age, I know exactly what she means. When I was small I was encouraged on icy mornings to go into my nursery school's playground and do slides, even though I couldn't and always fell over. I spent hours climbing on precariously balanced haystacks, stealing rhubarb from the local nuns and playing Hide and Seek in various bits of 1960s farm equipment. The teachers would look on and squeal with delight as blood spouted from our severed arteries, and you could barely hear the screams of pain because of all the breaking bones.

Like all old people, I can sit here now saying it never did me any harm and rolling my eyes at the news that the best-selling toy this Christmas is likely to be a £35 drone that can be flown from the comfort of your sofa. But only if there's experienced adult supervision, because the blades could cause light bruising. Tragic.

Certainly, if Enid Blyton were to write a Famous Five

book today, there'd be no ginger beer because Red Bull is nicer, no Uncle Quentin because he'd be in jail for child abuse and no smugglers because, obviously, that would be racist in some way. The kids would just sit around smoking weed until one day Timmy made George pregnant. No, hang on. Timmy was the dog. I meant Julian.

I used to encourage my children to play in the fields when they were young, but they looked at me as though I might be mad. They simply couldn't see how a field could possibly compete with *Call of Duty*, and I fear they may have had a point.

I'd wail about how we'd moved out of London so they could get rosy cheeks and make dens in all the fresh air and they'd look wistfully at the wi-fi router, wondering if any of the lights would ever turn as green as they'd been in Battersea.

So I wonder. If nursery schools were to follow Mrs Spielman's advice and keep climbing frames and all those things that used to fill our childhood with pain and misery, how much would they be used? How would you get a child to stop Snapchatting their mates and get on a seesaw? I'm not sure you could.

Or should. Because let's just paint a picture of how things would turn out. Little Johnnie would have his telephone confiscated, which in itself is bound to contravene some kind of human right, and then he'd be forced to play on the climbing frame. And because he's fat, he's going to fall off and break his wrist.

Now, in the past, the parents would have taken the child to hospital, they would have been strapped up and that would have been that. But not any more. Today the parents would take him straight to a lawyer, who would explain that the enormous orb of fat and tears would have become a Wimbledon champion were it not for the school's insistence that

he play on a climbing frame under the supervision of someone who that morning had arrived in Britain on the underside
of a Eurostar train.

And so, yes, he would gladly take the case on a no-win
no-fee basis. The parents will hug him and sob and express
their gratitude, not realizing that there is literally no chance
in hell he will lose and that when he wins he will take about
all the money that the court awards. Which will be a lot.

The school will have known the lawyer's letter was on its
way because the fat kid's father will have said as he picked up
his blubbing, blubbery son that he'd sue it for every penny it
had, so it will have launched an investigation. Translators
will have been found for the woman in charge of the playground that day, and counsellors found for the children who
heard the fat boy's wrist snap. The headmistress, meanwhile,
will be outside giving her fortieth interview of the day to a
reporter whose initial soppiness will have turned into mock-
incredulity: 'Are you seriously suggesting you didn't know
that a climbing frame would be . . .' and so on.

Eventually, after the head has been sacked and the teaching assistant deported and the school closed down, the case
will reach court, where the lawyer will deploy yet more mock-
incredulity, wondering out loud and with a lot of pomposity
how on earth a school could possibly have been so reckless
as to install a death trap in its playground. And having heard
from a 'tennis coach' that the fat kid could have beaten Roger
Federer, the court will award the parents about eleventy million pounds. Which will have to be sorted by the taxpayer.

So I'm afraid Mrs Spielman is fighting a war on all fronts
here. Children don't want climbing frames because they
prefer Snapchat, and schools don't want climbing frames
because they know that, sooner or later, no matter how many
precautions they take, they'll get sued.

So if Mrs Spielman really wants kids to get off their fat arses and party like it's 1961, she's going to have to address the root cause of all the safety and health nonsense that's keeping them glued to their screens.

And the only way of doing that is by explaining to the nation's no-win no-fee lawyers that, if they lose, they'll be taken to the nearest zoo and fed to the lions.

2 November 2017

Sorry, kids, but Britain will be the next Vietnam, with you as the cheap labour

When you go out these days you are picked up by an Uber driver who's Syrian and taken to the restaurant, where a pretty young Latvian woman shows you to your table and introduces you to your French waiter, who explains what specials the Italian chef has prepared.

On the way home you buy some milk from a Pakistani shopkeeper and then find the Estonian babysitter has broken the lavatory, so you call the Polish plumber and, as you sit waiting for him to arrive, you find yourself wondering when you last spoke in normal, non-enunciated English with anyone you encountered in your workaday life.

The man who runs my off-licence is French, my cleaning lady is from Estonia, the traffic warden with whom I have a daily row is Nigerian, the man at the garage is Indian, the chap who mends my wi-fi is Armenian . . . I cannot remember the last time I spoke to someone in a London shop or restaurant where I didn't have to speak slowly and clearly, like it's 1970 and I've just gone abroad for the first time.

I should point out that I don't really care about any of this. Why should I be the slightest bit bothered about what language the girl at the supermarket checkout uses when she gets home? Just so long as she's quick at her job and pays her taxes, it's irrelevant.

What's interesting, however, is that the vast majority of people who live in Britain are actually white British. There are regional differences, of course – it's less than half in London and more than 99 per cent in the Lake District or northern Norfolk – but the fact is that the last time anyone counted, there were more than 51 million white British people in the UK, and I have a question. What the bloody hell are they all doing with themselves?

We are told by the government that, despite Theresa May's best efforts to make everything worse, there are now more people working than at any time in the country's history. Well, I'm sorry, but that's about as believable as its claims that Brexit is going very well and the Cabinet is united on all fronts.

Yes, my accountant is white British and so, despite a French-sounding name, is my lawyer. But not everyone can be a lawyer or an accountant. Not everyone has that sort of mind. Some are fit only to be cobblers, but there's no such thing any more. We don't mend shoes because we don't keep them long enough to break: they get thrown out when they go out of fashion, which is every three months.

We don't mend anything, so you can no longer earn a living with a television-repair shop or an under-the-arches garage. Heavy industry used to soak up the masses but, by and large, that's gone, as are all the mines. And who works on the land? Well, I have quite a big farm and it's all looked after by one man, except at harvest time, when he gets a mate to help out.

The armed forces? Hmmm. I listened to a senior officer on the radio last week and, from what I could tell, the Royal Navy today has a smaller, less powerful fleet than the row-boat hire company on the Serpentine in Hyde Park.

It's not even possible these days, really, to be a shop assistant because in the first half of this year fourteen high-street stores closed down every day. Because why go to town when it can come to you?

Hairstyling will survive, naturally, because only James

May has worked out how this can be done remotely – and the results are not successful. But this line of work is only for those who are too dim even to get a job in a nail salon.

I did actually encounter a young white British person in a working environment recently. I was staying in a hotel in Yorkshire, he was working as a waiter and he was completely useless.

He wore his supposedly smart black trousers in the manner of a Los Angeles remand prisoner, with his underpants sticking out over the top of the belt line, and he leaned on everything when he wasn't doing anything, which so far as I could tell was all the time.

When he did finally arrive to take my order he said in a completely flat, nasally way, 'Do you want a cooked breakfast or owt like that?' Since I couldn't think of anything that was 'like' a cooked breakfast that wasn't a cooked breakfast, I had one of those.

And off he went to lean on a wall while the chef made it. I suspect he'd only managed to get the job because his mum and dad knew the hotel's owner. And secretly, I suspect, she would rather have employed a Hungarian.

I look at my friends' kids who are now leaving university and, while many have used nepotism to get a job, the job in question is invariably an internship. Which means they are working twelve hours a day for no money and can only exist on their parents' backs.

A lot of them, however, have decided that they don't want to work for other people, for no money, and have started blogs, which means they are now working for themselves, for no money. I feel for that generation, I really do, because it is becoming used to this state of affairs.

And think about it. When Britain has left the EU and we can no longer offer the bosses of foreign manufacturing companies a nice place to live and lots of golf courses, as well as access to the single market, we will have only one fiscal way of attracting investment: cheap labour. We will become the next Vietnam.

Your kids, then? They're at university now, studying hard for a 2:1 in archaeology. But if they want a job that pays money down the line, their only option will be in a factory, putting the laces in training shoes for a gigantic Chinese corporation.

19 November 2017

Stick to pretty fish, Sir David Attenborough, and stop blubbing about dead whales

We have learned in recent weeks that people in a position of power should never use that power to influence their underlings. Many people have been caught up in this sea change and the latest, tragically, is none other than Sir David Attenborough.

I am a huge fan of his new fish programme and I'm in awe of the people who make it. They sailed for four thousand miles to film some grouper fish – which once a year spawn wildly before being eaten by sharks – and they missed the moment. So the next year they sailed all the way back to try again. That sort of devotion to the cause is almost beyond comprehension in today's televisual world of orange and pink, that'll-do, bish, bash, bosh.

Then there's Sir David himself, a towering colossus, a giant among naturists. Or is it naturalists? I can never remember. But, whatever, his enthusiasm and passion for the fish, no matter how puny or how stupid they look, leaves me begging for more each week. And I salute him as a broadcasting god because, if it were me behind the mic, I'd be tempted once in a while to say, 'God almighty, that's an ugly f*****.'

However, it seems he has been in trouble for spouting a lot of Greenpeace eco-babble instead of moving on to the next sea cucumber that can open tin cans with its hairstyle. People have been saying that it's a Sunday night and, while they are sitting in front of the fire with a glass of sherry, they don't want to be told by an old man that they should sell their Range Rover. And that using a BBC-funded show to get across his point of view is an abuse of power.

I can see where they are coming from. I certainly don't want to be told to sell my Range Rover because coral is so stupidly picky about what sort of temperature it likes the sea to be. If it heats up by so much as one degree, it squirts all its colour into the nearest current and dies. Well, diddums. If the sea's too warm off Barbados, why doesn't it come and live off Morecambe?

When I was cold as a kid and would ask my dad to turn up the heating, he'd tell me to put on a jumper. And frankly, that's what Sir David should be telling the coral to do.

He was at it again a week later, showing us a whale swimming around with its dead calf and saying it may have died because its mother's milk had been poisoned by plastic. That may have been the case, but scientists have been saying that he couldn't possibly have known. It may have been shot by a fisherman, or died of boredom, or cancer.

Yes, plastic is a problem in the sea. But, again, I don't want to hear about it on a programme about pretty fishes. It'd be like Mary Berry popping up in the middle of a show about pastry to tell us that cargo ships should be fitted with hydrogen fuel cells.

And, anyway, it's an easy fix. I analysed all the plastic that washed up on the beach at my place in the Isle of Man recently and found that it's mainly deposited by people who like milk chocolate Bounty bars and Flora spread. Tackle those two things and, hey presto, everything is tickety-boo. This is what Attenborough should have said: that poor people who eat spreads and milk chocolate are killing whales. But he didn't. He said we are all to blame because we want easy, comfortable, disease-free lives.

He's been getting stick for that, and I understand why. Though at this point I should admit that I once concluded a

TV programme in which I'd driven to the magnetic North Pole by saying there's no such thing as global warming because I hadn't fallen through the ice. But this wasn't really abusing my powers. I was simply saying it to annoy the BBC.

If you want to see the number-one abuser of his power in action, you should dig out a recent copy of *Country Life* magazine and have a look at what Prince Charles has to say about the British countryside. It's so miserable it makes the average Philip Larkin poem look like a commercial for DFS.

I was in the British countryside last weekend and it was so beautiful my knees kept buckling. The colours were spectacular, fieldfares danced about in the fruit trees, finches hopped hither and thither in the hedgerows and I saw a swarm – an actual swarm – of yellowhammers. I also saw some pretty partridges, which I shot and later ate.

Somehow, though, when Prince Windsor looks at our green and pleasant land, he sees disease and pestilence. He sees withered oaks and fallen elms, and immigrant moths and beetles chomping their way through the woods, and he knows who's to blame. You. And me.

He says that when we go to the garden centre we don't check to make sure the plant we are buying isn't riddled with some foreign disease – and that because of this laziness on our part the country and the world will become a desert. I'm not quite sure how he's worked this out, but he reckons trees cause rainfall. Maybe they do. Maybe I haven't been paying attention but, whatever, without them we all die of thirst.

I don't doubt that, as Harvey Weinstein emptied his seed into a plant pot and Mr Spacey Invader did his thing, they thought that their power and fame would allow them to get away with it. But one day the little people reared up and said, 'Actually, you know what, you bloody well can't.'

And that's what Charles needs to remember. He needs to stick to opening cricket pavilions and stop scolding us for not recognizing Asian longhorn beetles or potato brown rot when we are buying shrubs at the garden centre. Because frankly, we have better things to do.

26 November 2017

Eat your heart out, Dyson – the Surrey space cadets are hoovering the galaxy

Last week my stern words about Sir David's eco-preaching on the fish programme went down badly with one reader, who wrote to say that Sir Richard is a national treasure and that I was just a smartarse. That made me laugh. But the truth is Sir David – as opposed to his brother, who has no opinion on the matter because he's dead – is quite right to say we are dropping too much junk in the sea. We are. But it's nowhere near as disturbing as the amount of junk we are dropping in space.

When we watched the space shuttle take off, we saw its solid rocket boosters fall away a couple of minutes after launch and, if we thought anything at all, we assumed they'd burn up on re-entry. But they didn't. They fell back into the sea, and then they were recovered, rinsed out and used again. So that's all very lovely.

The space shuttle, meanwhile, would drift about doing science until it was time to come home. And that's lovely too. The idea that Johnny Astronaut was up there lobbing crisp packets and fag butts out of the window is preposterous. But, actually, he sort of was.

Somewhere in the heavens is a hammer that someone dropped a while back. An actual hammer. And there are countless nuts and bolts as well. Today, the faecal matter of astronauts is bagged, compressed and brought back to Earth, but that wasn't always the case. In the past it was chucked overboard to float around for decades in the big nothing. Urine too. One astronaut described a sunset pee dump as the most beautiful thing he'd seen.

Over time, some of that crystallized pee crashed into the Mir space station, causing a fair bit of damage. And that's the nub of the problem.

A problem that's getting bigger. In 2007 China destroyed one of its own satellites with a missile, and the mess – from both the satellite and the missile – is still up there somewhere. Then, two years later, a US communications satellite hit a Russian one, and all the flotsam and jetsam from that crash is still having to be monitored.

It's estimated that there are currently about 5,500 dead satellites and more than 20,000 bits of debris bigger than four inches across whizzing round the Earth, and you probably think this is no big deal because space is really huge and the chances of crashing into someone's lost spanner are quite remote.

Not so. One shuttle returned to Earth with a chipped window after hitting something we'd left behind. Another was actually holed. A European space agency satellite has a big dent in one of its solar panels caused when it hit a bit of dust.

You may think a bit of dust is no big deal. But when it's travelling at 17,500mph in one direction and you're travelling at 17,500mph in the other – trust me on this – it's going to sting. Dust? No one knows how much of that's up there.

What we do know is that soon we'll get to the point where there's a very real risk that every launch will fail because the spacecraft is bound to hit something. And when it does, and it shatters, you're going to end up with more bits of debris. You've seen the film *Gravity*. Well, it's like that.

And then there's the business of this rubbish coming back to Earth and landing on someone's head. The chances are remote, of course, but it has happened. A Turkish woman was hit on the bonce once by a bit of heat shield that hadn't burned up properly. If we don't watch out, we'll need to start walking around under steel umbrellas because it'll be raining Neil Armstrong's matter pretty much constantly.

Naturally, the problem will be solved at some point by Norwich Union, which will refuse to insure space launches. So they won't happen any more. Which will mean we have no internet, or satellite navigation, and that, if you're twenty, will be like going back to the Dark Ages.

We need the sea to be clean and shampoo-advert fresh so we can enjoy snorkelling when we are on holiday. But we need space to be clean too because, if it isn't, everything we hold dear these days will not work any more.

Happily, help is at hand from the Surrey Space Centre – no, me neither. But, whatever, it has built an orbital vacuum cleaner that will be launched next year and is designed to whizz about up there being Wall-E.

Like everything made in a British shed these days, it doesn't look very impressive – think twin-tub washing machine from 1964 – but the Borg's spaceship was pretty cool and that wasn't exactly sleek either. It's called, imaginatively, the RemoveDEBRIS, and what it does is tow a net around, like a trawler, collecting rubbish. When it gets to a big bit, it uses a harpoon to spear it and reel it in. Then, when it's full, it will deploy a sail and float back into the atmosphere, where it and everything it's collected will be turned to ash.

It sounds very simple, and I hope it works. It'll be nice to think that, while the Russians and the Americans and the French are busy making a mess up there, a bunch of space-men from Surrey will be hoovering it all up. Maybe that's a metaphor for what Britain will become post Brexit: the world's cleaning lady.

If it doesn't work, I see two possible solutions. First, stop employing clumsy astronauts. We really can't have people up there who can drop a hammer and then not notice.

Or introduce a one-way system. At present, satellites go in whichever direction the maker chooses, which means they can have head-on crashes.

This is madness, so why not force them all to go the same way? Just a thought.

3 December 2017

The girls, the gambling, the gin – I've gone galloping mad for horse racing

When you watch horse racing on the television you're told by hieroglyphics on the screen and by the commentator that the action is coming from the 3.20 at Lingfield. But is it? Because Pontefract and Lingfield and Wetherby? Only a very small number, of very small people, would be able to tell the difference.

I've thought for a long time that when colour television was invented a horse race was filmed and they just use the same footage over and over again. Because can you tell Graphic Decapitation from Telltale Skidmark? Of course not. Claiming that horses are all different is like saying ants have recognizable faces. They're all just milk bottles. Identical.

And there's more. We are expected to believe that a television cameraman or cameraman woman spends years being an assistant. He or she humps tripods up and down hills, drives vans through the night and learns about all the latest breakthroughs in digital technology so that one day they can sit in the mist, on top of a Citroën, filming a sport being watched by only half a dozen red-nosed drunks in betting shops in the north.

Think about it. Every single horse race is filmed, apparently. That means at least six sound recordists and six cameramen at four different courses, six days a week. If that were really happening, there would be no crews left for anyone else. David Attenborough would have had to film his nature programmes on a cameraphone.

This Friday you will not be able to watch Fleetwood Town play Gillingham on the television, but you will – we are told – be able to watch the action from Uttoxeter and Wolver-hampton. And that makes no sense. Because in horse racing there never is any action. It's just meat running about. As a sporting spectacle, it's even more dreary than Formula One.

Of course, it works if you have some money on Womble Boy and it's leading by a nose with a furlong to go. But if you are betting on a race in Wolverhampton, on a Friday even-ing, then you are a friendless drunk and you should get some help. What's weird, though, is that horse racing does work extremely well if you watch it live.

I went to Newbury the other day and had lunch in the royal box with various owners who were competing with one another to see who had the fastest pet.

I'd like to say this was all rather tragic, but the truth is that I have a shoot and I've been known to just fire my gun repeat-edly into the air so people who run neighbouring shoots think, 'Clarkson's having a better day than me so I'd better kill myself.'

It's all part of growing up and being a man and having an ego. Which is why, in horse racing, people will spend millions – lots of millions – on a horse with a fast dad. Just so they can have a faster pet than Sheikh Hakeem Makeem Dhakeem. Or Mr O'Reilly from Kildare.

Outside the royal box, it was a scrum of tweed and red noses and people queuing for the cash machine. It was an alloy of hope and drink and fur. And at one point I was taken into the paddock so people could take my picture.

After a little while, some horses were brought out and, somehow, we were expected to be able to tell which ones stood a chance and which ones were going to limp home last in the race after the one they'd started. They all looked exactly the same to me. So I picked one that was running at 8–1 – I always do that, even though it has never, ever worked – and went off to give Honest John from Liverpool some of my money. He took it gratefully and gave me some banter and a bit of paper, which I put in the bin because it would never be worth anything. And then the race began.

There's no getting round the fact that it's all very brilliant. Fuelled by sloe gin and whisky and beer, people begin to make noises that rise in volume to become, in the final few moments, like the sound of 4 million startled geese. And then it's done and Jeremy Kyle is dancing around because his pet has won and no one hears the vet shoot the 8–1 outsider that fell over at the first fence.

All this noise and excitement and gunfire is infectious. And that's before we get to the summertime events such as Royal Ascot or the Melbourne Cup in Australia, where women decide that, in order to watch a horse running along, they must not wear knickers and should fall over in the paddock every five minutes.

I don't know why they do this. I think it's because they have it in their minds that horse racing is posh, which it is, of course. But what makes it posh is that you have the lords and the ladies and the groundsmen and the dry-stone wallers and none of the idiots in between. You and me? We are just there to make a noise and fill the tills.

And it works. We go there, into the olden days, and we have no idea what's going on. We place our bets for reasons that make no sense, which gives us something to cheer about when the race happens, and then we have an egg sandwich and some more sloe gin and then another girl falls over and, when it's all finished, it's cost us whatever we chose to spend and that, for an exciting day out, is not bad value.

When we get back we don't feel compelled to watch the highlights on television because the sport's not important – and it wasn't really televised anyway. No. It's because we could spend a day dressing up and sounding like geese and having a drink with our friends. And there's always a chance that you could go home with a wallet so full that it's actually uncomfortable to sit on. This, I'm told, is the most wonderful feeling in the world, because winning £50 is better than earning £100.

Thanks to tax, actually, it amounts to the same thing.

17 December 2017

I had fun with acids at school; now I want them kept under military guard

I used to enjoy chemistry lessons at school because there were never-ending opportunities to cause explosions and 'accidentally' drop big lumps of sodium into a bucket of water. Plus, whenever a master noticed yellow nicotine stains on my fingers and accused me of smoking, I could claim I'd been handling potassium permanganate and the stains had come, in fact, from that.

But by far the best way of enlivening the lessons would be to pour a cup full of sulphuric acid into one sink, wait a moment and then get a friend to pour a cup of nitric acid into his sink. And then all we had to do was contain our mirth for a few seconds until the next sink along exploded, causing the boy standing beside it to get some detention.

My teachers would claim afterwards that I had learned absolutely nothing from my chemistry lessons, but this isn't true. I learned how to sleep with my eyes open and that acid is extremely weird and should never ever be thrown into someone's face.

Today, though, children are not allowed to play with acid when they are at school. They are too busy being told to stay at home because it's a bit chilly or too hot. So they have no idea about the havoc it can wreak, which means that in many parts of the country it's considered an amusing game to squirt it on to the head of someone who was looking at you funny.

Between 2012 and 2016 the number of acid attacks in Britain rose by 500 per cent. This is largely because of gang people who like to melt the arms off someone who's stolen their phone or their moped. Or their girlfriend, if she decides that, on balance, she'd rather go out with an estate agent.

The BBC is telling us that, contrary to what we thought, the acid problem in London isn't caused by Asian immigrants doing so-called 'honour' crimes on girls who won't marry them. Nobody thought it was, you halfwits.

We know that sometimes the attacks are for fun. At the Notting Hill Carnival this year it was used to mark out territories. And last week a man was sentenced to twenty years in jail for spraying the dancefloor with acid at an east London club. There was no suggestion he'd targeted anyone in particular.

Recently, in a shopping centre not far from the nightclub, gang members decided to have a water fight. That would have been quite a laugh if they really had used water. But they used acid. And that wasn't a laugh at all, as six passersby were caught up in the action.

And now, as a result, London is the world capital of acid crime. A title it hasn't held since Victorian times.

More recently, acid-throwing has been popular in Asia, but governments in that neck of the woods came up with successful solutions. If you threw acid at someone in Pakistan and were caught, the authorities would tie you down and drip acid into your eyes. In Bangladesh, they now go one step further and kill you.

I'm not certain either solution would be adopted here. Because if the warders at Belmarsh were to be caught dripping acid into the eyes of teenagers, the *Guardian* would have something to say about it. And there'd be calls for the police to concentrate on the real criminals such as Andrew Mitchell, Damian Green and various bankers.

Last week a young woman who'd been caught up in the London nightclub attack released photographs of her scars.

And they were horrible. I'd quite like to meet the man who caused them, for a laugh, and hammer my point across using an actual hammer.

I was slightly amazed to hear, though, that people who use acid as a weapon here can only be done for grievous bodily harm. Knives and guns will put you in court charged with attempted murder, but it's felt by someone that acid can only cause harm, not death.

Hmmm. I think if someone were to be lowered into a bath of acid, they would not be thinking as their legs melted, 'Well, it could be worse. I could have been shot.' Acid can kill. And acid attacks must be seen that way.

But before we get to the question of punishment, we must first address the problem of supply. Knives are tricky to deal with on this front because everyone needs them for chopping up vegetables or carving meat. Kids can get hold of one by going no further than their mum's cutlery drawer.

Acid is different. I have never once in fifty-seven years thought, 'Damn, we are low on hydrochloric acid. I must get some next time I'm in town.'

I appreciate there are various heavy industries that need acid to make bits for ships or fertilizers but, again, I bet they don't buy their supplies from the local chemist.

Bleach is the only issue, because that's something most households do need. But bleach in gangland is like a Ruger LC9 handgun. A bit wet. A bit lightweight. You're not going to rise up the ladder in the criminal underworld if all you have is a bottle of Domestos. In a gang, it's all about looking cool, and for that you need the AK-47 of acids, the full sulphuric. That stuff can melt bone, man.

So step one, I suggest, is simply to treat it, and all its nasty corrosive brothers, like we treat assault rifles, hand grenades and plutonium. They need to be kept on army bases and transported under heavy guard to places where they are really needed. They should not, ever, fall into the hands of Gazza from Dalston.

Instead, the government is talking about implementing measures that would reverse a recent decision that allows shops to sell corrosive substances without a licence. Whereas what it should be thinking is, 'Why does any high-street shop need to sell it at all?'

And on that cheery note, happy Christmas to everyone – except Tom Watson.

24 December 2017

Just remind me, please, why we think the world is becoming a better place

Over the Christmas period I was introduced by a friend to Amazon's Alexa device. It's amazing. You just say, 'Alexa, play "Long Train Runnin'"' by the Doobie Brothers,' and it goes into a record collection of everything ever written, finds what you want and plays it.

Now, I don't want to sound like an old man but, if *Tomorrow's World* presenter Judith Hann had said to me, as I was taking a record out of its sleeve, carefully dusting it and then placing it on a turntable, that in my lifetime the sky would become a giant voice-activated record player, I'd have laughed at her. And it would have been the same story if she'd said I could sit in a car, on a motorway, and watch a feature film on my telephone.

Thanks to technology, and improved medicine, we think the world is getting better but, if we look back at the events from the past year, we can see that, actually, it isn't. Not really.

For example, if Hann's colleague Raymond Baxter had said that in 2017 a Muslim would be so devoted to the cause of Islam that he'd strap some dynamite to his chest and walk into a pop concert that he knew would be full of children – and explode – I'd have thought, 'Oh dear. The breeze of insanity is blowing through the poor man's head.'

Especially if he'd gone on to say that people would one day drive their vans down the pavement trying to kill as many pedestrians as possible. We'd seen that in a film – *Death Race 2000* – but the idea that it could actually happen would have seemed completely idiotic.

Then there's the business of nationhood. After the First World War, it was decided that the lump of rock and ice in the Arctic Ocean that is now called Svalbard couldn't just belong to nobody because a villain might come along and build a rocket site there. So it was gifted to Norway. And with Antarctica buried under a mass of treaties, the world was all sorted out.

Now, though, there are countries throughout the world with no effective government at all. So instead of operating from bedsits in Cologne and Belfast, terrorist groups are able to really stretch their legs. And if they do eventually get pushed out of say, Syria, they simply up sticks and move to Libya.

As a child, I holidayed once in Tunisia and, if William Woollard had popped up and said one day, on this very beach, a man will walk along shooting tourists, I'd have called the police and said a madman was on the loose.

Predicting where the next actual war would come from has always been easy. It was Germany. So who would have said, in the late 1970s, that Britain's next big scrap would be with Argentina? Or when we were yomping over the Falklands, that twenty years later it'd be Afghanistan? Or that the next big nuclear threat would come from North Korea?

A threat so severe, it seems, that Japan is about to circumvent its pacifist constitution and accept that its collection of grey boats staffed by efficient and uniformed sailors is actually a navy. And not a department of the police force.

And then there's Africa. I would have assumed that, by now, it'd have all been sorted out. But no. Just last month a coup in Zimbabwe saw the lunatic Mr Robert Mugabe ousted and replaced with a chap called Mr Emmerson Mnangagwa. Who, apparently, is even worse.

There might have been a time when Britain would have flexed its muscles over such a move. But this is not possible any more because our army is on a course, learning to no longer say 'Ladies and gentlemen' when addressing a crowd, and the navy's aircraft carrier has no planes and a leak.

Also, the politicians in London are all consumed with how we are going to leave the EU. That's all they are doing, all of them. All of the time. It makes you wonder how they fill their days when they don't have the border between Northern Ireland and Ireland to sort out.

There are similar issues in Spain, which everyone thought had been fixed after General Franco went west. Seems not. As nobody at all predicted, Catalonia decided it wanted to break free and organized an election in which the only people who voted were secessionists.

And lo, when they won, the leaders of the campaign decided that it was all too complicated and fled to Belgium. Anyone see that coming?

Meanwhile, in America – well, what can I say about that? In 2016 the Democrats fielded someone so useless that the election, with some help from the Russians, was won by a dotard who thinks 'bigly' is a word.

Everyone predicted that Trump's victory would herald the end of days but, as he approaches the end of his first year in office, there's no getting round the fact that the Dow Jones is higher than ever, that his tax cuts will boost the economy and that so far, at least, no actual war has started. It'll be hilarious if he goes on to become the most successful president yet. Would you bet against it?

Really? In this world? Where no one can predict anything? Harvey Weinstein, for example, could not have predicted this time last year that in the next twelve months he'd have fallen so low that he could never again show his face in public.

Or that by inviting young actresses to watch him shower, he would set in motion a chain of events that would see more

than thirty high-ranking people in the entertainment industry and beyond accused of being alleged sexual nuisances
and cause a sea change in the way the world works. Now it is
pretty much illegal to ask a young woman out.

Who knows where this one will end? Will the stone continue to roll down the hill, until it becomes socially impossible
for men and women to converse? Or will the pendulum
swing the other way so that next year the big comedy hit will
be a remake of *Carry On Camping*?

The fact is that we don't know what will happen next. No
one ever has done. A point proved by *Tomorrow's World*. Every
week it was full of the latest innovations that would shape our
lives in the future. And it didn't see the internet coming.

31 December 2017